The Horror Comic
Never Dies

The Horror Comic Never Dies
A Grisly History

MICHAEL WALTON

McFarland & Company, Inc., Publishers
Jefferson, North Carolina

LIBRARY OF CONGRESS CATALOGUING-IN-PUBLICATION DATA

Names: Walton, Michael, 1970– author.
Title: The horror comic never dies : a grisly history / Michael Walton.
Description: Jefferson, North Carolina : McFarland & Company, Inc., 2019 | Includes bibliographical references and index.
Identifiers: LCCN 2019002647 | ISBN 9781476675367 (paperback : acid free paper) ∞
Subjects: LCSH: Horror comic books, strips, etc.—United States— Hitory and criticism.
Classification: LCC PN6725 .W293 2019 | DDC 741.5/3164—dc23
LC record available at https://lccn.loc.gov/2019002647

BRITISH LIBRARY CATALOGUING DATA ARE AVAILABLE

ISBN (print) 978-1-4766-7536-7
ISBN (ebook) 978-1-4766-3512-5

© 2019 Michael Walton. All rights reserved

No part of this book may be reproduced or transmitted in any form or by any means, electronic or mechanical, including photocopying or recording, or by any information storage and retrieval system, without permission in writing from the publisher.

Front cover illustration by Don Heck, 1953 (Comic Media)

Printed in the United States of America

McFarland & Company, Inc., Publishers
　Box 611, Jefferson, North Carolina 28640
　　www.mcfarlandpub.com

Table of Contents

Preface	1
Introduction	5
1. The History of the Comic Book	7
2. The Birth of the Horror Comic Genre	23
3. Seduction of the Innocent	36
4. The Comics Code Authority	60
5. Horror Comics in the Silver Age of Comic Books	67
6. Horror Comics in the Bronze Age of Comic Books	80
7. The Modern Resurgence of the Horror Comic	87
8. Crossover Hits	132
Afterword: Whatever Happened to…?	137
Chapter Notes	161
Bibliography	167
Index	169

Preface

I admit that I have a deep and abiding love for all things horror. Halloween is a major holiday in our household—a fact that I'm sure my neighbors will testify to. It's probably best that I take this opportunity to publicly apologize to our new neighbors for the fact that my yard display last year was "a bit intense" for their young daughter. In all honesty, I'm pretty sure that was what they said since it was difficult to hear over the crying. Sorry about that and welcome to the neighborhood! It's also fitting that I take the opportunity here to mention how grateful I am to have such a gracious, patient, and long-suffering wife who has borne with quiet dignity my aforementioned love of all things horror. There are not many wives in the world who would put up with the fact that their husband has a strong opinion on the fast zombie vs. slow zombie debate (slow all the way) and a detailed Zombie Apocalypse House Fortification Plan. In fact, the only resistance I ever get to my (admittedly) eccentric tastes would be the suggestion of "maybe not another horror movie" when it is my turn to pick the entertainment on Movie Night. For what I have given her to put up with, I certainly can't complain about that.

My love for horror is only eclipsed by my love for comic books. I, like many other boys, started reading and collecting comic books at an early age. Unlike many other boys, I never really stopped. One of my earliest memories is sitting on the floor of a family friend's house and demonstrating to them that I could actually read at my young age by reading aloud from a ghost story comic book. They were so impressed that they let me keep the comic. If there was a word for a sense of pride mixed with trepidation—I'm sure that's what my parents felt that day. I imagine that they believed I would eventually grow out of the "horror phase" or the "comic phase" (or preferably both), but that never happened. In fact, my "comic phase" lasted throughout my childhood and teenage years into early adulthood. It was at this point that I selected a few hundred comic books from my own personal collection that I felt I could part with and, armed with the headstrong bravado that only comes with youth, I opened my own comic book store. The venture went quite well considering I had absolutely no experience in starting or running a business. I started out selling comic books on a table at a flea market and in less than a year had a lease on a storefront on the main street of my hometown. I was fortunate to have done this when I was young enough that the long hours, extra work, added stress, and the abject terror of throwing everything you have into a small business without any type of safety net didn't affect me in the least. I was either too young, too stubborn, or too stupid (or most likely a combination of all three) to let it stop me. Running the store taught me invaluable lessons about operating a business, establishing relationships with customers, establishing relationships with the local community, and the business end of the comic book industry. My store closed in the late 1990s. Of course, my pride feels the need to mention that I closed the store of my own volition and not as a result of the devastation brought on to the comic book industry as a result of the bursting of the Speculator Bubble of the late 1990s. A special shout-out goes to anyone reading this who ever visited the Adventurer's Guild in Marion, Virginia, during the time it was in business. Those were halcyon days.

This book was born from a serendipitous event. There is a saying that goes "old comic collectors never die, they just disappear behind stacks of longboxes." While this may be true, I learned that old comic collectors with wives (patient and longsuffering as they may be) will learn to pick up on the subtle hints that there may be a few too many boxes of comics just sitting around and it might just be time to prove how valuable of an "investment" all those old books are. That time had come for me so I bought table space at a local comic convention one weekend in October. With Halloween looming large on my mind, I thought I could differentiate myself from the other vendors by selling only horror comics. Lucky for me, I had plenty!

The weekend was a rousing success! Not only was I able to demonstrate that those boxes and boxes of dusty old books were actually worth something (if memory serves, I was able to pay for a couple rooms of carpet with the weekend's proceeds), but I was also able to connect with many other fans of horror comics. Several people told me stories of reading some of the grisly "classics" late at night by flashlight under the covers. Younger collectors discovered books, writers, and artists they had never encountered before. Older collectors were reunited with treasures from their youth. Talking with collectors both young and old led me to discover the vast and storied past of the horror comic genre.

In researching this book, I discovered things about the horror comic genre that I had never known. I was also able to discover hidden treasures of comic books that I never read and some that I had never heard of. It was

Preface 3

impressive to be able to follow the birth of an entire genre and watch it grow and expand by just flipping through pages of old comics. Sure, titles like *Tales From the Crypt* and *Vault of Horror* were the grandfathers of the genre, but just like the mainstream comic industry has changed and evolved from the 1950s until today, the horror comic genre had its own set of twists and turns. Driven almost to the brink of extinction, villainized, demonized, and practically staked in the heart, the horror comic genre managed to cling to life in the shadows and eventually claw its way back to the surface. This book tells the story of the birth, death, and reanimation of the horror comic genre. Just like the monsters in the classic films, you can chase it away with torches and pitchforks and even trap it in a burning windmill, but just as soon as you think you're all safe and sound in your bed—there will come that bump in the night and deep down inside you will wonder what you'll see if you were to look over your shoulder.

This book will focus specifically on the horror comic genre—from its origins through its trials and tribulations all the way through to today. While there are many good books on the history of comic books in American popular culture and the history of the famous men and famous companies that made up the comic book industry—this book is not designed to be one of those. The horror comic book genre has been present since the earliest comic books were published, so it is impossible to talk about the birth of the horror comic genre without also talking about the birth of comic books in general. Many of the most famous names in the comic book industry have worked within the horror comic genre in the same respect that nearly all of the major comic book publishers have, at one time or another, published horror comic books, so it would again be impossible to have a study of the horror comic genre without touching on some of the best-known names and companies in the industry. That being said, this book is not intended to be an overarching history of the comic book in American popular culture.

Likewise, the horror comic genre has seen its share of censorship. It would be impossible to write about the horror comic genre and not give some detail on Dr. Fredric Wertham, his writings, and the Comics Code Authority. Dr. Wertham, the Comics Code Authority, and comic book censorship are all touched on within this book in as much as they relate to the horror comic genre, but that is also not the primary focus of this work.

This book, I believe, stands alone. It is unique in the fact that its primary focus is the overall history of the horror comic genre and how that intersects with and interacts with American popular culture in the last 70 or 80 years. I hope that this book will be educational and enlightening and that it prompts you (as the research did me) to seek out some of the comic books mentioned and explore for yourself the wonderful, grisly history of the horror comic genre. Many of the books I mention here have been reprinted or collected into trade paperbacks so they can be picked up at a minimal expense. Comic conventions are a great place to find them, but, as a former comic shop owner, I would be remiss not to suggest that you support your local comic shop!

Introduction

People love to be scared. From the earliest Gothic horror novels to the Victorian tradition of telling ghost stories at Christmastime, tales of horror have been a part of human culture nearly as long as humans have told stories to one another. Who among us does not know by heart the famous urban legend of the two teenagers parked in Lover's Lane who hear a radio report about an escaped maniac? The girl hears something outside the car and prompts the boy to take her home. Frustrated (in more ways than one), the boy speeds off in his car. He pulls into the girl's driveway and gets out of his car to do the gentlemanly thing and open the girl's door—only to find a bloody hook dangling from the door handle. The idea of the horror story as scary ghost story or cautionary tale has been with us since two people first sat down by a fire. Horror has found its way into all areas of our culture—from books to television shows to movies. The comic book is no exception to this.

Comic books have been a part of American popular culture since the late 1930s, and amidst all of the tales of costumed superheroes, detectives, soldiers, and spies, there have been tales of horror. With this book, I attempted to piece together a complete history of the horror comic book genre.

In this book, I shed some light on the birth of the horror comic book genre in the late 1940s and its increasing popularity through the 1950s. At one point in the 1950s, the popularity of the horror comic genre grew to the point that there was a public outcry against it on the grounds that children reading horror comic books could bring about the ruination of American society. Noted experts took up the anti-horror comic book banner and there was even a Senate subcommittee tasked with investigating the issue. The fallout from this set the tone for the art and writing during the Silver Age of Comic Books. Horror comic books themselves were nearly eradicated, but a small, dedicated group of horror aficionados kept the genre alive through the 1960s and 1970s until the stage was set for a return beginning in the 1980s. Today horror comics are so popular as to have inspired television shows and major motion pictures—a fact which seems hard to believe when you remember how hard they were campaigned against not that long ago.

The trials and tribulations of the horror comic genre have had profound effects on the comic book industry as a whole. Many of the things we, as comic book collectors, consider just "the way things are done" today were actually brought about as a result of the comic book industry professionals working for the freedom to create their own things—and more than a few of those were horror comic books. American society was forced to rethink its ideas of art and cultural criticism. Comic book industry professionals became empowered to act against censorship and the changing roles of their medium in society. Comic book readers themselves changed as they matured and their tastes evolved. All of this is set on a backdrop of an American society which was itself in transition.

A great deal has changed in the nearly 80 years since the publication of the first comic book, but the one thing that has remained constant is the reflection of American society and culture in its art and media. Comic books are a part of this reflection and horror comics are even more so.

1

The History of the Comic Book

Very few things are more typically American than the simple comic book. Once hailed as cheap, disposable entertainment for children, the comic book has brought us such household names as Superman, Batman, and Spider-Man. Generations of people have believed that a man could fly or learned that with great power comes great responsibility. Comic books have influenced and inspired literature, popular culture, television programming, and even major motion pictures. As deeply ingrained into the fabric of society as they are, it would be easy to think that comic books have always been around. Of course, this is not the case. There was a time that such recognizable names like Superman, Batman, Wonder Woman, or the Avengers were nothing more than an idea in the creator's mind or a series of doodles in a high school student's notebook. Just like all of the great comic book heroes have an origin story which details their humble beginnings, comic books themselves also have an origin story of their own.

The earliest ancestors of modern comic books began to appear in the late 1920s and early 1930s when newspaper publishers began to collect reprints of popular newspaper comic strips and bound them together as small eight- to twelve-page booklets. These booklets were to be used as tabloid inserts into the newspapers themselves or as promotional items.[1] These "proto-comics" were printed on the same plain newsprint as the newspapers they were inserted into. Some of them featured comic strips printed in color, while the vast majority of them were printed in plain black and white. A few of them offered new and original comic strips in them, but most were simply reprints of the more popular newspaper comic strips of the times. While these "proto-comics" clearly laid the earliest groundwork for the modern comic book, these publications actually bore closer resemblance to the Sunday comic insert in most modern newspapers.[2]

It wasn't until 1933 when Eastern Color Printing Company sales manager

Harry I. Wildenberg and salesman Maxwell Gaines set up a collaboration with Dell Publishing to produce a 36-page "one shot" book entitled *Famous Funnies: A Carnival of Comics* that the first true American comic book was created.[3] The book was distributed through the Woolworth's department store chain although it remains unclear whether the comic was available for sale or used as a promotional giveaway. The comic itself did not have a price printed on the cover; however, rumors exist of Maxwell Gaines claiming to have stuck ten-cent price tags on them by hand. In 1934, Dell published *Famous Funnies: Series 1*, a 68-page collection of previously published comic strips printed with a ten-cent cover price—so this book was clearly designed to be sold. This book, which was also printed by Eastern Color Printing, had a print run of 35,000 and had impressive sales on the newsstands.[4] Despite the sales success, Dell did not publish any further issues. Instead, Eastern Color went ahead on its own and started publishing an ongoing monthly series starting with *Famous Funnies* #1. This comic book was also a 68-page collection of comic strips with a ten-cent cover price. This time the book was distributed to newsstands across the country through the American News Company and met with outstanding success. *Famous Funnies* #1 had an initial 200,000-copy print run and it sold over 90 percent of the copies that were printed. This is quite exceptional considering *Famous Funnies* #1 was published right in the middle of the Great Depression when many Americans were out of work and money was tight. Couple that with the fact that the ten-cent cover price is equivalent to nearly two dollars in modern currency and it adds even more weight to its unexpected success. Quite possibly the difficult circumstances people were living in added to its success. Where else could some light-hearted entertainment for the whole family be found for such a reasonable price? By issue #12, Eastern Color was making over $30,000 in net profit on each issue[5] and so the comic book as an entertainment medium was born. The phrase "comic book" itself was born as well around this time. Since the publications were literally books made up of reprinted strips from the comics section of the newspapers, describing them as a "comic book" wasn't a stretch of the imagination—although some publishers took the more sophisticated route of referring to their works as "comic magazines."

The birth of the comic book as a medium for entertainment also ushered in a paradigm shift in the way people thought about children as consumers. The idea of children's literature as its own separate and distinct field of literature didn't come about until the 1920s. Before that time, there wasn't "children's literature" and "adult literature"—there was just "literature." Literary works were written and it was up to the parent to decide whether or not a particular work was suitable for their child to read. In the 1920s library schools started offering specialized courses in children's literature, which began the distinction between the two separate fields. Now there were children's literature specialists as well as a new wave of authors who primarily wrote works for the burgeoning field.[6]

By the time the comic book debuted on newsstands, the supervision of children's reading material had been effectively turned over to teachers, schools, and professional librarians. At the time, the only real problem that these professionals had with comic books was the fact that they were considered to be "poor literature." The comic book introduced the concept of the "child consumer." Comic books were readily available on newsstands and at retail establishments like drug stores and grocery stores—places where children were likely to be and not necessarily in the company of their parents. Price was another factor. The relatively high price of books meant that it generally fell onto an adult to choose and purchase a book for a child. Even magazines specifically aimed at children relied on annual subscriptions (again chosen and paid for by an adult) for their main source of revenue. This is in contrast to the typical magazine of the time, which saw the sale of individual issues on newsstands as its primary revenue stream. Comic books were priced much lower than books or magazines—generally ten cents or less. This meant that comic books were at a price point that was affordable to the average child. Who couldn't pick up a few cents here and there by mowing lawns, doing chores, or even delivering newspapers? Comic books were cheap and readily accessible which placed them in the perfect place to provide children with an alternative to the "parent approved" or "teacher approved" reading. Children could now use their own judgment and their own purchasing power to make their own choices as to which comic books to buy and so the idea of the child as a consumer was also born.[7]

The Golden Age of Comic Books

For general points of historical reference to comic book collectors, the history of comic books has been divided up into "eras" or "ages." The first of these was known as the Golden Age of Comic Books which generally refers to the period of time from the late 1930s up through the mid–1950s.

The Golden Age of Comic Books is the time in which the comic book as we know it is born. It is also the beginning of the superhero comic book genre as many of the most well-known superheroes had their origins during the Golden Age of Comic Books. Most comic book historians designate the beginning of the Golden Age of Comic Books with the 1938 publication of

Action Comics #1. Published by Detective Comics (the company later to become better known as DC), *Action Comics* #1 featured the debut of Superman. Created by Jerry Siegel and Joe Shuster, the Man of Steel would go on to establish the superhero archetype and become one of the most popular and recognizable characters in the world[8]—not bad work for a couple of teenagers from Cleveland!

Superman may have been the first superhero, but he soon had plenty of company. Over the next few years, Detective Comics introduced the world to Batman and Robin, Wonder Woman, the Flash (Jay Garrick to be precise), Green Lantern, the Atom, Hawkman, Green Arrow, and Aquaman. Timely Comics (which would later become Marvel Comics) introduced the Human Torch (the android—not Johnny Storm), Sub-Mariner, and Captain America and all of them became runaway hits as well. Captain America, for example, was selling over one million copies a month by its second issue.[9] If you judge popularity by overall circulation numbers, far and away the most popular superhero from the Golden Age of Comic Books would have to be Captain Marvel. Introduced in Fawcett's *Whiz Comics* #1 (February 1940), the adventures of young Billy Batson (who could transform into the adult superhero Captain Marvel by uttering the magic word "Shazam!") would become so popular that by 1943 *Captain Marvel Adventures* was selling over a million and a half copies a month. Demand for the book was so strong that Fawcett began publishing the title twice a month. If you think you remember this particular hero by a different name, that is understandable. In 1941, Detective Comics brought a lawsuit against Fawcett on the grounds that Fawcett's character of Captain Marvel was too similar to Detective Comics' own Superman character. The lawsuit drug on through the 1940s and into the 1950s until the courts eventually ruled in favor of Detective Comics. Fawcett was forced to cease all publication of Captain Marvel, with the final issue of *Whiz* being published in 1953 and the last issue of *Captain Marvel Adventures* being published in 1954. Detective Comics brought the character of Captain Marvel back in 1973 in a title called *Shazam!* The character's name change being due to the fact that, in the intervening years, Marvel Comics had introduced (and more importantly trademarked) their own character called Captain Marvel.[10]

The amazing popularity of the new comic book medium led publishers to branch out beyond just superhero comics. Dell Comics would have great success publishing comic books based on licensed movie and popular literary characters such as Mickey Mouse, Donald Duck, Roy Rogers, and Tarzan.[11] Some of these titles would be so popular they would go on to outsell many of the superhero comics of the day.[12] The "teen humor" comic genre would also gain popularity after the debut of America's favorite teenager, Archie Andrews in *Pep Comics* #33 (December 1941).[13]

In the years following the end of World War II, comic book readers' taste began to change. Sales for superhero comics began to decline. The American consumer had new ways to spend their entertainment dollars and they had more expendable income to spend. Paper was strictly rationed during wartime and the end of the war saw the relaxation of these rations. Cheap paperback books—including pulp magazines—became widely available. The American consumer also had access to the radio and the new entertainment medium of television. In response, comic book publishers diversified their offerings and began publishing other genres like war, true crime, Westerns, romance, science fiction, and horror. Superheroes lost their popularity and many existing superhero titles were converted to another genre or cancelled altogether.[14]

For the purpose of this book, I demark the end of the Golden Age of Comics and the beginning of the Silver Age of Comics with the publication of Dr. Fredric Wertham's book *Seduction of the Innocent*, his testimony before the Senate Subcommittee on Juvenile Delinquency, and the formation of the Comics Code Authority in 1954.

The Silver Age of Comic Books

The Silver Age of Comic Books is the term used to denote the period of time between 1955 and 1970. The term itself was coined by a letter from a comic fan. The Silver Age of Comic Books saw a new resurgence in the popularity of superheroes. DC was leading the field in this by relaunching updated versions of its popular Golden Age superheroes. In a letter published in the letter column of *Justice League of America* #42 (February 1966), Scott Taylor of Westport, Connecticut, wrote, "If you guys keep bringing back the heroes from the Golden Age, people 20 years from now will be calling this decade the Silver Sixties!"[15] Comic fans quickly adopted the phrase and began to differentiate between Golden Age comics and Silver Age comics. Dealers also picked up on the phrasing and began describing their books for sale as either Golden Age books or Silver Age books.[16]

The Golden Age of Comics effectively ended after Dr. Fredric Wertham testified before the Senate Subcommittee to Investigate Juvenile Delinquency. Dr. Wertham testified that children who read comic books regularly would be more likely to become juvenile delinquents.[17] Parents were understandably concerned and wanted something to be done. There was a great public outcry.

Communities banned the sale of comic books while others went as far as to gather them up and burn them in large public bonfires.[18] The Senate Subcommittee to Investigate Juvenile Delinquency in the end did not endorse Dr. Wertham's findings, although it was recommended that the comic book industry take steps to reduce the violent, gory, and (perceived) sexual nature of their content. The message that was sent to the comic industry was clear—either they cleaned up their act or the government would step in and do it for them.[19] The comic book industry responded by forming the Comics Code Authority—an agency used to self-regulate the content that comic book publishers were allowed to print. Comic book publishers would submit their books to the Comics Code Authority (CCA) and would receive feedback as to what elements of the story or art would need to be changed in order to meet "the Code." If the publisher adhered to the Comics Code Authority rules, then the comic book could be released with the Comics Code Authority "Seal of Approval" on the cover. While comic book publishers were not technically required to submit their books to the Comics Code Authority for approval, distributors outright refused to sell any comic books without the Comics Code Authority Seal of Approval on the cover, due to pressure from parent groups to only allow their children to purchase a "wholesome" product. This means a comic book without the Comics Code Authority seal on the cover would most likely never be placed out for sale, so there was a very strong incentive for publishers to conform to the Comics Code Authority and their standards.

The Comics Code Authority placed severe restrictions on what could be shown in a comic book—even going as far as to ban certain words from the titles. The words "terror" and "horror" were strictly forbidden, for example.[20] In response, the writing in comic books was toned down to the point of campiness as the industry focused itself to target a younger audience. During the Golden Age of Comic Books, readership spanned in ages from adults to teenagers and younger children. During the Silver Age of Comic Books, comics began to be targeted towards a pre-teen market almost exclusively. The horror and true crime genres had all but been eliminated. Comic book publishers either changed direction or simply went out of business. By 1962, there were less than a dozen comic book publishers still in business—a drop of over 50 percent from just ten years before.[21]

Despite this gloomy outlook, there was still innovation in the comic book industry. The Silver Age of Comic Books saw a resurgence in the superhero genre. DC still remained a viable player in the market with Superman comics still selling around one million copies per issue. These sales were bolstered in no small part by the *Adventures of Superman* television show which aired from 1953 through 1957 and served to keep DC's flagship hero in the public eye. DC breathed new life into another Golden Age superhero with the reintroduction of the Flash as police scientist Barry Allen in *Showcase* #4 (October 1956). This was quickly followed by Hal Jordan as the new Green Lantern in *Showcase* #22 (October 1959), Ray Palmer as the new Atom in *Showcase* #34 (October 1961), and a revamped Hawkman in *The Brave and the Bold* #34 (February–March 1961). These new Silver Age heroes teamed up with Superman, Batman, and Wonder Woman to form the Justice League of America.[22]

Marvel Comics was probably the company that came into their own the most during the Silver Age of Comics. The "dream team" at Marvel of Stan Lee, Jack Kirby, and Steve Ditko created some of Marvel's most memorable and enduring characters during this time. This includes the Fantastic Four, the X-Men, the Avengers, Iron Man, the Hulk, and Spider-Man. The Marvel team took a different approach to writing their stories. Marvel superheroes were, at heart, regular people. They didn't always get along. They had squabbles and fights. They had "real world" worries like getting good grades or wondering where the rent was going to come from this month. Sure, they had awesome powers, but they each had their own personal demons to contend with. This approach was drastically different than DC's superheroes which were held up to be paradigms of human virtue—practically gods among men. Marvel comic titles sold well among college students and teenagers, as the idea of an "everyman hero" resonated with the youth of the time.[23]

The Bronze Age of Comics

In keeping with the Olympic medal theme, the period of time following the Silver Age of Comic Books is commonly known as the Bronze Age of Comic Books. This generally refers to the period of time between 1970 and 1985. Unlike the Golden Age of Comic Books and Silver Age of Comic Books, there is no real clear-cut event that prompted the end of the Silver Age of Comic Books and the beginning of the Bronze Age of Comic Books. Comic historians refer to several events which happened in the early 1970s as events worthy enough to bring on the beginning of a new age of comic books.

In April of 1970, DC Editor Julius Schwartz turned creative control of *Green Lantern* over to the new creative team of Denny O'Neil and Neal Adams, due in no small part to the title's slumping sales. Starting with *Green Lantern* #76, the title became a team-up of Green Lantern and Green Arrow. Julius Schwartz was the editor at DC who started the reimagining of Golden

Age superheroes (Green Lantern among them), which kicked off the Silver Age of Comic Books. His leaving *Green Lantern* is often noted as the end of the Silver Age of Comics.[24] Also occurring in 1970, Jack Kirby left Marvel Comics after 12 formative years to go to work for Marvel's crosstown rival—DC. There were also big changes at DC where Mort Weisinger, editor of Superman titles since the mid-1950s, retired and was replaced by Julius Schwartz.[25]

Those people looking for an "in comic" change instead of a "real world" change often point to the death of Peter Parker's girlfriend, Gwen Stacy, at the hands of the Green Goblin in *Amazing Spider-Man* #121–122 (June/July 1973). This pivotal moment seemed to symbolize the death of the innocence of the Silver Age of Comic Books and the onset of a darker tone for the storylines in the Bronze Age of Comic Books. Aside from Gwen Stacy's shocking death, the Denny O'Neil/Neal Adams creative team behind *Green Lantern/Green Arrow* wrote unflinching stories dealing with racism, income inequality, political corruption, and even had a storyline entitled "Snowbirds Don't Fly" in *Green Lantern/Green Arrow* #85–86 (September/October 1971) in which Green Arrow's sidekick, Speedy, became addicted to heroin.[26] Marvel Comics had the Uncanny X-Men, a group of mutants who were hated and feared by society because they were different—a thinly veiled metaphor for the struggles of minorities in America. This was also the era of the famous "Demon In a Bottle" storyline in *Invincible Iron Man* #120–128 (March–November 1979) where Tony Stark battles with his alcoholism.[27]

This increase in social relevance isn't all "doom and gloom." The Bronze Age of Comic Books also saw a dramatic increase in the number of minority superheroes as well as several new female characters who weren't just relegated to the roles of girlfriend or sidekick. Marvel introduced Black Panther (the first mainstream black superhero) in *Fantastic Four* #52 (July 1966). Black Panther was joined by Falcon in *Captain America* #117 (September 1969), Blade in *Tomb of Dracula* #10 (July 1973), Storm in *Giant Size X-Men* #1 (May 1975), Misty Knight in *Marvel Premiere* #21 (March 1975), and Luke Cage in *Luke Cage, Hero for Hire* #1 (June 1972), who was also the first black superhero to star in his own title.[28] DC introduced their first African American superhero, Green Lantern John Stewart, in *Green Lantern* #87 (December 1971).[29] They would also debut Black Lightning in *Black Lightning* #1 (April 1977) and Cyborg in *DC Comics Presents* #26 (October 1980).

The Bronze Age saw the beginning of the hobby of comic book collecting and the growth of specialized comic book stores. Comic books began to grow and be recognized as a legitimate literary medium. No longer considered cheap, disposable entertainment for kids, comic books now began to attract an older audience. Comic book conventions began to crop up more and more frequently. While sporadic during the 1960s, comic book conventions became a regular, annual event in many cities in the United States and throughout the world. While early comic book conventions would be lucky to see a couple of hundred attendees, by 1980 comic book conventions in major cities were bringing in tens of thousands of attendees.

The Modern Age of Comic Books

The Modern Age of Comic Books is typically referred to as the period of time spanning 1985 until the present day. I don't think this is particularly accurate, though. Previous comic "ages" have lasted roughly ten to fifteen years and so I think it would be ignoring a lot of comic history to lump the last 30 years into one classification. I think the following classifications make more sense:

The Speculator Age of Comic Books (1985–1996)

The Speculator Age of Comic Books begins with the publications of Frank Miller's *Batman: The Dark Knight Returns* (March 1986), Alan Moore's *Watchmen* (September 1986), and DC's *Crisis on Infinite Earths* (April 1985). These three works set the tone for the darker, grittier stories which became popular throughout the Speculator Age of Comic Books. In *Batman: The Dark Knight Returns*, Bruce Wayne (now in his 50s) has given up the mantle of the Bat and Gotham is overrun with crime. He resumes the role of Batman and is forced to face the idea of his own mortality and the more jarring fact that the city—*his* city—may have moved on without him. *Watchmen* tells the story of a bleak future where costumed vigilantes have been outlawed and the remaining superheroes have either retired or become government agents. A group of older, world-weary former heroes tries to find out who has started killing off retired heroes—all the while trying to keep the world from sliding into World War III. In *Crisis on Infinite Earths*, DC attempted to clean up 50 years of continuity by eliminating the multiverse in a universe-shaking battle in which vast swaths of characters were killed off—including Supergirl and Barry Allen.

Storylines would tend to take a more dark and gritty tone. Superheroes themselves would be rewritten to be less "black and white" and more psychologically complex. Supervillains were given similar treatments. Batman's longtime nemesis, the Joker, was portrayed as a mentally-ill psychopath instead of a giggling, evil criminal mastermind. Longtime foe of the Fantastic Four, Galactus became more of a force of nature controlled by hunger instead of an entity who willingly targeted populated planets for consumption. Magneto went from being a mere villain for the X-Men to fight to a person who was driven to fight for the oppressed people by whatever means necessary. Given a background story as a survivor of the Holocaust, Magneto's motives to fight and his methods became more sympathetic. Writers during this time also played up the parallels between Professor X and Magneto in comparison to Dr. Martin Luther King and Malcolm X—with Professor X professing peace between mankind and mutantkind being a product of goodwill and understanding, whereas Magneto had the desire to force peace between the two sides through whatever methods he saw fit and was clear in the idea that one side would come out the victor and the other side the loser.

As if morally troubled superheroes weren't enough, the Speculator Age also gave rise to the antihero. Whereas Superman and Captain America were motivated to do the right thing because it was the right thing to do, antiheroes found themselves in less altruistic light. An antihero may do the "right thing," but it is typically out of self-interest instead of some grand idealism. This concept completely turned around the concept of the superhero as a cheerful humanitarian willing to sacrifice everything for the greater good. Marvel Comics introduced the Punisher—a damaged Vietnam veteran turned vigilante by the murder of his wife and children, Wolverine—surly and brooding with razor-sharp claws and unbreakable bones thanks to being the subject of medical experimentation at the hands of a secret government agency, and Frank Miller's darker version of Daredevil—who changed from "the sightless swashbuckler" to the self-proclaimed protector of Hell's Kitchen fighting against everyone from the Kingpin of Crime to ninjas from the organization known as the Hand. DC reshaped Catwoman from a burglar with bullwhip and a cat costume to a master criminal who wasn't afraid to change allegiances (even in the middle of a fight) and wrapped up in a love-hate relationship with Batman. Harley Quinn was introduced as the Joker's therapist, Dr. Harleen Quinzel, but enough time around the Clown Prince of Crime transformed her into his part-time accomplice/part-time girlfriend. The unstoppable (and unkillable) alien bounty hunter Lobo was created as a parody of the "grim and gritty" heroes of the time, but his character grew so popular that he became a regular in the DC Universe. Finally, a list of DC Comics' antiheroes wouldn't be complete without a mention of John Constantine—a hard-drinking, chain-smoking conman who also happens to be a powerful sorcerer. John Constantine has fought back demons and devils and saved the world more than a few times, but the jury is still out as to whether he does it for humanitarian reasons or just to keep his own posterior out of the fire. Image Comics debuted their own antihero, the Todd McFarlane creation Spawn. Al Simmons was a Marine and a CIA agent who began to ask too many questions about the "black OPs" portion of his job, so he was killed for his trouble. After his death, Simmons made a deal with the devil to allow him to return to the land of the living and see his wife again. Like all of such deals, the outcome wasn't exactly what Simmons had in mind. He was living again, but he had returned five years after his death. His wife had remarried his best friend and they had a daughter together. As if that wasn't enough, Simmons had been changed into Spawn—a disfigured demonic being who was returned to Earth to do the devil's work. Spawn lived up to the antihero role, brooding in dark alleys and attacking street gangs and other thugs. In the sense of purest vigilante justice, Spawn hunted down a known pedophile and child murderer and brutally killed him.

All of these "heroes" existed in a moral grey area where the concept of right and wrong wasn't set in stone—indeed it could change on a daily basis. For the antihero, rules and laws were constructs that applied to other people, whereas they had their own moral compass (regardless how twisted) to follow. While it would be easy to dismiss the antihero as a product of the angst of the 1980s, the cultural cynicism of post–Vietnam America, or merely a pushback against the previous age's larger-than-life, squeaky-clean superheroes, nearly all of the titles were developed by strong creative teams. The writing was usually quite well done and the characters themselves ended up as more thought provoking than just simple backlash. In fact, many of these characters enjoy tremendous popularity even today. Both Daredevil and the Punisher have ongoing television series broadcast on Netflix. Wolverine has been the subject of several major motion pictures as well as being an integral part of the X-Men movie franchise. John Constantine enjoyed a short television series and the character still makes regular appearances in DC Comics. *Hellblazer* was Vertigo's longest running title before it was finally cancelled. *Constantine*, *Harley Quinn*, and *Spawn* are still being published.

It's impossible to talk about the Speculator Age without actually mentioning the speculators. By the beginning of the Speculator Age, comic book collecting was a well-established hobby and there was a thriving market for older comics. "Key" issues, or issues where something prominent happens (such as the first appearance of a character, the revelation of a character's origin, the first issue of a popular series, or the debut of a famous artist or writer), began to fetch larger and larger prices in the collectors market. The mainstream media eventually discovered this fact and began reporting on the record prices these books were demanding, with all of the hype and hoopla that mainstream media could afford. Comic books were reported to be a good financial investment.[30] This began to fuel the fire for speculators who would buy comics (sometimes multiple copies of the same issue) on the hopes that the comics would increase in value. Comic book publishers did little to discourage this practice. Instead, they would release "gimmick" covers like foil-embossed covers, die-cut covers, glow-in-the-dark covers, hologram covers, and variant covers. A variant cover is a comic that is printed with multiple covers, each with unique cover art. Typically variant covers are sold to comic stores as sales initiatives—for example, if a store would order ten copies of the regular issue of a comic, they would be allowed to purchase one variant cover. This introduced a certain amount of scarcity for the variant covers and drove the demand even higher for speculators.

The 1992 "death" of Superman played a big part in the speculator boom. In the months leading up to the event, DC Comics had been dropping hints that something major was going to happen to the Big Blue Boy Scout. When the rumors were confirmed that Superman was about to meet his match, there was a media frenzy. National periodicals ran headlines about the "Death of Superman." Editorial columns ran articles with weeping, wailing, and gnashing of teeth bemoaning Superman's fate and what such a shocking turn of events could mean to the very soul of America. Superman was DC's most profitable title and so it should have been obvious that there was absolutely no chance that DC was actually going to kill the character off and cancel several long-running comic series. That fact did very little to stop the hype machine once it got rolling, however. Initial orders for *Superman* Vol. 2 #75 (January 1993) were over five million strong before the book even hit comic store shelves. On the day of the book's release some stores had lines around the block and other stores instituted a "one copy per customer" limit.[31]

DC quickly followed this up with the "Knightfall" storyline in which Batman is attacked and beaten by the chemically-enhanced villain Bane. The "Knightfall" storyline culminated in *Batman* #497 (July 1993) in which Bane triumphed over Batman by breaking his back and ending Bruce Wayne's career as Batman forever.

Of course, comic book fans realize there really isn't such a thing as "forever" in comic books. Within a few months' time, Superman was back in the sky over Metropolis and Bruce Wayne was fully healed from his injuries and had resumed the Mantle of the Bat. Just as quickly as the status quo returned to Metropolis and Gotham City, speculators began to realize that their "investments" weren't producing the quick returns that they had expected and they began to sell off. On top of that, in order to feed the speculator frenzy, comic book publishers had published an unprecedented number of titles and essentially flooded the market with their own product—to the point that some stores did not have enough room to display all the new books that were released each week. This made for a recipe for disaster or, in stock market terms, a "contraction." Speculators sold off their comics—often at a loss—just to get rid of them. This caused the values of collectible comic back issues to fall. Speculators in turn stopped buying new comics which hurt overall sales at comic shops. Lower circulation numbers caused comic book publishers to cut titles and produce the remaining titles in lower numbers. The speculator bubble had burst and the repercussions were devastating to the comic book industry. Between 1993 and 1997, two-thirds of all specialty comic book stores went out of business.[32] Comic book publishers were not immune to this either. Broadway Comics, Comico, Continuity Comics, Defiance Comics, Eclipse Comics, First Comics, and Malibu Comics were some of the major comic book publishers to close during this time.[33] Even the mighty Marvel Comics—the House that Stan Built—was forced to file for Chapter 11 Bankruptcy Protection in 1997.[34]

The Creative Age of Comic Books (1997–2007)

The end of the Speculator Age left the comic industry as a whole in a very low place. Speculators had abandoned the market. Many collectors, unhappy with the comic industry, had left as well. This is not an unfounded claim, either. In the rush to feed the speculator frenzy, there was a lot of product released to the market that was, to be kind, not the highest of quality. Comic book publishers realized that readers would be drawn to well-written stories and began to reach outside of the traditional comic book industry for new writing talent. A few comic book writers were already established authors. Neil Gaiman had a long and successful tenure writing *The Sandman* for DC/Vertigo with the series winning several awards over its seven-year publication run. Peter David enjoyed a 12-year run at Marvel Comics writing some of the most memorable storylines in *The Incredible Hulk*. Pulitzer Prize–winning author Michael Chabon has written for both DC and Dark Horse. It is worth mentioning that Michael Chabon won the Pulitzer Prize for Fiction in 2001 for his novel *The Amazing Adventures of Kavalier and Clay* which is about the beginning of the Golden Age of Comic Books. Brad Metzler wrote the *Identity Crisis* miniseries for DC as well as *Green Arrow* and an Eisner Award–winning run on *Justice League of America*. Outside of the comic book industry, Metzler has written best-selling fiction, non-fiction, and children's books. The comic industry has also attracted more than just novelists. Hit TV show *Babylon 5* creator J. Michael Straczynski wrote a well-received, six-year stretch of Marvel's flagship title *Amazing Spider-Man* before spending time writing *Fantastic Four* and *Thor*. Filmmaker Reginald Hudlin, director of *House Party* and *Boomerang*, wrote *Black Panther* for Marvel from 2005 until 2008 including the storyline *Bride of the Panther* in which Black Panther married Storm of the X-Men. Joss Whedon (creator of *Buffy the Vampire Slayer*) wrote *Astonishing X-Men* and *Runaways* for Marvel. DC also took advantage of this influx of creative talent as Richard Donner (director of the *Superman: The Movie*) took over as writer for *Action Comics* in 2006 and Paul Dini, producer and writer of both *Batman: The Animated Series* and *Superman: The Animated Series* began writing *Detective Comics* in 2006 as well.

The Creative Age also saw a change in the way readers would access comic books. Sales of individual comic books bottomed out after the speculator bubble burst and never really recovered. In the early 1990s, a successful comic book title could expect to sell upwards of 100,000 copies per month. By the mid-2000s, a comic title selling 20,000 copies a month was considered to be successful.

While sales for individual monthly comic books were declining, sales for trade paperbacks were on the increase.[35] A trade paperback is a collection of stories which were originally published in monthly installments that are reprinted in a square-bound book format. This is in contrast to regular comic books which are essentially folded and stapled. Trade paperbacks typically collect a single story arc or a collection of stories sharing a story arc or common theme. Typically, a comic book publisher would release a few trade paperbacks a year, reprinting older story arcs which were long out of print, and so the individual back issues were not easily available to the average reader. In the early 2000s, comic book publishers began to produce trade paperbacks more frequently, collecting more recent story arcs. It was not unheard of for a publisher to release a trade paperback collecting a story arc within a month of the last issue of the story arc being published in the monthly comic series. Publishers saw this as a way to draw new readers to the title instead of leaving the reader to have to scrounge around to find all of the back issues of the individual comic books. Some trade paperbacks are given volume numbers so a reader could potentially read an entire comic book series by just reading the trade paperbacks—almost like a serial. Trade paperbacks have become so popular that there are some comic titles that have been saved from cancellation due to the sales of their trade paperbacks.

This has changed the way comic book writers develop their stories as well. In previous comic ages, a story arc could potentially last as long as a writer had creative control of a title. If the writer wanted one long, overarching story that stretched out over many years, this could be done provided the book's sales figures held up. Comic book writers during the Creative Age have learned how the readers expect to be able to consume their product and so most writers now write story arcs that can be told over the course of six to twelve issues—just the right size to be collected in a trade paperback.

Since trade paperbacks are typically collected in a book format with a square spine, a consumer is much more likely to find trade paperbacks on shelves in libraries or for sale in bookstores or even department stores. This fact, plus the influx of more mainstream writers, have gone a long way in helping the comic book industry to survive the dark times brought on by the end of the Speculator Age of Comic Books and still evolve and change for the future.

The Digital Age of Comic Books (2008–present)

Comic books have come a long way from their humble beginning in the 1930s. Once considered "fringe," "lowbrow," or "nerdy" forms of cheap, disposable entertainment, comic books have now grown to become a part of American pop culture. The Digital Age of Comic Books marks the time in which comics have grown beyond the pages of books and made the transition into television, feature-length movies, and other forms of digital media.

While the comic-to-film crossover started gaining traction (and financial success) with the 2000 release of *X-Men*, the tipping point didn't really come until the 2008 release of *Iron Man* and the launch of the multi-movie Marvel Cinematic Universe. Never before has a studio attempted such a bold undertaking. The plan was to have dozens of movies all set in one shared universe with one larger overarching story connecting them all. For die-hard comic fans, this is nothing new. As a matter of fact, this was what comics have done for years. The gamble has paid off for Marvel Comics in a big way. The total box-office gross for all of the films in the Marvel Cinematic Universe at the time of this writing has just exceeded $12 billion! Not to be left out, DC is steadily picking up steam for its own DC Extended Universe with the release of *Man of Steel* (2013), *Batman v Superman: Dawn of Justice* (2016), *Suicide Squad* (2016), *Wonder Woman* (2017), and *Justice League* (2017) as well as upcoming movies for Aquaman, Shazam, and a Wonder Woman sequel to be released by 2019.

Marvel Comics has crossed over into television as well with *Marvel's Agents of S.H.I.E.L.D.*, and *Marvel's Agent Carter*, plus the Netflix exclusives *Marvel's*

Jessica Jones, Marvel's Luke Cage, Marvel's Iron Fist, Marvel's Defenders, and *Marvel's Punisher.* Marvel Comics has also promised television shows for the Runaways, Cloak & Dagger, and the New Warriors. DC is in the TV game as well with *Flash, Arrow, Gotham, Supergirl,* and *DC's Legends of Tomorrow.*

Comic books themselves have evolved in the way they are being made available. In the Golden Age of Comics, the only way a person could buy a comic was to purchase one from a newsstand. By the Bronze Age of Comics, the rise of the specialty comic books store made it easier for comic collectors to find what they wanted. In the Digital Age of Comics, you don't even need to leave the comfort of your house as comics can be bought and read digitally on a computer, tablet, or smartphone.

Marvel Comics offers several options to get digital versions of their comic books. Many of their print comic books have a special code inside which the reader can redeem for a digital version of that book. Trade paperbacks and single comic issues are also available for purchase from Marvel's own digital comic store. Marvel Comics also has the Marvel Unlimited service which is a subscription-based service that allows a reader to have access to over 20,000 digital Marvel comics for a small monthly fee.[36] DC also offers its own service for the purchase of individual digital comics although DC does not offer a subscription-based service like Marvel Unlimited. For more publisher-neutral options, ComiXology is one of the more popular distributors of digital comics. The ComiXology service has over 100,000 comic books available for purchase from Marvel, DC, Dark Horse, Image, and well over 100 different publishers—both large and small. ComiXology also offers ComiXology Unlimited, their own subscription-based service which also gives subscribers access to thousands of comics for a monthly fee. As of April 2014, ComiXology became a subsidiary of Amazon as the powerhouse Internet retailer tries to get a piece of the digital comic book pie.[37]

Comic book conventions have also grown dramatically. Early conventions were fortunate to have a few hundred attendees with a few dozen vendors. Today comic conventions have become huge multi-day celebrations of everything comics and pop culture. Comic conventions now have hundreds of dealers selling comics, books, DVDs, clothing, and other geeky collectibles. Comic book industry professionals are in attendance and fans can meet their favorite comic book writer or artist. Movie and TV stars are available for pictures and autographs. Fans dress up in elaborate "cosplay" costumes—either for fun or to win prizes. The largest comic book convention in America, the New York Comic Con, set an attendance record in 2017 with over 200,000 fans in attendance over the four days of the event.[38]

2

The Birth of the Horror Comic Genre

Comic books have been a part of American culture since the Golden Age of Comic Books in the 1930s, and horror comics have been right there from the very beginning lurking in the shadows. By and large, the most famous comic book from the Golden Age of Comic Books would be *Action Comics* #1 (June 1938) which introduced the world to Superman. Jerry Siegel and Joe Shuster created Superman in 1933 while they were both still in high school in Cleveland, Ohio. They sold the concept of the Superman character to Detective Comics (which would later become DC) and the rest is history. Superman and his fight for "truth, justice, and the American way" created the superhero archetype and would go on to become a cultural icon.[1] It didn't take long for Superman to have plenty of company, either. Over the next few years, other superheroes would be introduced and would go on to become household names as well. Boys and girls alike would save up their pennies and nickels to be able to read of the larger-than-life adventures of Superman, Batman, Wonder Woman, Captain America, Captain Marvel, and the Flash as they beat up on bad guys and left the world a brighter place. While this is all well and good, as fans of the horror genre, we know that you can't have a bright, shining new world without casting some shadows. From these shadows, the first horror comics began to slither into America's consciousness.

Horror comics (and comics in general for that matter) can trace their origins back to pulp magazines or "the pulps." Pulp magazines were fiction magazines which were published as quickly and as cheaply as possible. The "pulp" in the name refers to the low-quality wood pulp paper that was used for the pages of the magazines. In contrast, more "legitimate" magazines were published on high-quality paper and often referred to as "glossies" or "slicks" due to the slick texture of the glossy pages. The average pulp magazine was 128 pages in length. It was also smaller than a "glossy," being only seven inches wide and ten inches tall. The interior pages were printed on thick, coarse wood pulp and the edges of the cream-colored pages were generally left untrimmed and ragged. This obviously gave the magazine a cheap look. That look, plus the pulp magazine's reputation for publishing sensational, lurid, and occasionally exploitative subject matter led to the rise of the term "pulp fiction" to mean any type of low-brow, low-quality literature. While pulp magazines may have deserved the reputation they had, this is not to say that they were all without merit. Some very well-known authors had their work published in pulp magazines. A few of the most recognizable names are: Isaac Asimov, Ray Bradbury, Edgar Rice Burroughs, Agatha Christie, Arthur C. Clarke, Joseph Conrad, Philip K. Dick, F. Scott Fitzgerald, Zane Grey, Robert Heinlein, O. Henry, Frank Herbert, L. Ron Hubbard, Rudyard Kipling, Louis L'Amour, Fritz Leiber, Jack London, H. P. Lovecraft, Upton Sinclair, E. E. Smith, Mickey Spillane, Mark Twain, H. G. Wells, and Tennessee Williams. "Pulp fiction" may have had a bad reputation, but this is some pretty good company to keep!

The first pulp magazine in America was *Argosy*, which began publication in 1896 and by 1902 was selling over half a million copies per month. *Argosy* was a perfect example of a pulp magazine. It was 192 pages long, printed on the off-white pulp paper and sold with the pages left untrimmed. There were no illustrations of any kind—not even on the cover![2] Seeing the success of *Argosy*, publisher Street & Smith, known at the time for publishing boys' weekly and dime novels, entered the pulp magazine business in 1903 with *The Popular Magazine*. It was described as "the biggest magazine in the world" due to the simple fact that *The Popular Magazine* had two more pages of content than *Argosy*. This was solely because *The Popular Magazine* printed content inside the front and back covers whereas *Argosy* did not. Street & Smith continued to up the ante in the pulp magazine market by producing the first pulps with color covers. They also were the first publisher to feature a select group of consistent authors for each magazine. That way if a reader enjoyed reading Zane Grey, for example, they would know which magazine to pick up each month in order to read his work.

Pulp magazines were the most popular during the 1920s through the 1930s. During this time, popular pulps could easily sell over one million copies a month. Popular Publications, a publisher of pulp magazines, reported publishing over 300 different pulp magazines and, at their peak in popularity, more than 42 different titles per month.[3] Pulp magazines began to be separated into different genre magazines instead of having different authors and styles all lumped into a single magazine. Pulp magazines were published in a wide variety of genres including: adventure, detective/mystery, fantasy, crime, humor, romance, science fiction, "spicy" (essentially softcore pornography), war, and Western. The writers in pulp magazines introduced readers to characters who would go on to become household names—even today. Characters like Doc Savage, Hopalong Cassidy, Ka-Zar, Nick Carter, the Shadow, Buck Rogers, Conan the Barbarian, John Carter of Mars, Kull, Tarzan, and Zorro were all featured in pulp magazines.

Of course you couldn't have all of those great writers putting out so much content into that many pulp magazines without there being a horror element. Horror genre pulps (also known as "shudder pulps" or "weird menace") were being published to an eager audience as well. Shudder pulps originally grew out from the detective pulp genre. In the early 1930s, detective pulps started publishing stories with eerie, weird, or even supernatural elements. As the stories grew in popularity, pulp magazines were launched just to print the new "weird menace" stories. *Dime Mysteries, Horror Stories,* and *Terror Tales* were among the most popular shudder pulps. Their sales were just as brisk as the most popular pulp magazines for several years. The stories published in many of the shudder pulps eventually became so lurid and graphic that people began speaking out against the increasingly disturbing content, and the shudder pulp genre began to lose popularity (and circulation numbers) in the early 1940s. The entire pulp magazine genre itself would not fare much better. Paper shortages due to rationing during World War II and the rising costs of printing and publication caused a dramatic decline in pulp magazines. Street & Smith ceased publication of all of their pulp magazines in 1949 in order to concentrate on the more upscale "slicks." In 1957, American News Company, the primary distributor of pulp magazines, went out of business and effectively ended the pulp magazine era. The pulp magazines that remained in print switched over to the smaller "digest" size magazine. The famous *Analog Science Fiction and Fact* remains one of the few publications to start as a pulp and survive until present day—although *Analog Science Fiction and Fact* is now published as a bi-monthly magazine as well as an ebook. Many of the pulp's contributing authors switched to writing full-length books after the collapse of the pulp magazines while others still began writing for the fledgling television industry.[4]

The comic book industry, another industry in its infancy at this time, also drew from the popularity of the shudder pulps and started introducing vampires, monsters, mad scientists and other horror and supernatural elements into their stories.[5] In 1935, National Periodicals (which would later become DC) published the first story of Doctor Occult in *New Fun Comics* #6 (May 1935). Created by Jerry Siegel and Joe Shuster (of Superman fame), Doctor Occult, also known as the Ghost Detective, was a magic-using private detective who specialized in cases involving the supernatural—think of him as a magic-wielding Sam Spade. It is worth noting that Doctor Occult's first appearance in 1935 technically does predate the first appearance of Superman in *Action Comics* #1 which was released in June of 1938. That means that Doctor Occult has the distinction of being one of the very first superheroes—even beating out the Big Blue Boy Scout! In another interesting technicality, Doctor Occult also made an appearance in *The Comics Magazine* #1 published by Centaur Publications as "Dr. Mystic" due to copyright restrictions. This story was continued in DC's *More Fun Comics* #14–17 (October 1936–January 1937). During this story, Doctor Occult/Dr. Mystic travelled to a mystic realm where he flew and wore a cape. Since this story also predates Superman's origin, Doctor Occult was technically the first caped superhero.[6]

Batman even had a run-in with the supernatural around this time. In *Detective Comics* #31–21 (September/October 1939), Batman meets a hooded villain known as the Monk. As it turns out, the Monk was Niccolai Tepes—a vampire. Tepes is never revealed to be related to Vlad Tepes—Dracula himself—but the reader can only assume some type of relation due to the shared last name and penchant for blood drinking. Batman tracks the Monk all the way to Hungary where they clash for the last time. The Monk subdues Batman using his vampiric power of hypnosis and leads Batman into a deadly trap. Of course, the Monk does not stay to make sure that the trap is indeed fatal. Instead, he goes to sleep in his coffin, assured in the notion that Batman has met his doom. Batman, of course, escapes the trap and returns to Tepes' castle where, finding Tepes asleep, he melts down a silver statue and makes a silver bullet which he then uses to shoot Tepes to death while he sleeps.[7] A different take on both the vampire mythology and the character of Batman as we know him to be sure!

Early comics would draw from classic literature for horror elements as well. *Prize Comics* #7 (December 1940) ran the eight-page feature "New Adventures of Frankenstein." Written and drawn by Dick Briefer (under the pseudonym "Frank N. Stein"), "New Adventures of Frankenstein" took Mary Shelley's famous creature and set him loose in 1930s New York City. Pedants will note that the creature in "New Adventures of Frankenstein" is actually called "Frankenstein" whereas the creature in Mary Shelley's novel does not have a name—Frankenstein being the surname of the doctor that created the creature. "New Adventures of Frankenstein" ran through *Prize Comics* #52 (April 1945). During the series, Frankenstein developed an archenemy in Denny "Bulldog" Dunsan; battled Prize Comics' superheroes the Black Owl, the Green Lama, and Dr. Frost; and (like so many other superheroes of the time) even joined the war effort travelling to Europe to assist the Allied troops in fighting Nazis. The title was then converted to a humor series with the publication of *Frankenstein Comics* #1 (undated, 1945). The humorous take on Frankenstein ran through *Prize Comics* #68 (March 1948) as well as through *Frankenstein Comics* #17 (February 1949). Like so many other returning veterans, Frankenstein (now dubbed "The Merry Monster") bought a house in the suburbs and sat about adjusting to peacetime life, complete with homeownership woes and backyard barbecues. The primary difference between Frankenstein and his suburban neighbors is that The Merry Monster's work buddies who came over for his barbecues were the likes of (also humorous takes on) Dracula and the Wolfman. After a three-year hiatus, Briefer brought back the *Frankenstein Comics* series with issue #18 (March 1952) and returned the series to its horror roots. *Frankenstein Comics* remained a horror title until its final issue, #33 (November 1954).[8]

Classic Comics #12 published by Gilberton Publications in June of 1943 adapted the Washington Irving short story "The Legend of Sleepy Hollow." The next issue, *Classic Comics* #13 (August 1943) adapted the Robert Louis Stevenson novella "Strange Case of Dr. Jekyll and Mr. Hyde" as a full-length story—making it the first comic book to feature full-length horror content.[9] It wasn't until 1946 that a comic book was published that contained all original horror content—not a superhero comic with horror elements or an adaptation of a literary work. Avon Publications' *Eerie Comics* #1 was published in late 1946 (with a January 1947 cover date) and had a ten-cent cover price. For one thin dime, anyone picking this book up off the newsstand would have held in their hand the first true horror comic and the origin of the horror comic book genre.[10]

Eerie Comics #1 was a 52-page, full-color comic book. The cover featured a sinister-looking fiend (bearing no small resemblance to Count Orlok from the movie *Nosferatu*) wielding a wicked-looking knife while a young woman lies helplessly bound in front of him on the floor of a ruined building. The entire scene is silhouetted by the full moon behind them. Very sinister stuff! The book is an anthology of six different stories of the supernatural and macabre. "The Eyes of the Tiger" tells the tale of a man haunted by the ghost of a stuffed tiger. "The Man-Eating Lizards" is a story of an island which was inhabited by carnivorous lizards (as one would expect). This story was written by Edward Bellin and drawn by Joe Kubert. Very little is known about Edward Bellin, but Joe Kubert would go on to have an illustrious career as a comic book artist—doing work for both Marvel and DC, but probably best known for his work at DC on *Sgt. Rock* and *G.I. Combat*. In 1976, he would found (and teach at) the Joe Kubert School of Cartoon and Graphic Art—a technical school which teaches the principles of sequential art and the craft of the comic book industry and that has produced some of the biggest names in the modern comic book industry. "The Strange Case of Henpecked Harry" was a story of a man haunted by the bloody corpse of his murdered wife. This story was drawn by Fred Kida who drew the Golden Age of Comics aviation hero Airboy as well as *The Amazing Spider-Man* newspaper comic strip. Other feature stories include "Dead Man's Tale," "Proof," and "Mystery of Murder Manor," with a two-page humorous tale starring Goofy Ghost to finish out the issue. Very little is known about the rest of the creative team who contributed to the book.[11]

Horror fans had to wait a long time for *Eerie Comics* #2, though. The title ran for exactly one issue and then was not published again until 1951 when it was restarted with issue #1. *Eerie* #1 reprinted "The Strange Case of Henpecked Harry" from *Eerie Comics* #1 changing the title to "The Subway Horror!." New features included "The Werewolf of Warsham Manor" in which the last remaining member of the Warsham clan discovers a terrible family secret (HINT: it involves a werewolf), "King of the Living Dead" in which a kidnapping leads to the discovery of a zombie army, and "The Monster From the Pit" in which a pair of Transylvanian policemen try to stop a mass murderer as only they know how.[12] The series would continue for 17 issues with the final issue being published in September of 1954. The title was then changed to a science fiction anthology title and renamed *Strange Worlds*.[13]

While Avon Publications' *Eerie Comics* #1 was the first horror comic book, it was technically a "one-shot" and since Avon Publications didn't launch the ongoing series *Eerie* until 1951, the distinction of the first regularly published ongoing horror comic series goes to American Comics Group's *Adventures Into the Unknown*.[14] *Adventures Into the Unknown* #1 was published in September of 1948 and ran for a total of 174 issues with the last issue being published in August of 1967. *Adventures Into the Unknown* #1 featured an adaptation of Horace Walpole's novel *The Castle of Otranto*—generally regarded as the first Gothic novel. It is a very abbreviated adaptation as the story in *Adventures Into the Unknown* is only seven pages in length.[15] *Adventures Into the Unknown* would fill its nearly 20-year run with tales of werewolves, vampires, ghosts, haunted houses, ax-wielding maniacs, killer puppets, demons, escaped lunatics, and other supernatural excitement. It also had the distinction of being one of the few horror comic titles to survive the backlash brought on by the Comics Code Authority later in the 1950s.

In the same month that *Adventures Into the Unknown* debuted, comic publisher Entertaining Comics (more commonly known as EC Comics) published their first horror story entitled "Zombie Terror" as a short feature in their superhero comic *Moon Girl* #5.[16] "Zombie Terror" was written and drawn by the (at the time) relatively unknown Johnny Craig. Within a couple of years, EC Comics would rise to prominence as the most prolific and well-known publisher of horror comics and Johnny Craig would go right along with them. He would bring his own unique style to the genre and become one of the industry's most recognizable horror comic artists.

Superhero comic books had been extremely popular from the beginning of the Golden Age of Comic Books until the end of World War II. As America adjusted to peace, reader's taste began to change. Sales for superhero comic books dropped off and comic book publishers started branching out into new genres—with horror, of course, being one of them. With the publication of *Adventures Into the Unknown*, the horror comic boom had started. Over the next several months, many other comic book publishers would either launch new horror titles or convert existing titles to horror titles.

In November of 1948, Trans-World Publications published the one-shot *Mysterious Traveler Comics* #1 based on the Mutual Broadcasting Network's radio show of the same name. The comic was an anthology of crime and science fiction stories, but it also featured a comic adaptation of Edgar Allan Poe's "The Tell-Tale Heart" which was reprinted from Charlton Comics' *Yellowjacket Comics* #6.[17]

Atlas Comics (which would eventually become Marvel Comics) took their existing superhero title *Sub-Mariner Comics* and converted it to the horror comic genre, renaming it *Amazing Mysteries* starting with issue #32 (May 1949). Atlas changed their superhero anthology book *Marvel Mystery Comics* to the horror title *Marvel Tales* starting with issue #93 (August 1949). Atlas even went as far as changing *Captain America Comics* to *Captain America Weird Tales,* making it into a horror fiction title without Captain America appearing in it at all.[18] Harvey Comics also reformatted their superhero book *Black Cat* into the horror title *Black Cat Mysteries* with issue #30 (August 1951). *Black Cat Mysteries* delved deep into the horror line to the point that panels from issues #36 and #39 were actually featured in Dr. Fredric Wertham's book, *Seduction of the Innocent* (obviously not as a good example). Issue #51 even has one completely black panel where the entire panel had to be censored due to restrictions as to what could be displayed in a comic book after the Comics Code Authority came into existence. *Black Cat Mysteries* became a Western comic with issue #54 (February 1955) where it was retitled *Black Cat Western Mystery* before going fully over to *Black Cat Western* for issues #55 and #56 (April 1955 and October 1955). *Black Cat Western* lasted all of three issues before the title reverted to *Black Cat Mystery* with issue #57 (January 1956) and then changing again to *Black Cat Mystic* and becoming a supernatural title with issue #58 (July 1956). *Black Cat Mystic* lasted until issue #62 (March 1958), at which point the title reverted back to its superhero origins and became *Black Cat* again until its final issue #65 (April 1963).[19]

It is impossible to mention the horror comic boom of the Golden Age of Comics without the most famous horror comic publisher: EC Comics. EC Comics was a powerhouse of the industry and changed the face of comics forever. They are known for producing possibly the best-known and most popular horror comics ever published and launching the careers of some of the best-known names in the industry. Their rise and untimely collapse is one of the pivotal stories of not only the horror comic genre, but of the comic industry itself.

EC Comics was founded in 1944 by Max Gaines. Gaines had been a part of the comic book industry since its birth. In 1933, when Gaines was a salesman for Eastern Color Printing Company, he and sales manager Harry I. Wildenberg worked in tandem with Dell Publishing to produce a collection of previously published newspaper comic strips bound into a 36-page booklet. This booklet, with the title *Famous Funnies: A Carnival of Comics* was distributed through the Woolworth's department store—possibly as a promotional giveaway. *Famous Funnies: A Carnival of Comics* is more famously known by comic historians as the first comic book.[20] By 1944, Max Gaines was the editor of All-American Publications, a comic book company that was merged into DC that same year. When the merger happened, Gaines left All-American Publications while retaining the rights to the comic book *Picture Stories from the Bible*. Gaines started EC Comics (which at the time stood for Educational Comics) with the intention to create comics about science, history, and Bible stories and market them to churches and schools. Max Gaines ran the day-to-day operations of EC Comics until his untimely death in 1947 when he was killed in a boating accident on Lake Placid at the age of 53. Max's son, William Gaines, had served four years in the Army Air Corps and by 1947, he was a senior at New York University pursuing a career as a chemistry teacher. Upon his father's death, William Gaines returned home to arrange his father's funeral, to help out his widowed mother, and to ultimately sell off EC Comics. William had worked for his father when he was younger and found the experience to be less than enjoyable. Max Gaines was a hard-nosed, loud aggressive man with a vicious temper and, like many other men of this time, was harder on his son than he was anyone else. William Gaines had no experience in the comic book business and even less desire for it. His plan was to find a buyer for EC Comics and sell it for a fair price to make sure that his mother was taken care of. His mother convinced him not to sell off the company as it was all they had left of his father. She persuaded William to take over the company and run it for a little while until it was back on its feet. Then he could step away from the business and leave the day-to-day operations to Max's longtime circulation manager, Sol Cohen. William would be free to finish his degree at NYU and get a job teaching chemistry at a local high school. His mother would live off the income from EC Comics and everything would work out fine.[21]

It wasn't until William began looking more closely at the situation that he discovered how dire it actually was. No company would have been interested in buying EC Comics at any price. EC Comics itself was struggling. The company was over $100,000 in debt. Its titles were not selling and its characters had no market value. In an attempt to copy Wonder Woman, EC had a title called *Moon Girl*. In an attempt at a "celebrity comic," EC had Blackstone the Magician—a low-rent Houdini rip-off. Max Gaines' ideas for selling science, history, and Bible comics just weren't panning out. The company (and William's mother's financial security) was in serious trouble.[22]

In an effort to help revitalize the company, Sol Cohen introduced William Gaines to Al Feldstein, a comic artist who was working on "teen humor" comics for Fox Comics. Feldstein was young, talented, and (most importantly) would work cheap. Sol Cohen also introduced William Gaines to the EC Comics' Art Department. The introduction couldn't have taken too much time as the Art Department consisted entirely of artist Johnny Craig. EC Comics had a serious hole to dig themselves out of. Obviously, sales had to increase. William Gaines knew that their lineup of titles was all wrong. Crime comics were popular in 1947 and EC Comics wasn't publishing any, so William Gaines and his crew threw everything they had into crime comics. *Moon Girl* became *Moon Girl Fights Crime*. *Blackstone the Magician* became *Blackstone the Magician Detective Fights Crime*. William Gaines had decided that he was going to save his father's company, but he was going to do it in his own unconventional way. Even Sheldon "Shelly" Mayer, comic artist, writer, and editor (and longtime family friend) once said, "I got the feeling that Bill went into the business as a joke to see if he could screw up things, change them for his own private amusement, and still manage to make money doing it."[23] Oddly enough, that's exactly what happened. EC Comics titles sales improved. William Gaines found he was able to attract new, young talent and added artists Johnny Severin, Wally Wood, and Will Elder to the EC stable.[24]

In 1950, William Gaines took EC Comics in a bold new direction. He launched the "EC New Trend," a line of new titles aimed directly at teenage and adult readers. By this time, the horror comic book genre was quickly growing in popularity and EC Comics capitalized on this in a big way. They launched *Haunt of Fear, Vault of Horror, Tales From the Crypt, Weird Science,*

Weird Fantasy and *Crime SupenStories*—a crime comic title with a spooky edge to it. Gaines and crew were all fans of the radio suspense programs and they patterned their new line of horror comics on them. Complex plots, lurid descriptions, cruelly funny twist endings, and packed with some of the most intense and graphic artwork ever seen on newsstands, EC's New Trend line was a breakout hit. Sales increased and teenage (and adult) fans began sending in fan letters. The company's new direction wasn't for everyone, though. Sol Cohen was so disgusted with the trend that he quit EC Comics altogether. At one point, the FBI even opened a file on Gaines and the company, considering their publications to be subversive. Gaines and EC Comics thrived on the attention.[25]

EC Comics thrived on the attention of the fans as well. EC Comics was one of the first comic book publishers in the industry that printed fan's letters in the pages of the comic itself. Not only did this allow the fans to develop a relationship with the artist and writers, but it also allowed fans to develop relationships with other comic book fans. Letters to the editor were printed with the writer's address listed so fans could correspond with each other. At a time when comics were sold on newsstands and there were no such things as comic conventions, this provided a unique way for comic fans to find people sharing similar interests. EC Comics also had the first official comic book fan club—the National EC Fan-Addict Club. For the low cost of one quarter, EC Comics fans would get a membership certificate ("suitable for framing"), a wallet-sized membership card, a membership patch, and "a very distinguished-looking membership pin."[26] Many of these items are sought after by collectors still today.

EC Comics also took a very different approach with their artists. At this point in time in the comic book industry, most major comic book publishers had a "house style." In other words, any artwork in any comic book by the publisher was going to have a particular look to it. Artists were expected to conform to the house style and make their work look as close as possible to it. It also goes without saying that artists were not recognized for their work. It was very rare indeed that an artist's name was ever credited in a comic book. EC Comics would have none of this. Each and every EC Comics artist was encouraged to develop and draw to their own style. Not only were they allowed to be credited as the artist of their work, but they were given full-page biographies in the comics.[27]

EC Comics is most well-known for its famous (or infamous) trilogy of horror books: *Tales From the Crypt*, *The Vault of Horror*, and *The Haunt of Fear*. *Tales From the Crypt* ran 27 bi-monthly issues from 1950 through 1955 (with the first three issues titled *The Crypt of Terror*). *The Vault of Horror* ran

29 bi-monthly issues from 1950 through 1955. *The Haunt of Fear* ran 28 bi-monthly issues from 1950 through 1954.

Each title was a horror anthology and so each issue contained several different stories—usually written and drawn by the same creative team. Each title had its own "horror host" (or "GhouLunatic") to set up the stories, introduce the book, and to interact with the reader, breaking the fourth wall in an irreverent, pun-filled commentary to lighten the gruesome stories. *Tales From the Crypt* had the Crypt Keeper. *The Vault of Horror* had the Vault Keeper. *The Haunt of Fear* had the Old Witch. While each title had its own particular horror host, the overall hosting duties were split between all of the GhouLunatics so an issue of *Haunt of Fear* would contain two stories told by the Old Witch, one by the Crypt Keeper (host of *Tales From the Crypt*), and one by the Vault Keeper (host of *The Vault of Horror*). The three GhouLunatics would quarrel with each other in a professional rivalry which was played up for comic effect. This light-hearted (sometimes irreverent) back-and-forth interaction would influence many others in the comic industry. The most famous example of this influence would have to be the writing style of Stan "The Man" Lee and the Mighty Marvel Bullpen at Marvel Comics during the 1970s.

All of the EC Comics horror books told morality stories—granted, they were horrifying and gruesome morality stories, but the main protagonist would always get their comeuppance in some truly grisly fashion. For example:

"And All Through the House"—originally published in *Vault of Horror* #35 (March 1954)
    In this tale, a woman murders her husband on Christmas Eve. Unbeknownst to her, a raving maniac has escaped from the local asylum and (dressed in a Santa costume) decides to pay her a holiday visit. The woman knows that she can't call the police or her own crime will be discovered so she must defend herself as best as she can—with predictable results.

"Trapped!"—originally published in *Vault of Horror* #21 (October 1951)
    A robber is on the run from the law with his suitcase full of stolen cash. Desperate to get away, he doesn't allow anyone or anything to stand in his way. Could a lowly fly possibly be his downfall?

"A Strange Undertaking…"—originally published in *Haunt of Fear* #6 (March 1951)
    A cemetery caretaker takes revenge on his enemies by desecrating their bodies and refusing to bury them. Unfortunately for him, the dead have an opinion about this.

"Squash......... Anyone?"—originally published in *Tales From the Crypt* #32 (October 1952)

A circus elephant trainer murders his wife and makes it look like a part of his act. Imagine his surprise when his dead wife and the elephant make a surprise appearance at his next show!

"Foul Play"—originally published in *The Haunt of Fear* #19 (May-June 1953)

A baseball team is looking for revenge after a member of a rival team murders one of their own. They lure the murderer to a secluded baseball field late at night and get their revenge. They kill him and, in typical EC Comics horror fashion, dismember his body and play one last game of baseball with him—literally. His intestines are the lines for the bases. His lungs and liver mark the bases themselves with his heart taking the place of home base. The batter uses a severed leg as a bat and the pitcher, of course, uses the head as a baseball.

Stories in EC Comics' horror anthologies were influenced by the works of Edgar Allan Poe, H.P. Lovecraft, Oscar Wilde, Robert Bloch, W.W. Jacobs, Bram Stoker, and Maurice Level. Although sometimes the "influence" was stronger than others. EC Comics *Weird Fantasy* #13 ran a story called "Home to Stay!" that was a combination of two of science fiction author Ray Bradbury's short stories: "Kaleidoscope" and "The Rocket Man." Bradbury personally contacted Gaines and praised him for EC's treatment of his work. He also mentioned that Gaines seemed to have "inadvertently" neglected to send him the check for the use of secondary rights on the stories. Gaines immediately got in touch with Bradbury (and paid him) and then worked out an arrangement so that EC Comics could publish official adaptations of Bradbury's work. This led to even more popularity for EC Comics' horror and science fiction titles.[28]

Horror comics vaulted EC Comics to astounding success. At their height of popularity, EC Comics' horror "big three" would sell nearly half a million copies of each issue every time it would hit the newsstands.[29] Other comic publishers that saw EC Comics' success with the horror titles quickly brought their own horror comic offerings to the newsstands. Ziff-Davis released *Weird Adventures* and *Weird Thrillers*.[30] St. John Publications released *Weird Horrors*.[31] Key Publications released *Weird Chills*, *Weird Mysteries*, and *Weird Tales of the Future*.[32] Comic Media released *Weird Terror*.[33] Star Publications released *Ghostly Weird Stories*.[34] Quality Comics released *Web of Evil*.[35] Ace Comics released *Web of Mystery*.[36] Premier Magazines released *Horror From the Tomb*.[37] Harvey Comics released *Tomb of Terror*, *Witches Tales*, and *Chamber of Chills Magazine*.[38] Avon Comics released *Witchcraft*.[39] Ajax-Farrell Publications released *Fantastic Fears*.[40] Fawcett Publications released *Worlds of Fear* and *This Magazine is Haunted*.[41] Charlton Comics released *The Thing*.[42] Atlas Comics (which would become Marvel Comics) released several horror titles including *Adventures Into Weird Worlds, Adventures Into Terror, Menace, Journey Into Mystery,* and *Strange Tales*.[43] Horror comics were everywhere. Between 1949 and 1955 Atlas published 399 issues of 18 separate horror titles, American Comics Group (ACG) published 123 issues of five horror titles, and Ace Comics published 98 issues of five horror titles.[44] In comparison, EC Comics published 87 issues of *Tales From the Crypt, Vault of Horror,* and *Vault of Fear* during the same timeframe.

Horror comic books hit their peak of popularity between 1950 and 1955. Publishers were racing to get new horror comics titles on the newsstands and horror comic fans were buying them just as quickly as they could be published. Unfortunately, things were about to get much worse for horror comics as a drastic shift in public perception was happening.

3

Seduction of the Innocent

Post–World War II America did have a growing problem with juvenile delinquency. This fact is undeniable. In 1942, New York City reported 3,691 arrests of juveniles under the age of 16. By 1959, this figure had skyrocketed to 11,365 and similar trends were being seen all across the country.[1] Juvenile Delinquency is classified as any sort of crime committed by an offender under the age of 18. The law doesn't take into account the severity of the crime so anything from petty theft to attempted murder is viewed by the law to be a juvenile delinquent office. This means a five-year-old kid who shoplifts a ten-cent pack of chewing gum is no more or less a juvenile delinquent than a seventeen-year-old who flies into a rage and beats someone so severely that they have to be admitted to the hospital. It is also worth pointing out that children under the age of 18 are also subject to "status crimes" or acts that are illegal simply due to the fact that the person committing them is a juvenile. These "status crimes" would be things like underage consumption of alcohol, curfew violations, driving a vehicle without a license, truancy, purchase of cigarettes, disorderly conduct (which most municipalities would charge runaways with), and the famous "incorrigible behaviour" (essentially acting out in an uncontrolled manner—pretty much a job description for the average teenager).[2]

Juvenile delinquency, like most societal problems, is a complex issue. It is impossible to find one basic cause for the rise in the rate of juvenile delinquency throughout the 1950s. In fact, it is still impossible today to name a single cause even looking back through nearly 70 years of historical data. There were several factors that most likely contributed to the trend. Teenagers during the 1950s were an increasingly marginalized group. Adults had returned home from serving in World War II, settled down, and started families. This, of course, prompted the post–World War II "baby boom." A teenager during this time would be stuck in a type of limbo—they weren't adult enough to have jobs and families, but they were too old to be the children of the "baby boom." Teenage culture as we know it in today's society didn't exist and so teenagers of this time were forced to struggle to find not only their own identity, but their place in society. Their beliefs, values, fashion, musical tastes and speech were different from their parents, teachers, and other adults. This was puzzling and distressing to parents and they began searching for an explanation for this. One of the more prevalent ideas was the thought that the rapidly changing forms of mass popular culture (movies, television, radio, and comic books) had led to a "misshapen generation of boys and girls."[3]

Not being recognized as a unique cultural group meant that teenagers were not targeted by advertisers nor were there any forms of media (newspapers, radio, or television) that were aimed directly at them. This was complicated by the fact that American society was moving towards more urban population centers. Families were moving away from farms and rural areas into cities and suburbs in order to find better paying employment. A move away from the rural way of life meant that young boys were not expected to start work as soon as they had been and young girls were no longer expected to marry until they were older. More focus on education meant more encouragement for children not only to attend school, but to also complete school and graduate before they were expected by society to get a job and get married. Now a young person wasn't considered to be a full-fledged adult until they were 18. America was prosperous in the years after World War II and so jobs were plentiful—so plentiful, in fact, that school-aged boys and girls were encouraged to get part-time jobs after school and on weekends in order to ease their transition into the workforce and to teach them the "value of a dollar." This put more purchasing power than ever before in the hands of teenagers. Despite not being officially targeted by the media, teenagers in the 1950s had more access to news and information than had previously been possible for other generations. Newspapers, movies, radio, and the new media of television brought the outside world right to a teenager's doorstep. Just like the rapid growth of the Internet in the early 2000s, this access to a wealth of nearly instant information was both a blessing and a curse. New information was flowing in so rapidly and from so many different sources, it was very difficult for parents to have full control over what their children saw and heard. This rapid influx of information also served to help fan the flames of the juvenile delinquency issue. Just like today's news, there was a great deal of news coverage about the "hot topic" of the day—which, of course, was the growing juvenile delinquency problem. As juvenile delinquency rates increased, the media spent more time reporting on the issue and so the issue loomed larger and larger in everyone's mind. Parents, rallied to action by the increased news coverage, called for a greater police presence in their communities. Responding to the request of the parents of a community, law enforcement more closely monitored the activities of local teenagers. This, in turn, led to more teenagers being arrested. More teenagers being arrested caused the juvenile delinquency rates to continue to increase, which caused sensationalist news agencies to dedicate even more time to covering the ever-increasing juvenile delinquency rates—essentially catching themselves in a vicious cycle.[4]

The "generation gap" was a real issue as well. Adults in the 1950s had grown up either serving in World War II or living on a wartime home front. Many of them either lived through or had memories of the Great Depression before that. This was a generation that was used to sacrifice and "make do or do without." America survived World War II essentially unscathed. No major battles were fought on American soil and so the country and its infrastructure as a whole remained intact. Unlike countries in Europe and the Far East, America didn't have to struggle with rebuilding houses, roads, factories, bridges, and sea ports. This meant that the American economy became very prosperous in the post-war years. Americans had modern houses with electricity, running water, kitchen appliances, radios, televisions, and other luxuries. American workers had easy access to well-paying jobs in the booming manufacturing sector and they got to work driving their new cars on the new freeway system. A teenager coming of age during this time would only know prosperity and growth. Things like food rationing, gasoline rationing, scrap metal drives, air raids, citywide blackouts, the draft, and hundreds of other wartime sacrifices were only a memory to them at best. Teenagers in the 1950s had a totally different childhood than their parents. On its face, this seems quite obvious, but the experiences of the two generations were so widely different that it hardly seems likely that there wouldn't be some type of intergenerational friction.

The 1950s was the beginning of the American Dream of a house in the suburbs with a white picket fence and 2.5 children. Television shows like *Leave It to Beaver*, *Father Knows Best*, and *Adventures of Ozzie & Harriet* reinforced these ideals. Adults at the time, growing up in the times that they did, held to the strict adherence of society's rules. Rules were what kept things running smoothly. A man had to look a certain way. If he worked in an office, he wore a suit and tie to work every day. Likewise, boys and girls were expected to look and behave in a particular way. A boy was expected to keep his hair cut short. A boy's hair touching the collar of his shirt was simply out of the question. Likewise, when going out—even to school—a boy was expected to dress appropriately, so a nice collared shirt and slacks—blue jeans were generally discouraged. Girls were held to similar standards. A girl was supposed to wear a dress or a skirt to school or downtown and not pants. Boys and girls were often encouraged to address their teachers or elders with "Sir" or "Ma'am." "Children should be seen but not heard" was a popular mantra, but what was society supposed to do with the group of young people who were neither children nor adults? The term "teen-ager" (later shortened to "teenager") only started to see widespread use during this time to describe this group.[5]

The 1950s was a decade of fear. America and the Allied forces had triumphed over the Axis powers in World War II, but they saw a worldwide conflict which brought civilization right up to the brink of total and absolute destruction. The horrors of the war only served to demonstrate how truly evil mankind could be. Even in victory, Americans still had to worry about the new enemy—Communism. In 1947, President Truman signed an executive order to screen federal employees for associations deemed "totalitarian, Fascist, Communist, or subversive" or advocating "to alter the form of Government of the United States by unconstitutional means." In 1949 a high-level State Department official was convicted of perjury in a case of espionage. The Soviet Union (a former ally during World War II and now on the other side of the Iron Curtain in the increasingly tense Cold War) tested their first atomic bomb and the very next year the Korean War started. In 1950, Senator Joe McCarthy presented a list of Communist Party members who were actively working at the State Department. Senator McCarthy's insistence that members of the Communist Party had infiltrated the very fabric of American society only served to fan the flames of paranoia. Americans had their "Other"—their bogeyman, the target for all of their pent-up fear. As long as someone followed the rules and was a good red-blooded, God-fearing American, they were fine. Complicate this by adding in a group of alienated, isolated, marginalized youths who were in the throes of adolescence and, by nature, were a ball of angst, rebellion, and out-of-control hormones and now your own teenage son or daughter could also be an Other. Movies of the time like *Blackboard Jungle, Reefer Madness, High School Hellcats, The Delinquents, Girls Town, Crime in the Streets*, and *Rebel Without a Cause* only served to sensationalize and exploit the issue.

The 1950s definitely had a dark undercurrent. While everything appeared to be squeaky-clean on the surface, neighbors were encouraged to watch their neighbors for signs that they could be a Communist sleeper agent. Children didn't fare much easier. Granted, there was a growing problem with juvenile crime in America at the time, something as simple as chewing gum in class, talking back to your parents, or even driving a souped-up "hot rod" car could get a teenager accused of being a juvenile delinquent. The issue had clearly spun out of control, but instead of trying to quell the hysteria, parents, police, and government officials wanted to find the cause. Nearly all of the professional social workers, psychologists, sociologists, and criminologists of the time openly denied any link between juvenile delinquency and comic books specifically or mass media in general. The consensus was that juvenile delinquency was a product of the family environment. This, of course, was not a popular opinion because there was no easy fix for environmental issues, so the general public found it much easier to lay the blame on comic books and mass media since it was a relatively easy target.[6]

By the late 1940s, crime and horror comic books were starting to come under public scrutiny. A growing number of people were concerned that the images presented in horror and crime comic books were having adverse effects on children. Some groups were beginning to put forth the idea that horror and crime comic books were responsible for the county's increase in the rate of juvenile delinquency.[7] Several cities throughout the United States began to institute bans on comic books. In 1948, Bellingham, Washington, passed a binding prohibition against the sale of 50 specific comic book titles and on September 23, 1948, the County of Los Angeles banned the sale of crime comics to minors. The American Municipal Society reported that in 1948 alone, nearly 50 municipalities had instituted some type of ban against the sale of certain comic books.[8] Some schools and parishes went as far as to host bonfires for the burning of comic books.[9] Lawsuits regarding the banning of sales of comic books made it to the United States Supreme Court. On March 29, 1948, the United States Supreme Court ruled that any law outlawing publications of "pictures and stories of deeds of bloodshed, lust, or crime" was unconstitutional thus overturning the local bans on the sale of comic books.[10]

In March of 1948, a discussion regarding the effects comic books on children was broadcast on the ABC Radio program *America's Town Meeting of the Air*. The program featured a debate between John Mason Brown, the drama critic for the weekly magazine *Saturday Review of Literature,* and Al Capp—a lecturer and "wisecracking cartoonist" who drew the popular comic strip *Li'l Abner*. Brown argued against comic books and he was supported in his argument by author and *Vogue* editor Marya Mannes. Capp adopted the pro-comic stance and he was supported in his argument by *Parents' Magazine* publisher George Hecht. Brown's argument was that comic books contaminated children's culture. Brown referred to comic books as the "lowest, most despicable, and most harmful form of trash, designed for readers who are too lazy to read." He went on to call comic books "the marijuana of the nursery, the bane of the bassinet, the horror of the house, the curse of the kids, and a threat to the future." Capp would defend comics by pointing out the fact that the murder, crime, and violence depicted in crime and horror comics was no different than what was written about daily in the newspapers. Children have had ready access to newspapers for years and nobody has ever tried to link reading a newspaper to juvenile delinquency. Capp would continue to say that comic strips themselves were "as old a form as the written word itself." The airing of the broadcast generated a record response of over 6,000 letters. The opening statements and highlights of the debate were published in the March 20 *Saturday Review of Literature*.[11]

The tide had already turned against horror comic books, though. On March 18, 1948, noted psychiatrist Dr. Fredric Wertham hosted a symposium at the New York Academy of Medicine called "Psychopathology of Comic Books." Speaking at the symposium were author and folklorist Gershon Legman; author and psychiatrist Dr. Hilde Mosse; Paula Elkisch, a psychoanalyst specialized in child psychology and the psychoanalytical analysis of literary works; and child psychiatrist Marvin L. Blumberg. The speakers were universally against comic books. They spoke out against comic books as an unhealthy escape mechanism and stated that comic books taught children that violence was the only solution to their problems. Comic books, they contended, stirred primitive impulses that retarded the development of socially desirable behavior and attitudes. Dr. Wertham did invite some comic book industry professionals to the symposium to present their point of view. Present were cartoonist and Airboy creator Charles Biro, comic book artist Alden Getz, and cartoonist (and eventual editor of *Mad*) Harvey Kurtzman. Biro, Getz, and Kurtzman were given a chance to speak, but their speaking opportunities were very abbreviated. When criticized about this, Dr. Wertham unapologetically said, "I am even more guilty than that: once I conducted a symposium on alcoholism and didn't invite a single distiller." Each speaker's opening remarks as well as a summary of the symposium was published in the *American Journal of Psychotherapy*.[12]

In the March 25, 1948, issue of *Collier's Weekly*, film critic Judith Crist published the article "Horror in the Nursery" in which Crist interviewed Dr. Wertham and gave him an avenue to present his findings from the symposium to a wider audience. Crist illustrated Dr. Wertham's major points by introducing anecdotal evidence from his case studies—a technique Dr. Wertham himself would come to use in his later articles and books. Dr. Wertham would reiterate several points—interspersing his points with stories of children who acted out the comic book stories they read for dramatic effect. Dr. Wertham pointed out exactly how pervasive comic books were. He estimated there were approximately 60 million comic books published each month with some children admitting to reading as many as 20 comic books a week. In his defense, Dr. Wertham described himself as "a voice for the thousands of troubled parents who, like myself, are primarily concerned with their children's welfare." Wertham went on to attack those members of his profession who worked as consultants to publishers—a fairly common practice of the time. Dr. Wertham dismisses these individuals saying, "The fact that some child psychiatrists endorse comic books does not prove the healthy state of comic books. It only proves the unhealthy state of psychiatry." Dr. Wertham continued to state that comic book reading was an influencing factor in the case of every delinquent or emotionally disturbed child he studied. He concluded the article by calling for formal legislation against comic books. "The time has come to legislate these books off the newsstands and out of the candy stores."[13]

Soon after the ABC radio broadcast aired, Dr. Wertham was given another opportunity to present his views to a broad audience. Norman Cousins, the editor for the *Saturday Review of Literature*, asked Dr. Wertham to write an article for the publication. The article entitled "The Comics ... Very Funny" was published in the May 29, 1948, issue of the *Saturday Review of Literature*.[14] In the article, Dr. Wertham reinforced his views regarding the harmful effects of comic books on children. The article essentially rehashed Dr. Wertham's presentation from his "Psychopathology of Comic Books" symposium and his article in *Collier's Weekly*. Dr. Wertham began the article with a long list of more anecdotal evidence which he claimed demonstrated that children were acting out the violent acts that they read about in comic books. The article also provided some illustrations including two comic book panels—one showing a woman being attacked by an ape and another showing a woman, bound and helpless, with a needle about to be plunged into her eye (an example of Dr. Wertham's "injury to eye" fixation). Also shown was the cover of *Jo-Jo: Congo King* #15 (May 1948) which showed a scantily clad woman in the foreground being pursued by a man dressed only in a loincloth and riding a water buffalo. Dr. Wertham borrowed a turn of phrase from John Mason Brown in labeling the illustrations "Marijuana of the Nursery."[15] The *Saturday Review of Literature* article was also to be published in a condensed form in the August 1948 *Reader's Digest*.

In response to the increasingly bad press, several comic book publishers banded together and formed the Association of Comics Magazine Publishers (ACMP). The ACMP was an industry trade group formed in June of 1948 with the intent to regulate the content published in comic books.[16] Founding members of the ACMP were: Phil Keenan of Hillman Periodicals; Leverett Gleason of Lev Gleason Publications; William Gaines of EC Comics; Harold

Moore, publisher of *Famous Funnies*; Rae Herman of Orbit Publications; distributors Frank Armer and Irving Manheimer; and with George T. Delacorte, Jr., founder of Dell Publications serving as president.[17] In 1948, the ACMP released their "Publisher's Code" which drew heavily from the Hollywood Production Code (or the "Hays Code") which was also constructed to stave off external regulation. The 1948 ACMP Publisher Code was a simple six points:

1. Sexy, wanton comics should not be published. No drawing should show a female indecently or unduly exposed, and in no event more nude than in a bathing suit commonly worn in the United States of America.

2. Crime should not be presented in such a way as to throw sympathy against the law and justice or to inspire others with the desire for imitation. No comics shall show the details and methods of a crime committed by a youth. Policemen, judges, Government officials, and respected institutions should not be portrayed as stupid, ineffective, or represented in such a way to weaken respect for established authority.

3. No scenes of sadistic torture should be shown.

4. Vulgar and obscene language should never be used. Slang should be kept to a minimum and used only when essential to the story.

5. Divorce should not be treated humorously or represented as glamorous or alluring.

6. Ridicule or attack on any religious or racial group is never permissible.[18]

The ACMP hired a team of reviewers to review the art and dialog of the comic books submitted to them. Comic books that complied with the code were awarded the ACMP's "Seal of Approval." Despite the strong initial support, the ACMP ran into problems very early on. Comic book publishers quickly broke ranks and began withdrawing from the ACMP. Some publishers left because they didn't want to be associated with the publishers of what they considered to be "inferior" comic books. Some publishers left due to objections regarding the ACMP code and their methods of enforcement. Other publishers left due to the time and expense involved in the prepublication review process. Some publishers chose to ignore the ACMP altogether. Despite having the founder of Dell Publications as the ACMP's president, Dell Comics never joined the ACMP. By 1950, there were just three comic book publishers left participating in the ACMP review process and those publishers had discovered that they could make use of the ACMP Seal of Approval with little or no prepublication review process—thus fully defeating the entire purpose of the ACMP in the first place. By the end of 1950, the ACMP had completely disbanded.[19]

Dr. Wertham was never a fan of the ACMP Code. In August of 1948, he denounced the code and took another opportunity to attack comic books while speaking at the 78th Annual Congress of Correction of the American Prison Association. He followed this attack up with a paper entitled "The Betrayal of Childhood: Comic Books" which was a five-part analysis consisting of case studies, content analysis, an evaluation of effects, an examination of the industry, and a proposal for action. In the paper, Dr. Wertham listed seven ways in which comic books were harmful to children. His list included:

1. Comic books may suggest criminal or sexually suggestive ideas.
2. They create mental preparedness or readiness for temptation.
3. They suggest forms a delinquent impulse may take and supply the latest techniques for its execution.
4. They may tip the scales in behavior of an otherwise normal child and act as the precipitating factor of delinquency or emotional disorder.
5. They supply the rationalization for a contemplated act which is often more important than the act itself.
6. They set off a chain of undesirable or harmful thinking.
7. They create for the child an atmosphere of deceit, trickery, and cruelty.

The failure and subsequent disbanding of the ACMP only served to drive Dr. Wertham's anti-comic book crusade forward. He responded to the ACMP's failure by once again calling for legislation—this time calling for a total ban on the sale of comic books to anyone under the age of 16.[20]

Dr. Wertham collected his essays and studies into a book. His editor suggested the book's title, *All Our Innocence*, be changed to *Seduction of the Innocent*. The book was published in 1954, although excerpts were published in the November 1953 *Ladies' Home Journal* in an article titled "What Parents Don't Know About Comic Books." This article drew from three chapters from *Seduction of the Innocent*: "What Are Crime Comic Books," "The Effects of Comic Books on the Child," and "The Struggle Against the Comic Book Industry."[21] Within the pages of *Seduction of the Innocent* Dr. Wertham expanded on the topics he originally brought forth in his 1948 symposium "The Psychopathology of Comic Books"—those ideas being that reading violent comic books led to violent behavior in children. Dr. Wertham suggested that reading "crime comics" (his catchall phrase for not only crime comics, but horror comics and even superhero comics) caused behavior problems in children and ultimately led them to become violent, drug-addled, juvenile delinquents. While Dr. Wertham's ire was particularly directed at horror and crime comics, superheroes weren't immune to his criticism. Dr. Wertham postulated about the rampant sexuality in comic books—going as far as to say that Batman and Robin were a closeted homosexual couple and that Wonder Woman had her strength and independence because she was a lesbian.[22] Even Superman was not able to avoid Dr. Wertham's notice. The champion of truth, justice, and the American way was reviled by Dr. Wertham as being un-American and even promoting fascism, stating, "Superman has long been recognized as a symbol of violent race superiority." Dr. Wertham furthermore objected to the advertisements in comic books. He felt that things like knives and air rifles should not be advertised alongside such violent content. In fact, about the only group who escaped Dr. Wertham's criticisms were the newsstands where comic books were sold. He claimed that a retailer could not refuse to sell a comic book it felt was objectionable. If it did, the distributor would not allow the retailer to sell any of its other periodicals. Even the artists themselves, Wertham claimed, were forced to produce lurid content against their will.[23]

Dr. Wertham presented data that 95 percent of children he interviewed in reform schools admitted to regularly reading comic books and concluded from this that reading comic books led to children becoming juvenile delinquents. This, of course, is a textbook example of how correlation does not imply causation. In this case, Dr. Wertham neglected to mention that 95 percent of *all* children at the time regularly read comic books and, obviously, all of those children were not in reform schools. He would go on to suggest that comic books made children into scheming little creatures who would openly read the "harmless" funny animal comic books in front of their parents and then switch to horror comic books as soon as their backs were turned. He hinted at seedy storefronts with nefarious backrooms where the most awful kinds of comic books were sold directly to children. The images of their bright-eyed, God-fearing children prowling around dark back alleys looking for their "fix" of violent comic books in the same way that a dope fiend looks for their next score made parents feel helpless in the face of an evil industry.[24]

Wertham's graphic descriptions of sex and violence in comic books were accompanied by illustrations. These illustrations were typically individual panels of artwork from comic books. The panels chosen were all taken out of context and picked for shock value and they certainly did their job in that respect. One early reviewer of *Seduction of the Innocent* wrote: "In a shocking gallery, including a landscape in which the phallic symbolism could scarcely escape an observant six-year-old; a baseball game played with a corpse's head for the ball and with entrails for the base paths; pictures showing men and women being hanged, dragged face down and alive behind cars, branded, having their eyeballs pierced with needles (a favorite motif), and their blood sucked by beautiful female vampires; representatives of nudes in all shapes and conditions (this is apparently known in the trade as 'headlight' art), usually being bound of beaten, or both; and helpful diagrams illustrating the latest methods of breaking into a house or fracturing an Adam's apple with the edge of a hand. These examples appear in black-and-white, but it is explained that they are considerably more effective in the three-color [sic] originals."[25]

Dr. Wertham's arguments may seem ridiculous now—especially since many of us have heard similar arguments throughout the years about the horrible effects that heavy metal music, Dungeons & Dragons, or subliminal messages on records would have on children. At the time, though, Dr. Wertham's book sold briskly and generated a great deal of uproar. It even spent some time as an alternate selection for the Book of the Month Club. Parents and teachers were outraged. After all, Dr. Wertham was a noted psychiatrist. If he were raising these allegations, then how could they not be true? The public outcry against horror comics and the comic book industry had begun in earnest.

Dr. Wertham's article, "What Parents Don't Know About Comic Books," published in the November 1953 issue of *Ladies' Home Journal* also coincided with the announcement of the formation of the Senate Subcommittee on Juvenile Delinquency. Originally chaired by Robert C. Hendrickson, a Republican senator from New Jersey, the committee was established to "furnish leadership and stimulate activity at the state level." The Senate Subcommittee on Juvenile Delinquency was officially established on April 27, 1953.[26] Senator Hendrickson was the chairman of the subcommittee when it was formed and during the comic book hearings, but following the 1954 elections, the chairmanship of the subcommittee was given over to Senator Estes Kefauver—a Democratic senator from Tennessee. Senator Kefauver was chair of the subcommittee and it was under his direction when the final report on the comic book industry was written. Estes Kefauver was first elected to the United States House of Representatives in 1939 and won the Tennessee senate seat in 1948. He rose to national prominence for heading up the Senate Special Committee to Investigate Crime in Interstate Commerce in 1950 which became popularly known as the Kefauver Committee. The Kefauver Committee held hearings in 14 different cities and heard testimony from more than 600 witnesses—including several high-profile Mafia crime bosses including Willie Moretti, Joe Adonis, and Frank Costello. The committee hearings made Senator Kefauver a household name as the hearings were televised live right when many Americans were first buying televisions. Senator Kefauver became so popular as a result of the televised hearings that he even made an appearance on the popular television show *What's My Line?* in 1951.

Senator Kefauver attempted to leverage his newfound popularity and made a bid for the Democratic presidential nomination in 1952, but he lost this bid to Adlai Stevenson. Senator Kefauver signed on with the Senate Subcommittee on Juvenile Delinquency with the hopes that serving as chair of that subcommittee might help provide him with the political capital to make another presidential bid.[27]

Even before the official formation of the Senate Subcommittee on Juvenile Delinquency, Senator Kefauver was working with Dr. Wertham. In August of 1950, Dr. Wertham and Senator Kefauver put together a questionnaire which was sent to judges of juvenile and family courts, probation officers, court psychologists, public officials, social workers, comic book publishers, cartoonists, and officers of national organizations who showed interest in the idea of juvenile delinquency. The questionnaire consisted of seven questions:

1. Has juvenile delinquency increased in the years 1945 to 1950? If you can support this with specific statistics, please do so.

2. To what do you attribute this increase if you have stated that there was an increase?

3. Was there an increase in juvenile delinquency after World War II?

4. In recent years, have juveniles tended to commit more violent crimes such as assault, rape, murder, and gang activities?

5. Do you believe that there is any relationship between reading crime comic books and juvenile delinquency?

6. Please specifically give statistics and, if possible, state specific cases of juvenile crime which you believe can be traced to reading crime comic books.

7. Do you believe that juvenile delinquency would decrease if crime comic books were not readily available to children?

Of those responding, nearly 60 percent felt there was no relationship between comic books and juvenile delinquency and almost 70 percent felt that banning crime and horror comic books would have little effect on juvenile delinquency.[28] A similar questionnaire was sent out in April 1953 in preparation for the subcommittee hearing scheduled for late that year. The questionnaire went out to nearly 2,000 experts, social workers, and representatives of service organizations, church groups, and others expressing concern about the problems of the youth. This questionnaire requested the recipient's opinion on the extent and causes of juvenile delinquency and more than 50 percent of the responders placed some blame for juvenile delinquency on films and comic books. Over the course of its existence, the subcommittee received thousands of unsolicited letters and over 75 percent of those expressed concern over comic books, television, radio, and movies. Most of the letters expressing concern over comic books were received after the publication of excerpts of Dr. Wertham's book. This growing concern over the influence of the media prompted the subcommittee to schedule a series of hearings on the effect of media on juvenile delinquency. The investigation began with the comic book industry starting in April of 1954.[29]

The initial groundwork of the subcommittee was done by Richard Clendenen—the executive director of the subcommittee. Clendenen was the chief of the juvenile delinquency branch of the United States Children's Bureau and the bureau's leading expert on the subject of juvenile delinquency. Before that, Clendenen was a probation officer in a juvenile court and administrator at various institutions for emotionally disturbed children. In 1952, Martha Eliot, the new director of the United States Children's Bureau, made juvenile delinquency a priority and formed a Special Delinquency Project headed by none other than Richard Clendenen. Eliot loaned Clendenen to the Senate Subcommittee on Juvenile Delinquency partially because the subcommittee was underfunded, but also so that the Children's Bureau would have a voice in the investigation. Clendenen joined the Senate Subcommittee on Juvenile Delinquency in August of 1953.[30]

Clendenen immediately set to work by requesting from the staff of the Library of Congress a complete summary of every study published on the effects of comic books on children. He also sent several prominent individuals some samples of the comic books under investigation in order to solicit their opinion on the effects of the material contained in them. The Post Office Department was given an extensive list of comic book titles along with the names of comic book publishers, writers, and artists with the instructions to determine whether any of the comic book titles had ever been classified as "unmailable" or whether any named individual had ever come under Post Office Department scrutiny for any reason. This line of investigation turned up nothing of any interest and was summarily dropped. Comic book publishers were asked to provide the subcommittee with copies of the comic book titles that they published as well as their circulation figures so that the subcommittee could learn more about their operations. Members of the subcommittee were particularly interested in how a comic book was made—from the creation of the story through the execution as well as what the procedure was for reviewing the manuscripts and artwork.[31]

Once the preliminary investigations were completed, staff members drew up a list of witnesses who would be testifying before the subcommittee. The list of witnesses was finalized on Wednesday, April 21, 1954—one day before the first day of the subcommittee hearing was set to start. In all, the subcommittee accepted 33 exhibits as evidence and called 22 witnesses—including experts on juvenile delinquency (among them Dr. Fredric Wertham), comic book publishers (among them William Gaines of EC Comics), distributors and retailers (to testify about the sale and distribution of comic books), and other witnesses who had been active in other investigations of comic books. This list would include James Fitzpatrick, chairman of a New York committee to study comic books, and E. D. Fulton, who engineered a ban on crime comic books in Canada. Committee members were provided with a list of all of the witnesses including an extensive background on each witness, details on the position each witness was expected to take, and suggested directions the questioning could take.

The Senate Subcommittee on Juvenile Delinquency opened the first of two days of public hearings on April 22, 1954, in New York City. The day was bright, sunny and unseasonably warm. The location of the public hearings was chosen for the simple fact that nearly all major comic book publishers had their headquarters in New York City, so committee members could have direct access to the comic book publishers to see first-hand how they operated. The committee consisted of Senator Robert Hendrickson from New Jersey as the chairman; Senator William Langer from North Dakota; Senator Estes Kefauver from Tennessee; Senator Thomas C. Hennings, Jr., from Missouri; and Senator Herbert J. Hannoch as chief counsel.

The hearings opened with a statement from Senator Hendrickson who outlined the purpose and goals of the committee. He stated that the hearings would only be concerned with crime and horror comic books and acknowledged that authorities agreed that the majority of comic books sold were "as harmless as soda pop." He went on to state that freedom of the press was not at issue and that the committee had no intention to become "blue-nosed censors." He finished by claiming that the committee had no preconceptions and was only tasked to determine whether crime and horror comic books produced juvenile delinquents.[32]

Richard Clendenen was the first witness to speak to the subcommittee on the morning of April 22 and his testimony quickly set the tone for what was to come. Clendenen began by showing the committee examples of comic books that were under investigation. Clendenen had originally planned to show a total of 29 slides with accompanying plot summaries of the comic books, but time constraints limited him to 13 slides and the discussion of seven comic book titles. The slides he showed consisted of both comic book covers and sample panels. Clendenen told the committee what he was showing was "quite typical" of crime and horror comic books. In reality, the comic book covers and panels Clendenen picked out were from titles that had been singled out by Dr. Wertham. The plot summaries Clendenen provided were creatively phrased to place emphasis on the violence in the stories—even going as far as to include a count of how many people died in the comic book.

One example Clendenen cites is the story of "Frisco Mary." This story was from *Crime Must Pay the Penalty* #3 (March 1954) and in relation to the story, Clendenen showed two slides—the cover of *Crime Must Pay the Penalty* #3 (which has nothing to do with the "Frisco Mary" story) and a single panel from the story which Clendenen described as a "shot of Frisco Mary using a submachine gun on a law officer." The story itself is about "Frisco" Mary Fenner and her gang of criminals. Far from the helpless victim, Mary takes charge of the gang and commits most of the violence associated with it. In the scene Clendenen described, Mary leads her gang in a bank robbery and the town sheriff shows up to stop the robbery. The sheriff is shot by one of the gang members and Mary steps up to finish him off. In the slide presented to the committee she remarks, "We could have got twice as much if it wasn't for this frog-headed rat! I'll show him!" Mary is actually chided by her gang for being too trigger-happy. Detectives later find the gang's hideout and the police take Mary and her husband Frank into custody. The rest of the gang, afraid that Frank will "rat them out," break into the jail where Frank is being held and shoot him dead. A gunfight happens and the police shoot the remaining gang members remarking, "Well—that finishes the Fenner gang—and saves the state the cost of a trial." Mary, the sole survivor, is tried and executed in the gas chamber. Clendenen's account of the story is a little different. His testimony reads: "One story in this particular issue called 'Frisco Mary' concerns and attractive and glamorous young woman who gains control of a California underworld gang. Under her leadership the gang embarks on a series of holdups marked for their ruthlessness and violence. Our next picture shows Mary emptying her submachine gun into the body of an already wounded police officer after the officer has created an alarm and thereby reduced the gang's take in a bank holdup to a mere $25,000. Now in all fairness it should be added that Mary finally dies in the gas chamber following a violent and lucrative criminal career."[33]

Clendenen next introduced the survey of literature on comic books and juvenile delinquency compiled by the Library of Congress, noting that expert opinions and findings of the study reflected a diversity of opinion regarding the effects of comic books on children. The remainder of the morning's session was taken up by the testimony of Dr. Harris Peck, the director of the Bureau of Mental Health Services Children's Court of New York City. Dr. Peck took a position he himself described as "middle of the road" on the issue. Dr. Peck made it clear that he was not an expert in the field of comic

3. Seduction of the Innocent   51

books. He claimed to have worked extensively in the psychiatric treatment of juvenile delinquents and did have some contact with the "comic-book situation," but not having made a systematic study of it he could not testify as an expert in that sense. He testified that, in his own general view, his experiences with children as seen in a court clinic would lead him to believe that comic books could not be viewed as a primary causative force for juvenile delinquency. Dr. Peck testified that he supported the view that normal children were not being led to crime because of reading comic books; however, Dr. Peck also testified that there were areas of the city with "deteriorating influences at work on children" and in those cases comic books could indeed be an influence to their actions. The last testimony of the morning of the first day was Henry Edward Schultz, the general counsel for the Association of Comic Magazine Publishers (ACMP). Schultz explained the failure of the ACMP code and presented the committee with a copy of the 1948 Comic Book Code from the Association of Comic Magazine Publishers.

Initially William Gaines of EC Comics was scheduled to testify during the morning session of the first day, but the other witness testimonies ran longer than expected and so Gaines was rescheduled to speak first in the afternoon session. When Dr. Wertham appeared to testify, the committee bumped Gaines again, allowing Dr. Wertham to give his testimony as the first witness in the afternoon session. Dr. Wertham opened his testimony by reciting his long list of professional credentials. Smartly dressed and speaking with his terse German accent, he spoke eloquently and passionately about the deleterious effect of comic books on children, openly citing comic books as a chief contributing factor to juvenile delinquency. Dr. Wertham produced a copy of the infamous "Foul Play" story [originally published in *The Haunt of Fear* #19 (May–June 1953)] and pointed out the images of men playing baseball with a corpse's dismembered body parts. "They play baseball with a dead man's head! Why do they do that?," he incredulously asked the committee. Dr. Wertham insisted that everything he was advocating was for the protection of the children and not censorship. He did warn, though, that "as long as the crime comic books industry exists in this present form, there are no secure homes."[34] From the onset, the committee took a very respectful position with Dr. Wertham. The committee allowed Dr. Wertham to make a long statement before even beginning his questioning and when the questioning finally started Dr. Wertham was presented with questions that were more meant to allow him to clarify his position instead of to challenge him. At one point Senator Thomas Hennings, Democratic senator from Missouri, told Dr. Wertham that he himself had a copy of *Seduction of the Innocent* and was "reading it with great interest."[35] Despite the topic of the subcommittee being crime and horror comic books, Dr. Wertham expanded his testimony to also denigrate all comic books. Dr. Wertham called out champion of truth, justice, and the American way stating that Superman comics "aroused phantisies [sic] of sadistic joy in seeing other people punched over and over while you yourself remain immune." Dr. Wertham referred to this as a "Superman complex." He concluded his testimony by stating without any doubt or reservation that comic books were an important contributing factor to juvenile delinquency.[36]

The next person to testify was William Gaines. By this time, Gaines had already been rescheduled from the morning session to the afternoon session and then furthermore unceremoniously bumped to an even later spot by Dr. Wertham. Gaines had been sitting all morning long listening helplessly to the testimonies and seeing the blatant bias of the committee and when the time came for him to speak, he was already fuming. He knew he was on his own and speaking to a hostile committee in defense of his company and the comic book industry as a whole, and it suited him just fine. He had his EC Comics attitude, his thick New York accent, and his notebook full of prepared statements and he was "really going to fix those bastards."[37] He was unapologetic in his opening statement, taking full responsibility for the horror comic books he produced and claiming to be the "first publisher in these United States to publish horror comics. I am responsible. I started them." He fully acknowledged that horror comics were not to everyone's liking. "It would be just as difficult to explain the harmless thrill of a horror story to Dr. Wertham as it would be to explain the sublimity of love to an old maid." Hitting at the heart of the matter, Gaines defended the rights of children as educated consumers. "Are we afraid of our own children? Do we forget that they are citizens too and entitled to select what to read or do?" He dismissed the idea that the children were so "simple minded that it takes a story of murder to set them to murder, or a story of robbery to set them to robbery." Gaines was adamant that "delinquency is the product of [the] real environment in which the child lives and not of the fiction he reads."[38]

The committee was surprised by Gaines' defiant attitude. They had never expected this young, outspoken New Yorker to mount such a vigorous defense for an issue that, in their opinion, was completely indefensible. Chief Council Herbert Hannoch asked Gaines if it did children any good to read his stories. Gaines replied, "I don't think it does them a bit of good, but I don't think it does them a bit of harm, either."[39]

As the proceedings went on, the committee's attitude towards Gaines did not soften, though. Gaines was peppered with questions from committee members about everything from the artwork in the comics, to the messages the comics allegedly sent, to editorial pieces Gaines had written. This led up to the most famous exchange of questioning from the hearing:

Senator Kefauver: (holding up a recent copy of EC's *Crime SuspenStories*) Here is your May 22 issue. This seems to be a man with a bloody ax holding a woman's head up which has been severed from her body. Do you think this is in good taste?
Gaines: Yes, sir. I do, for the cover of a horror comic. A cover in bad taste, for example, might be defined as holding the head a little higher so that the neck could be seen dripping blood from it and moving the body over a little further so that the neck of the body could be seen to be bloody.
Kefauver: You have blood coming out of her mouth.
Gaines: A little.
Senator Hendrickson: Here is another one I want to show him.
Kefauver: This is the July one. It seems to be a man with a woman in a boat and he is choking her to death here with a crowbar. Is that in good taste?
Gaines: I think so.
Chief Counsel Hannoch: How could it be worse?[40]

The questioning didn't get any better from there. Gaines knew he was done for. "I could feel myself fading," he would later admit. "They were pelting me with questions and I couldn't locate the answers." Gaines' "good taste" exchange made the evening news and was on the front page of the next day's *New York Times* with the glaring headline "No Harm In Horror, Comics Issuer Says." It was also featured in an article in *Time* magazine which was very critical of comic books and openly mocked Gaines' "good taste" comment while showing the *Crime SuspenStories* severed head cover. William Gaines spent the next two days in bed with stomach pains. He knew he had lost, but what was worse was that Dr. Wertham had won. Gaines, EC Comics, and horror comics were villainized and he knew the repercussions from this would have a long-lasting effect on the horror comic industry. Horror comic book publishers had now been made to look exactly like Dr. Wertham had alluded—a decadent, uncaring group of people who were out to make a profit at the expense of children with no regard for the impact crime and horror comic books had on them.[41]

The remainder of the day would see testimony from Walt Kelly, the president of the National Cartoonist Society and Disney animator who would go on to create the popular comic strip *Pogo*; Milton Caniff, artist for the comic strips *Terry and the Pirates* and *Steve Canyon*; and Joseph Musial, artist for *The Katzenjammer Kids*. The comic strip artists took this opportunity to distance themselves from comic books, with particular venom reserved for EC Comics artist Johnny Craig.

While the "severed head/good taste" exchange attracted the most media attention, the discussion regarding a story called "The Whipping" probably best demonstrates the extreme positions Gaines and Wertham held. Dr. Wertham accused Gaines of fostering racial hatred due to the fact that the story used the racial slur "spick" in it several times. The story was originally published in *Shock SuspenStories* #14 (May 1954). In the story, a Mexican family has moved into a suburban neighborhood. One resident of the neighborhood, Ed, becomes outraged when his daughter Amy becomes involved with the son of the Mexican family, Louis Martinez. Ed tries to turn the neighbors against the Martinez family to no avail, so Ed resorts to deception. He riles up the men in the community by lying to them and telling them that Louis tried to rape his daughter. The men opt for some good old-fashioned vigilante justice, so they put hoods over their heads and break into the Martinez house in the middle of the night. They throw a large sack over the head and body of the first person they encounter inside the dark house then proceed to drag their captive outside and beat them to death. In the next-to-last panel, Louis races into the yard calling out for Amy. In the last panel, the mob discovers they had mistakenly killed the girl whom Louis had just married.

Dr. Wertham summarized the story by saying, "I think Hitler was a beginner compared to the comic-book industry.... They teach them race hatred at the age of four before they can read." He offered the story "The Whipping" as an example of this, noting that the integration of Puerto Ricans into New York City neighborhoods was "a great social problem." He pointed out that the racial slur was used in the story a total of 12 times and commented, "Is it pointed out that a Spanish Catholic family moved into this neighborhood—utterly unnecessary. What is the point of this story? The point of the story is that then somebody gets beaten to death. The only error is that the man who must get beaten to death is not a man; it is a girl." Gaines was furious with the way Dr. Wertham represented the story. He told the committee that Dr. Wertham had to have completely read the story "to have counted what he said he counted." He said, "Dr. Wertham did not tell you what the plot of the story was. This is one of a series of stories designed to show the evils of race prejudice and mob violence, in this case against Mexican Catholics.... This is one of the most brilliantly written stories that I have ever had the pleasure to publish. I was very proud of it, and to find it being used in such a nefarious way made me quite angry." Wertham, like many of the other experts, took comic panels and dialog out of context in order to misrepresent the story and twist it to their own ends. The surprise ending, which was common for EC Comics, was meant to shock the reader with the consequences of racism. Amy's bound and gagged body was meant to symbolize victims' helplessness—symbolism made explicit in the caption "a victim unable to defend himself against that fantasy ... unable to cry out ... unable to be heard ... a victim like all victims of intolerance."[42]

The second day of testimony started with Gunnar Dybwad, the executive director of the Child Study Association of America. Dybwad was considered to be on the side of the comic book publishers, but his testimony wasn't exactly a resounding success. Dybwad testified that the Child Study Association of America had conducted a study of comic strips in 1937 and surveys of comic books in 1943 and 1949. When Herbert Beaser, chief counsel to the subcommittee asked Dybwad directly about his opinion on the effects that reading crime and horror comic books would have on children, Dybwad refused to take a stand either way. He felt that widespread distribution of such literature was symptomatic of larger problems within society, but he could say little about individual effects. He said he personally knew of no cases linking reading comic books with a criminal offense and, while there could be a connection, "so far I have not seen the clinical evidence."[43]

Dybwad was followed by another witness who was considered to be pro-comic books—Dr. Laura Bender, a psychologist who was considered to be an expert on emotionally disturbed children. Dr. Bender testified that she did not find horror comic books shocking, instead she found them "unbelievably silly" and added, "The more an artist tries to show horror and the more details he puts into the pictures, which most poor artists do, the sillier the thing becomes, and the children laugh at it." Dr. Bender went on to claim that a child would throw away a comic book if it gave them anxiety—not keep reading it.[44]

Senator Kefauver harshly discounted the testimonies of both Dybwad and Dr. Bender. Senator Kefauver pointed out that the comic book studies for the Child Study Association were done by Josette Frank who was employed as a paid consultant for the comic book publisher National Comics Publications (National Comics Publications being better known as DC, or at the time "Superman-DC"). Senator Kefauver also pointed out that Dr. Bender was also a paid consultant for National Comics Publications. Senator Kefauver summarily dismissed both Dybwad and Dr. Bender as "paid apologists." The press took this story and ran with it. The April 23 *New York Times* carried the headline "Senator Charges 'Deceit' on Comics" and ran an article which read "Senator Kefauver charged that reports on comic books—which opposed censorship but urged self-regulation by publishers and more active interest by parents—had 'minimized' the crime and horror comic book problem. He contended this was the effect of publisher retainers."[45] In retrospect, the subcommittee had a wealth of witnesses to choose from and the fact that they chose these two particular witnesses would certainly appear to be because the committee could easily discredit them thus strengthening their own case.

The afternoon session of the second day of testimony saw representatives from comic book publishers make their statements. First up was Monroe Froehlich, Jr., business manager of Magazine Management Co. (parent company to Atlas/Marvel Comics). Froehlich began by reading letters from organizations that did not testify but were asked for their opinion. After the letters were read, Froehlich did not fare very well. Atlas/Marvel Comics had published a line of horror comics with rather gruesome covers and Froehlich found himself having to defend the comic book covers in much the same way that William Gaines had to do the previous day. Next was William Richter of the News Dealers Association of Greater New York. Richter was not a fan of crime or horror comics nor was he particularly fond of William Gaines. He called crime and horror comics "trash" and called for them to be banned altogether. Richter was followed by Alex Segal, president of Stravon Publications. Segal used his testimony to distance the "good" comic books Stravon Publications produced from the crime and horror comics. The last publisher to testify was Dell Comics represented by vice president Helen Meyer and editor Matthew Murphy. Dell Comics never published any crime or horror comics and Meyer was quick to emphasize that point. She suggested that Dr. Wertham was possibly ignoring the "good" comics to make a stronger case against the "bad" ones. She concluded with: "We abhor horror and crime comics. We would like to see them out of the picture because it taints us."[46]

Originally the public hearing portion of Senate Subcommittee on Juvenile Delinquency was scheduled to be only two days long. Initial witness testimonies ran longer than expected and so a third day was added. The third day was for the purpose of the committee getting more information on so called "tie-in" sales. Many anti-comic book experts (Dr. Wertham prominently among them) had long proposed that retailers were at the mercy of the distributors when it came to the types of comic books and magazines they sold. Dr. Wertham and others claimed that a retailer would be penalized by the distributor if they chose not to sell a particular comic book title due to the content or for whatever reason. The idea behind "tie-in" sales is that a retailer (a newsstand or drugstore) would receive regular weekly shipments of comic books and magazines from their distributor. If the retailer wanted to continue receiving their shipments, they had to put out for sale everything they were given. In other words, if a newsstand owner decided they didn't like the cover of this month's *Horrific* comic book and kept it hidden away under the counter and not for sale, the distributor could punish the newsstand by no longer sending them more popular magazines like *Time* or *TV Guide* and thus hurting the retailer's overall sales. Distributors were portrayed as some shadowy entity that was motivated strictly by profit. "So what if you don't like those horror comic books," the distributor would say, "We don't care that they are corrupting our children. You MUST sell them or we'll pull ALL of your inventory and then your children will starve," and the distributor would break out in demonic laughter before vanishing in a puff of sulfur-smelling smoke. Hyperbole aside, the concept of "tie-in" sales would have left the retailer in a rather helpless position having absolutely no say in what inventory they were required to sell. That is, of course, if "tie-in" sales even existed. Dr. Wertham and some other anti–comic book people insisted "tie-in" sales were real whereas many distributors insisted they were not. The Senate Subcommittee on Juvenile Delinquency wanted to get to the bottom of the "tie-in" sales issue once and for all as part of their hearing, so a third day of testimony was scheduled for Friday, June 4, 1954.

Day three of the Senate Subcommittee on Juvenile Delinquency was opened by a statement from Senator Hendrickson who once again spelled out the purpose of the hearings before introducing James A. Fitzpatrick, the chairman of the New York State Joint Legislative Committee to Study the Publication of Comics. Fitzpatrick, for whatever reason, decided to spend nearly all of his testimony picking apart—nearly page by page—*Panic #1* (March 1954). *Panic* is a humor comic book published by none other than EC Comics. To say that Fitzpatrick was not a fan of *Panic* would be an extreme understatement. He repeatedly referred to it as "salacious literature," "complete and utter perversion," "rot," "particularly obnoxious," "sacrilegious," and (my personal favorite) "pictorial prostitution."[47] The remainder of the morning session did get back onto the subject of "tie-in" sales with testimony from Benjamin Freedman, chairman of the board of the Newsdealers Association of Greater New York and America; Harold Chamberlain, circulation director of Independent News Co.; Charles Appel, owner of Angus Drug Store; and George B. Davis, President of Kable News Co. And the comic book distribution process was explained in detail to the committee. Comic book publishers were represented by one of 13 different national distributors, with each distributor handling a different line of comics. Each distributor would coordinate with the printer to make sure that the correct number of copies of a comic book were printed and shipped to the appropriate wholesaler. The wholesaler received the publications from the distributors and sorted them into bundles which would then be distributed to retailers (newsstands, drug stores, and other retail outlets) who would place the comic books on the shelf for sale. At the end of the month, the retailer would return any unsold copies to the wholesaler who shipped them back to the distributor. The distributor, in turn, would return the unsold comic books to the publisher for credit. Testimony from distributors, wholesalers, and retailers all denied the existence of "tie-in" sales and so no retailer ever had to sell a comic book that they didn't not feel completely comfortable selling. If a retailer ever received a comic book they didn't want to sell, they were under no pressure to display it for sale. They could simply return it to the wholesaler with no penalty to sales or future purchases.[48] The afternoon session of the last day of testimony was taken up by E. D. Fulton, a member of the House of Commons in Canada who made an attempt to pass a law banning the sale of crime and horror comics in Canada. He was followed by Samuel Black, the vice president of the Atlantic Coast Independent Distributors Association. Mr. Black was adamant that, while he wasn't particularly fond of horror comic books, he was against the idea of introducing any kind of legislation to ban them. The final testimony was from J. Jerome Kaplon, the chairman of the Juvenile Delinquency Committee and Union County Bar Association. Kaplon was in the process of a crusade to ban horror comic books in New Jersey. His testimony included several newspaper articles demonstrating how the media has been responding to crime and horror comic books. William Gaines is naturally interviewed in many of the articles that were introduced.

Senator Hendrickson concluded the final day of testimony by stating that the committee would continue to collect information about crime and horror comic books and would study the issue carefully before drawing up their conclusions and recommendations. In his closing remarks he summed up the hearings by saying, "I think I speak for the entire subcommittee when I say … [a] competent job of self-policing within the industry will achieve much."[49]

The final report from Senate Subcommittee on Juvenile Delinquency was approved in December of 1955. The report drew no link between comic books and juvenile delinquency. It stated, "Surveying the work that has been done on the subject, it appears to be the consensus of the experts that comic-books reading is not the cause of emotional maladjustment in children." The subcommittee report did call for action, saying "the nation cannot afford the calculated risk involved in the continued mass dissemination" of crime and horror comic books to children. The committee stopped short of calling for federal censorship, instead placing the responsibility firmly on the publishers by stating: "Within the industry, the primary responsibility for the contents of each comic book rests squarely upon the shoulders of its publisher … the publishers of children's comic books cannot discharge their responsibility to the Nation's youth merely by discontinuing the publication of a few individual titles. It can only be fully discharged only as they seek and support ways and means of insuring that the industry's product permanently measures up to its standards of morality and decency which American parents have the right to expect."[50]

4

The Comics Code Authority

In response to the recommendations of the Senate Subcommittee on Juvenile Delinquency, the Comics Magazine Association of America (CMAA) was incorporated on September 7, 1954. The Articles of Incorporation listed six directors: Elliot Caplin of Toby Press, Allen Hardy of Allen Hardy Associates, Harold A. Moore of *Famous Funnies*, Stanley Estrow of Stanhill Publications, Jack Liebowitz of National Comics Publications, and Monroe Froehlich of Magazine Management Company. The attorney was Henry Schultz who had previously been the executive director of the Association of Comics Magazine Publishers. The CMAA was designed to produce a self-policing "code of ethics and standards" for the comics industry and so the CMAA established the Comics Code Authority (CCA) as the governing body which would judge comic book content. Taking a cue from the film industry (another self-regulated industry) the CMAA sought out a "comics czar" with the proper credentials to administer their new code of standards. Leo Holland of the Independent News Company, a distributor subsidiary of National Comics Publications, announced on August 21, 1954, that a search for the new comics czar was underway. Interestingly enough, the first candidate approached for this position was Dr. Fredric Wertham, but Dr. Wertham flatly refused—which was probably the best possible outcome for the comic book industry as a whole. On September 16, 1954, the CMAA appointed New York Magistrate Charles F. Murphy as the CMAA comics czar. Murphy was given a two-year contract with an annual salary of $17,000 (this equates to nearly $150,000 in today's money) and a promise from the publishers that a code would be completed by November 15, 1954.[1]

Charles Murphy, age 44, was married with three children. When asked about his comics czar position, he said, "I have been given a free hand by the Association to act and make decisions in the public interest. I am using this free hand forcefully." Murphy took his comics czar position very seriously—

more seriously, in fact, than anyone had expected him to. Comic book publishers fully expected Murphy to be nothing more than just a figurehead. They expected him to essentially ignore all but the most blatant violations of the code. One industry representative described Murphy as "a not-very-bright political hack who was selected mostly because of his religious faith." Even the public relations firm brought on to handle the CMAA campaign referred to Murphy as "a practical man who would recognize the problems of selling comic books in a declining market." Whether Murphy knew of the industry's lack of confidence in him or not is not really known. What is known is the seriousness and determination Murphy showed in the position. His zeal was such that even the CMAA didn't renew his contract after it expired in 1956. During his tenure, he not only delivered the Comics Code on time, but he was fervent about upholding it.[2]

The Comics Code Authority based its code on the (largely ignored) code of the Association of Comics Magazine Producers which was drafted in 1948. This code was in turn loosely based on the 1930 Hollywood Production Code or "Hays Code."[3]

The Comics Code as approved in 1954 laid out the following rules for comic book content:

- Crimes shall never be presented in such a way as to create sympathy for the criminal, to promote distrust of the forces of law and justice, or to inspire others with a desire to imitate criminals.
- No comics shall explicitly present the unique details and methods of a crime.
- Policemen, judges, government officials and respected institutions shall never be presented in such a way as to create disrespect for established authority.
- If crime is depicted it shall be as a sordid and unpleasant activity.
- Criminals shall not be presented so as to be rendered glamorous or to occupy a position which creates a desire for emulation.
- In every instance good shall triumph over evil and the criminal punished for his misdeeds.
- Scenes of excessive violence shall be prohibited. Scenes of brutal torture, excessive and unnecessary knife and gunplay, physical agony, gory and gruesome crime shall be eliminated.
- No unique or unusual methods of concealing weapons shall be shown.
- Instances of law-enforcement officers dying as a result of a criminal's activities should be discouraged.
- The crime of kidnapping shall never be portrayed in any detail, nor shall

any profit accrue to the abductor or kidnaper. The criminal or the kidnaper must be punished in every case.
- The letters of the word "crime" on a comics-magazine cover shall never be appreciably greater in dimension than the other words contained in the title. The word "crime" shall never appear alone on a cover.
- Restraint in the use of the word "crime" in titles or subtitles shall be exercised.
- No comic magazine shall use the word horror or terror in its title.
- All scenes of horror, excessive bloodshed, gory or gruesome crimes, depravity, lust, sadism, masochism shall not be permitted.
- All lurid, unsavory, gruesome illustrations shall be eliminated.
- Inclusion of stories dealing with evil shall be used or shall be published only where the intent is to illustrate a moral issue and in no case shall evil be presented alluringly, nor so as to injure the sensibilities of the reader.
- Scenes dealing with, or instruments associated with walking dead, torture, vampires and vampirism, ghouls, cannibalism, and werewolfism are prohibited.
- Profanity, obscenity, smut, vulgarity, or words or symbols which have acquired undesirable meanings are forbidden.
- Special precautions to avoid references to physical afflictions or deformities shall be taken.
- Although slang and colloquialisms are acceptable, excessive use should be discouraged and, wherever possible, good grammar shall be employed.
- Ridicule or attack on any religious or racial group is never permissible.
- Nudity in any form is prohibited, as is indecent or undue exposure.
- Suggestive and salacious illustration or suggestive posture is unacceptable.
- All characters shall be depicted in dress reasonably acceptable to society.
- Females shall be drawn realistically without exaggeration of any physical qualities. NOTE.—It should be recognized that all prohibitions dealing with costume, dialog, or artwork applies as specifically to the cover of a comic magazine as they do to the contents.
- Divorce shall not be treated humorously nor represented as desirable.
- Illicit sex relations are neither to be hinted at nor portrayed. Violent love scenes as well as sexual abnormalities are unacceptable.
- Respect for parents, the moral code, and for honorable behavior shall be fostered. A sympathetic understanding of the problems of love is not a license for morbid distortion.

- The treatment of live-romance stories shall emphasize the value of the home and the sanctity of marriage.
- Passion or romantic interest shall never be treated in such a way as to stimulate the lower and baser emotions.
- Seduction and rape shall never be shown or suggested.
- Sex perversion or any inference to same is strictly forbidden.

The Comics Code also spelled out regulations for the types of ads in comic books and the products that could be sold.

- Liquor and tobacco advertising is not acceptable.
- Advertisement of sex or sex instruction books are unacceptable.
- The sale of picture postcards, "pinups," "art studies," or any other reproduction of nude or seminude figures is prohibited.
- Advertising for the sale of knives or realistic gun facsimiles is prohibited.
- Advertising for the sale of fireworks is prohibited.
- Advertising dealing with the sale of gambling equipment or printed matter dealing with gambling shall not be accepted.
- Nudity with meretricious purpose and salacious postures shall not be permitted in the advertising of any product; clothed figures shall never be presented in such a way as to be offensive or contrary to good taste or morals.
- To the best of his ability, each publisher shall ascertain that all statements made in advertisements conform to fact and avoid misrepresentation.
- Advertisement of medical, health, or toiletry products of questionable nature are to be rejected. Advertisements for medical, health, or toiletry products endorsed by the American Medical Association, or the American Dental Association, shall be deemed acceptable if they conform with all other conditions of the Advertising Code.[4]

Even by the standards of the conservative 1950s, the Comics Code was a very strict set of rules that comic book publishers now had to play by. It is worth noting that ads for liquor, tobacco, knives, guns, and sex products were expressly prohibited despite the fact that none of these products were ever advertised in comic books to begin with! This is how far the CMAA went with their regulations. Comic book publishers argued that a "Rated G" movie of the time wouldn't even stand up to the scrutiny of the CMAA without having to make changes to the script. The CMAA held the strictness of the Comics Code up as a badge of honor. Charles Murphy referred to the Comics Code as "the strongest code of ethics ever enforced by a mass media industry and incorporates recommendations made from all quarters." The CMAA held to their hard standard with the intent to show that the organization took very seriously its moral obligation to the youth of America. It also stands to reason that the CMAA also hoped that the extreme self-regulation would help discourage an outside organization from stepping in with their own regulation.[5]

Initially everything was reviewed by Charles Murphy and his staff of five reviewers. Murphy's five reviewers were: Sue Flynn, a publicist for 13 years with the Department of Agriculture and the radio broadcast Voice of America; Marj McGill, a resident graduate of Albertus Magnus College who had done social work while attending college and who specialized in the study of juvenile delinquency; Esther L. Moscow, a librarian and researcher; Dr. Joan Thellusson Nourse, a professor in the Department of English at Hunter College and lecturer and writer on theater; and Dene Reed, an editor in the story department of Metro-Goldwyn-Mayer for a number of years. Murphy originally interviewed over one hundred candidates for the reviewer positions, but ultimately decided on the five women because he "felt they were more sensitive to the situation."[6]

For the review process, material was submitted on "boards"—the basic drawings that were completed before any plates or engravings were made for publication. The reviewers would scrutinize every written word and every drawn panel for adherence to the Comics Code. The reviewers would make note of any objectionable material and return the panel to the publisher with a list of necessary changes. When a page was approved, it was stamped by the reviewer and the pages were photographed to ensure that no changes were made by the publisher once the approved artwork left the Comics Code Authority office. Each reviewer would examine on average nine comic books per day or more than 260 pages.[7] When a comic book met the standards and passed the review process, it received the Comics Code Authority Seal of Approval which would be printed prominently on the cover. The presence of the Comics Code Authority seal on the cover of a comic book meant to parents that the comic book had passed all of the stringent requirements.[8]

Knowing that the public's impression of the CMAA and the Comics Code was pivotal to their success, the CMAA flooded the media with public appearances to tout their successes. At a December 1954 press conference, Charles Murphy boasted that his office had already screened 285 different comic books and rejected 126 stories as well as 5,656 individual drawings. Murphy volunteered that nearly 25 percent of the changes made involved "reducing feminine curves to more natural dimensions" and altering drawings to have clothing "cover a more respectable amount of the female body."[9]

Comic book publishers were not technically required to submit their comic books to the CMAA for Code approval. However, the negative backlash against horror and crime comic books coupled with the unstoppable public relations machine of the CMAA created a scenario where comic book distributors refused to carry any comic book without the Comics Code Authority seal on the cover. That means that a while comic book without the Comics Code Authority seal might get published, the odds were very slim that it would ever be distributed to a newsstand and so it would likely never be available for sale. Only a handful of comic book publishers chose not to submit their comic books to the Comics Code Authority for approval. Dell Comics and Gilberton (publisher of *Classics Illustrated*) refused on the grounds that their comic books were never associated with the horror comic controversy. Dell Comics published a majority of their titles based on licensed television and movie products and so they were beholden to their licensors to maintain wholesome content. Gilberton published comic book adaptations of works of classic literature and so stayed above the fracas as well. EC Comics never submitted any of their comic books to the Comics Code Authority for approval for the simple reason that William Gaines detested the code and everything it stood for. Gaines felt that the Comics Code Authority outright banning the words "fear," "terror" and "horror" in comic book titles was directly targeting EC Comics and their best-selling titles.[10]

Gaines dug in his heels, but this was a fight that Gaines and EC Comics weren't going to win. The Comics Code Authority was in place to stay and they had the full backing and support of the general public. Unlike the ACMP in 1948, the Comics Code Authority rules had teeth and were being enforced and so the Comics Code Authority became the de facto censor for the comic book industry. Comic book publishers effectively had no choice other than to comply with the regulations laid out by the Comics Code Authority, which meant a radical departure from the material they had been publishing for years.

As restrictive and puritanical as the Comics Code Authority was, Dr. Fredric Wertham was ultimately disappointed in it. He felt that it was not restrictive enough and referred to it as "an inadequate half-measure."[11] Violence, in his opinion, had not been removed from comic books. Instead it had just been sanitized into a bloodless and painless exercise with very little actual consequence. A comic panel could be brought up to Comics Code Authority regulations, for example, by asking artists to reduce a puff of smoke from a fired pistol in order to make the gunshot seem less violent. This seems absurd, but this was actually requested by the Comics Code Authority in one instance.

When asked about the Comics Code Authority, Wertham replied, "Whenever people begin to show signs of doing something themselves about controlling crime comics, the publishers come out with a 'code' or something to divert attention and avert action." Dr. Wertham maintained that comics czar Charles Murphy was not a censor, but instead an employee of the comic book industry and so he had no real power to enforce a censorship code. Dr. Wertham read comics that carried the Comics Code Authority Seal of Approval on the cover and he observed they contained the same harmful ingredients—including murders, race prejudice, torture, crime, and pornographic sadism—and concluded "That is why a law to protect children is necessary."[12]

The magazine *Saturday Review* asked Dr. Wertham to write a follow-up to his 1948 article "The Comics........ Very Funny" after the formation of the CMAA and the implementation of the Comics Code Authority. Dr. Wertham took them up on their offer and wrote a scathing indictment of the Comics Code in an article entitled "It's Still Murder: What Parents Still Don't Know About Comic Books" which was published in the April 2, 1955, issue of *Saturday Review*. In the article, Dr. Wertham lambasts the Senate subcommittee for rejecting any legislation against comic book publishers. He claimed that the connection between comic books and juvenile delinquency was "now well established" and added, "It is easy to build a straw-man argument that comic books are the 'sole factor' and then demolish it. But nobody ever claimed that they are." He continued, "Of course there are other evil influences to which we expose children. That does not mean we should take for granted, and do nothing about any one injurious factor. The comic-book pest, which we can isolate, is one of the worst and most far-reaching." He provided several examples where published material violated the provisions of the code in comic books which still bore the Comics Code Authority Seal of Approval on their cover. To this point, he argued, "Surely this is not a counter-measure, but a cover-up continuation of the cruelty-for-fun education of children." He concluded the article by once again calling for legislation against comic books: "The comic-book publishers, racketeers of the spirit, have corrupted children in the past, they are corrupting them right now, and they will continue to corrupt them unless we legally prevent it. Of course there are larger issues in the world today, and mightier matters to be debated. But maybe we will lose the bigger things if we fail to defend the nursery." The CMAA responded to Dr. Wertham's article by threatening to sue him for libel.[13]

Dr. Wertham continued to crusade against violence in comic books and other media, but his sphere of influence (and his audience) was slowly shrinking. He had set out to be the crusader for children and, in turn, had been reduced to the Joe McCarthy of the comic book industry. In an attempt to be the protector, he had become synonymous with censorship.[14]

5

Horror Comics in the Silver Age of Comic Books

The Silver Age of Comic Books started as a very dark time for horror comics. Dr. Fredric Wertham's testimony before the Senate Subcommittee on Juvenile Delinquency and the subsequent news (or hype) surrounding it brought the anti-comic book hysteria to a fever pitch. The formation of the Comics Magazine Association of America and the establishment of the Comics Code Authority in 1954 helped assuage parent's fears that their children would be lured into a life of crime by nothing more than simply reading a comic book. Every drawn line and every written word of every comic book that was published would be scrutinized so that parents could be sure nothing harmful got through. Bowing to the relentless pressure, the comic book industry agreed to regulate itself and submit to the rigid standards. Horror and true-crime comic book titles were cancelled en masse as comic book publishers made the shift to more "Code-friendly" comic books. The superhero genre began to grow in popularity once again. This time, however, the storylines were much lighter, campier—almost to the point of becoming cartoonish. During the Golden Age of Comic Books, teenagers and adults made up a large portion of the comic book reading audience. The Silver Age of Comic Books saw a shift in this with comic book publishers beginning to target a younger market of pre-teens. The horror comic genre had definitely had a stake driven through its heart, but even through all of this it still managed to cling desperately to life.

Comic book publishers adapted to the new Comics Code Authority requirements in many different ways. In 1954, DC was publishing two horror titles: *House of Mystery* and *House of Secrets*. *House of Mystery* (published from 1951 until 1987) started out as a horror anthology filled with supernatural-themed stories as one would expect. Once the Comics Code Authority regulations came into being and most supernatural themes (vampires, werewolves, demons, ghosts, etc.) were no longer permitted in comic books, the storylines in *House of Mystery* were changed to feature more science fiction monsters and mystery/suspense type tales that would be allowed by the Comics Code Authority. In the mid-1960s, *House of Mystery* became primarily a superhero title. Starting with *House of Mystery* #143 (June 1964) and running through *House of Mystery* #155 (December 1965), the title would feature J'onn J'onzz—the Martian Manhunter. Starting in *House of Mystery* #156 (January 1966) and running through *House of Mystery* #173 (March–April 1968), the title would center on Dial H for Hero—a magical dial that transformed a normal person into a superhero for a short period of time by simply dialing the letters H-E-R-O. Towards the end of the Silver Age of Comics, *House of Mystery* would finally revert back to its horror roots. Joe Orlando (formerly of EC Comics) was hired by DC to become the new editor for *House of Mystery* starting with issue #174 (June 1968). By this time, both DC and Marvel were strongly challenging the Comics Code Authority in regards to their restrictions on content, and *House of Mystery* became a horror title again. Issue #174 featured five horror stories reprinted from earlier issues of *House of Mystery*'s sister title *House of Secrets*: "The Wondrous Witches Cauldron," originally printed in *House of Secrets* #58 (February 1963); "The Man Who Hated Good Luck!" originally printed in *House of Secrets* #17 (February 1959); "Museum of Worthless Inventions," originally printed in *House of Secrets* #13 (October 1958); "The Court of Creatures," originally printed in *House of Secrets* #43 (April 1961); and "Page 13," a one-page story drawn by Sergio Aragones. *House of Mystery* #175 saw the first appearance of Cain the "able care taker" of the House of Mystery. Cain would serve as the horror host for the title introducing nearly all of the stories from issue #175 until the final issue, #321 (October 1983). *House of Mystery* also has the distinction of being horror artist (and the creator of Swamp Thing) Bernie Wrightson's first professional comic book work. He debuted with the story "The Man Who Murdered Himself" in *House of Mystery* #179 (March–April 1969).[1]

DC's *House of Secrets*, the companion title to *House of Mystery*, also started as a horror anthology comic book with its first issue being published in December of 1956. Given the timing, the format was changed to a fantasy and superhero anthology book within the first few issues. It featured the sorcerer Mark Merlin who first appeared in issue #23 (August 1959) and the supervillain Eclipso who first appeared in issue #61 (August 1963). Prince Ra-Man the Mind Master debuted in issue #73 (July–August 1965). Prince Ra-Man was introduced as a replacement for Mark Merlin and bore no small resemblance to Marvel's Doctor Strange—both in look and in his line of work. In a strange Silver Age twist, the decision was made that Mark Merlin wasn't appealing any longer and that readers were interested in superheroes. Not wanting to alienate any fans by dropping an old character and introducing a new one, Mark Merlin just sort of "became" Prince Ra-Man. You can't really explain Silver Age logic, but we will try. Mark Merlin is banished to another dimension to the lost world of Ra by the masked villain the Gargoyle using the mystic oil lamp of Imhotep. While on Ra, Mark Merlin gains the power of mind over matter from an emerald six-sided jewel that hangs in the sky above the realm and grants everyone dwelling there immortality. Mark Merlin cannot return to Earth in his own body so a scientist/sorcerer named Kranak (who led his persecuted followers to Ra over 4,000 years ago) uses a potion to reincarnate Merlin's spirit and memories into the body and brain of a long-dead young wizard named Prince Ra-Man—a hero whom ancient legends proclaimed as the son of the sun god Ra for whom their planet was named. Ra-Man (with Mark Merlin's memories) returns to Earth and defeats the Gargoyle with his mighty "mental beam" which gives him control over virtually all non-living matter. Prince Ra-Man was a regular feature in *House of Secrets* until issue #80 (October 1966) at which point the series went on hiatus for three years before returning with issue #81 in September of 1969 as a full-blown horror title. *House of Secrets* #81 is the first appearance of Abel, the caretaker of the House of Secrets, the horror host who introduces the stories in *House of Secrets* and brother to Cain from DC's sister title *House of Mystery*. Like the good old-fashioned EC Comics horror hosts, both Cain and Abel would each make appearances in both titles. Like their Biblical namesakes, their relationship was, shall we say, tumultuous. Thin and drawn, Cain is always a pleasant host to the reader, but viciously cruel to Abel. Abel, nervous, stammering, and chubby, endures Cain's abuse (up to and including murder). Abel is accompanied by his "imaginary" (and possibly ghostly) girlfriend Goldie and by Gregory, his pet gargoyle. *House of Secrets* would run through issue #154 (November 1978). Along the way the title would sport several wonderful covers by Neil Adams, Bernie Wrightson, and Michael Kaluta. *House of Secrets* #92 (July 1971) would feature the first appearance of Swamp Thing in an eight-page story written by Len Wein and drawn by Bernie Wrightson.[2]

Marvel Comics horror titles *Strange Tales* and *Journey Into Mystery* were forced into transition as well. *Strange Tales* started out as a horror anthology title with its first issue being published in June of 1951. Starting with *Strange Tales* #68 (April 1959), the title changed to focus on the drive-in monster craze which was trendy at the time. Almost every issue would feature a monster story drawn by Jack Kirby (who had recently just returned to Marvel after a short stint with rival DC), a couple of thriller or science fiction stories, and typically end with a Stan Lee/Steve Ditko short. The title changed again beginning with *Strange Tales* #101 (October 1962) when the drive-in monster stories took a backseat to superhero stories. The Human Torch of Fantastic Four fame began a feature story with guest appearances by the rest of the Fantastic Four. *Strange Tales* #110 (July 1963) saw the introduction of Doctor Strange and the title would continue to feature Doctor Strange until #188 (November 1976), its final issue.[3]

Marvel Comics' *Journey Into Mystery* also started as a horror/fantasy anthology comic. Its first issue was published in June of 1952 and it also made the transition into giant monster/science fiction stories as the decade went on with *Journey Into Mystery* #23 (March 1955) being the first issue to bear the Comics Code Authority seal on the cover. The title also made a transition into a superhero book with the introduction of the Mighty Thor in *Journey Into Mystery* #83 (August 1963). The Thor stories became so popular that Thor's stories grew longer and longer while the remaining science fiction stories grew shorter and shorter. Eventually the book would just feature Thor. This would be reflected in the title as well. Thor's name grew larger until the title became *Journey Into Mystery with the Mighty Thor* with issue #104 (May 1964). Thor's name would continue to get larger on the cover while the *Journey Into Mystery* title would continue to get smaller until issue #125 (February 1966) after which the title is renamed *The Mighty Thor*.[4]

Comic book publishers were not required to submit their comic books to the Comics Code Authority and a few publishers did not—namely Gilberton, Dell Comics, Gold Key Comics, and EC Comics. The Gilberton Company was best known for publishing *Classics Illustrated* which adapted works of classic literature into comic book form. Despite never submitting any of their comics to the Comics Code Authority, citing the fact that their comic books were classical literary works presented in comic book form, Gilberton did redesign the covers of their adaptations of *Frankenstein* and *Dr. Jekyll and Mr. Hyde* to be less gruesome. Dell Comics relied on the fact that they published several comic book titles based on licensed characters and thus were beholden to their licensors to publish "clean" content. Dell Comics published comic books based on the animated characters from Walt Disney and Warner Bros. as well as television series including *The Twilight Zone, The Lone Ranger, Tarzan, Yogi Bear,* and *Howdy Doody*. No Dell comic book ever bore the Comics Code Authority seal on the cover. Instead Dell Comics took it on themselves to print inside every one of their comic books a "Pledge to Parents" promising that their editorial process "eliminates rather than regulates" any objectionable material and which finished with the motto of "Dell Comics Are Good Comics." Dell Comics even went as far as to take out full-page ads in the *Saturday Evening Post* in order to drive home the point of their wholesomeness.[5] Interestingly enough, Dell Comics did publish a *Drac-*

ula series which started as a horror series and then took an interesting turn. Dell Comics' *Dracula* ran eight issues with issue #1 being published in October of 1962 and issue #8 being published in July of 1973. Oddly enough, only the first issue was horror and based on the classic vampire tale. The rest were superhero books featuring a modern descendant of Dracula who gains "vampire-like" powers (superhuman hearing, superhuman sight, and the ability to turn into a bat) after using a serum derived from bat blood in an attempt to cure brain damage. He pledges to use his new powers to redeem the family name and to fight evil and superstition in all its forms. He puts on a purple costume with a red cowl and a bat-shaped belt and begins his superhero career. He is joined by his girlfriend B.B. Beebe, a blackbelt in judo, who also gains similar "vampire-like" powers. She dons a costume of her own and calls herself Fleeta (as in *fledermaus*—German for "bat"). Together they fight crime based out of an abandoned underground government radar installation that just happened to be located on Beebe's family's mountain estate.[6] As completely over-the-top and outlandish as this seems, this pretty much sums up the Silver Age of Comic Books.

Gold Key Comics released several comic titles in what passed for the horror genre by licensing television properties. They published *Boris Karloff Thriller* based on the TV show *Thriller*. The comic series lasted longer than the TV show, however, and was retitled *Boris Karloff Tales of Mystery* after *Thriller* went off the air in 1962.[7] Gold Key purchased the publishing rights to *The Twilight Zone* from Dell Comics in 1962 and published it until 1982.[8] Gold Key also had comic series for the licensed TV properties of *The Addams Family*, *The Munsters*, and *Ripley's Believe It or Not!*[9]

EC Comics was by far the comic book publisher that was hardest hit by the enforcement of the Comics Code Authority. EC Comics owner William Gaines flat out refused to submit any of EC Comics' books to the Comics Code Authority for their approval—probably because he knew there would be no way any of them would be approved. In a last-ditch effort, EC Comics ran a full-page editorial in the fall 1950 issues of all of their comics appealing to the readers to take action. "Due to the efforts of various 'do-gooders' and 'do-gooder groups,' a large segment of the public is being led to believe that certain comic magazines cause juvenile delinquency." Laying the blame on "a psychiatrist who has made a lucrative career of attacking comic magazines." and pulling no punches, the editorial stated that "many groups of adults … would like to blame their lack of ability as responsible parents on comic magazines instead of on themselves." Readers were implored to "write a nice polite letter" to the Subcommittee to Investigate Juvenile Delinquency in defense of comic books and warned readers that if the subcommittee didn't hear from actual comic book readers, then "the very existence of the whole comic magazine industry" would be in jeopardy. EC Comics fans answered the call as an estimated three to four hundred letters were written. The writers ranged in age from children to teenagers to adults and they all were overwhelmingly positive about comic books and urged the Committee to back off from the comic book witch hunt. One young man wrote, "How can anyone truthfully say that reading a magazine gives them an urge or an idea to kill? With all of the 'love magazines' being printed, I am surprised we are not all professional lovers, if that's the case." One mother offered her own opinion about the anti-comic book sentiment by stating, "I think the only thing they have against these comics is just the fact they can't get the kids to help around the house because they are too interested in the comics and the mothers get tired of picking up a bunch of books." Another young mother brought a different perspective, writing that reading comic books was one of the only forms of entertainment she and her children could afford and "the most enjoyment for us is to go to bed early in the evening and read a funny book or two."

Adding insult to injury, Gaines received a letter from Senator Hendrickson after his testimony before the Senate Subcommittee on Juvenile Delinquency. The letter was nothing but a routine communication thanking Gaines for his testimony, but it did not sit well with Gaines. Gaines immediately fired back a letter in response to Senator Hendrickson telling the senator that, in Gaines' opinion, the committee had been neither impartial nor scientific in its approach and that his own treatment at the hands of the committee had been particularly unfair. Gaines complained that he was originally told his testimony would take place in the morning of the first day then he was rescheduled to be the first person on the agenda in the afternoon only to be "shunted aside" when Dr. Wertham showed up and was forced to wait until nearly 4:00 PM before being finally allowed to speak. He went on to note that his four-minute speech was constantly and rudely interrupted stating, "I need not tell you that this was far from the kid-glove patience accorded to Dr. Wertham—who spoke for hours on end—much of his contribution being obvious gush designed solely to increase the sale of his book." Gaines continued, "The headline-seeking carnival staged by your Committee has given fuel to those in our society who want to tar with the censor's brush. As a result, my business together with the entire comics industry has been severely damaged. Since this was so obviously an objective of the Committee, I trust it will give you some satisfaction." Gaines never received a response from Senator Hendrickson.[10]

Gaines fought tooth and nail, but in the end the opposition was too strong. In September 1954, Gaines called a press conference to announce that

EC Comics was immediately cancelling all of their horror and crime comics and starting up a "clean, clean line" since that seemed to be "what the American parents want."[11] Gaines published a final editorial in *Tales From the Crypt* that seemed to more succinctly sum up his point. "As a result of the hysterical, injudicious, and unfounded charges leveled at crime and horror comics, many retailers and wholesalers throughout the country have been intimidated into refusing to handle this type of magazine." Gaines summed up the last hurrah of horror comics by sarcastically stating that "with comic magazine censorship now a fact, we at EC look forward to an immediate drop in the crime and juvenile delinquency rate of the United States."[12]

EC Comics announced the "New Direction" line of comics. This line included the titles *Impact!* (stories with shocking endings—often seen as a toned-down version of *Shock SuspenStories*), *Valor* (tales of action and adventure in various time periods including Ancient Egypt, the Roman Empire, the Middle Ages, the Crusades, the French Revolution, and the Napoleonic Era), *Extra!* (stories about the adventures of various journalists), *Aces High* (tales of air combat and frontline service of World War I and World War II), *Psychoanalysis* (stories about the day-to-day work of therapists), *M.D.* (medical stories, surgical practices, and the day-to-day work of doctors), and *Incredible Science Fiction* (a science fiction anthology book). Gaines initially refused to submit these books to the Comics Code Authority for their approval, but low sales and a lack of distributors forced him to. Even after being Code approved, sales for the New Direction line of titles were quite poor. The final straw for Gaines came when the Comics Code Authority rejected a reprint of the antidiscrimination story "Judgement Day." Originally printed in the pre–Code *Weird Fantasy* #18 (April 1953), "Judgement Day" was to be reprinted in *Incredible Science Fiction* #33 (February 1956) in place of another rejected story, "An Eye for an Eye." "Judgement Day" told the story of a human astronaut, a representative of the Galactic Republic visiting the planet Cybrinia which was inhabited by robots. The astronaut discovers the robots are divided into functionally identical orange and blue races, one of which has fewer rights and privileges than the other. The astronaut decides that, due to the robots' bigotry, the Galactic Republic should not admit the planet. In the final panel, the astronaut removes his helmet and reveals himself to be a black man. Judge Charles Murphy, without any authority in the code, insisted that the black astronaut had to be removed. "Judgement Day" was written by EC editor (and writer) Al Feldstein and drawn by Joe Orlando. The story was written as an allegory against racial prejudice and the driving point of the story would obviously be negated if the main character was not shown to be a black man. Al Feldstein appealed to Judge Charles Murphy in an attempt to convince him to reverse his position on the ruling, but Murphy dug in his heels and refused to reconsider his decision. Feldstein told William Gaines of the situation and Gaines immediately called Murphy. The phone call between the three quickly became quite heated. Gaines accused Murphy of intentionally attempting to sabotage EC Comics' business by making it impossible for them to publish anything. Gaines then threatened to hold a press conference at which he would make public all of his grievances against Murphy and the Comics Code Authority. There were also threats of a lawsuit. Murphy at this point made what he probably thought was a generous concession. The last panel of the "Judgement Day" story featured a close-up scene where the astronaut removes his full-face helmet revealing he was a black man. In this scene the man is shown to have several glistening drops of perspiration running down his face. Murphy suggested to Gaines and Feldstein to remove the drops of sweat from the man's face. At that, Gaines and Feldstein both went ballistic. "Fuck you!" they shouted into the telephone in unison. Murphy hung up on them, but the story ran in its original form in *Incredible Science Fiction* #23 (February 1956) which, despite the numbering, was the fourth issue in the series and the last comic book that EC Comics ever published.[13] Immediately afterwards, Gaines sent the Comics Code Authority office a letter telling them "to go screw," formally withdrew from the CMAA, and cancelled all of EC's comic titles.[14]

As the decade drew on, comic book publishers were beginning to publish the horror-like "supernatural mystery" titles again. Charlton Comics had a strong showing in this emerging genre. They published *Ghostly Tales*, a horror-suspense title that was published from May of 1966 through October of 1984 (although the title was only reprinting older stories from 1978 onward). *Ghostly Tales* has its own horror host, Mr. L. Dedd (later changed to I. M. Dedd), a middle-aged man with purple skin and horns who dressed like a vampire and who told his ghostly tales from the parlor of his haunted house. *Haunted* was another horror-suspense anthology book published from September 1971 through September 1984, although it also went reprint-only after 1978. *Haunted* was hosted by Impy—a pint-sized ghost dressed in a solid white superhero costume. Impy acted as horror host until *Haunted* #21 (April 1975) when Baron Weirwulf took over hosting duties and the title was renamed *Baron Weirwulf's Haunted Library*. *Ghostly Haunts* was published from September 1971 through April 1978 and was hosted by the blue-skinned Winnie the Witch. *The Many Ghosts of Doctor Graves* was published from May 1967 through March of 1983 (with the three-issue, all-reprint *Doctor Graves* running from September 1985 through January 1986). Hosted by Dr. M. T. Graves, this anthology title featured the artwork of Steve Ditko (following his falling-out with Marvel Comics) and Jim Aparo who would go on to be most well-known for his work on *Batman*. *Ghost Manor* was published from July 1968 through July 1971 and hosted by the Old Witch (not to be confused with the Old Witch who hosted EC Comics *Haunt of Fear*). Charlton also published a second volume of *Ghost Manor* from October 1971 through November 1984. This series was hosted by Mr. Bones—a masked, reanimated skeleton butler. Charlton also took advantage of the drive-in monster craze by releasing comics based on the movies *Konga*, *Gorgo*, and *Reptilicus*. Charlton's foray into the horror/suspense genre definitely took the approach of "quantity over quality" since nearly all of their horror titles eventually stopped publishing new content and instead just simply reprinted older, previously published stories.[15]

DC converted their series *The Unexpected* from a fantasy anthology to a weird horror anthology. Hosted by the Mad Mod Witch, *The Unexpected* ran from March of 1968 through May 1982. DC also launched the horror anthology title *The Witching Hour* in March of 1969. Hosted by the three witches Mordred, Mildred, and Cynthia, *The Witching Hour* was published until October of 1977.[16]

Marvel Comics also launched a new anthology book. In October of 1969, *Chamber of Darkness* debuted. Like all of the other horror anthologies, *Chamber of Darkness* had its own horror host, the undertaker Headstone P. Gravely. Stories were also sometimes introduced by Digger the gravedigger or, in Mighty Marvel fashion, one of the artists or writers themselves. *Chamber of Darkness* had quite an impressive list of artists and writers dedicated to it as well. Stan "The Man" Lee was the editor and also a writer. He was joined at the writing desk by Gerry Conway and Archie Goodwin. Gerry Conway would go on to co-create the Punisher as well as script the famous *Amazing Spider-Man* story where Gwen Stacy dies at the hands of the Green Goblin. Archie Goodwin would soon be known (in the horror world, at least) as the editor and lead writer for the horror magazines *Creepy* and *Eerie*. *Chamber of Darkness* would also host some amazing artists including Jack Kirby, Johnny Craig (of EC fame), John Buscema, Tom Sutton (*Vampirella* artist and writer), Barry Windsor-Smith, and Bernie Wrightson. Wrightson's first professional work for Marvel Comics was in *Chamber of Darkness* #7 (October 1970).[17]

Chamber of Darkness had original stories, but it also featured some great literary adaptations. Issue #2 (December 1969) featured writer Roy Thomas and artist Don Heck doing a comic treatment of Edgar Allan Poe's "The Masque of the Red Death" in a story called "The Day of the Red Death." Issue #3 (February 1970) had writer Denny O'Neil and artist Tom Palmer adapt Edgar Allan Poe's "The Tell-Tale Heart" in a story called "The Tell Tale Heart."

Issue #5 (June 1970) featured Tom Palmer and Johnny Craig with a comic adaptation of H. P. Lovecraft's "The Music of Erich Zann" in a story called "The Music From Beyond." *Chamber of Darkness* issues #4 (April 1970) and #5 (June 1970) also have the rare distinction of having stories written by Jack Kirby. Kirby, much more well known for his art, left Marvel Comics to work for rival DC in late 1970. Some of his last work at Marvel was scripting and drawing the story "The Monster" in *Chamber of Darkness* #4 (April 1970) and the story "And Fear Shall Follow" in *Chamber of Darkness* #5 (June 1970). Kirby also drew the cover for *Chamber of Darkness* #5. Despite all of the talent present on the creative team, *Chamber of Darkness* did not sell well. It ran for eight issues before being renamed to *Monsters on the Prowl* and converted into mostly reprinting old Atlas and "pre-superhero Marvel" stories. *Monsters on the Prowl* ran from February 1971 until October 1974. Each issue had one original story and the rest of the content was all reprinted material. *Chamber of Darkness* did get a swan song with the January 1972 release of *Chamber of Darkness Special* #1 which was an all-reprint issue.[18]

Marvel also launched the horror anthology book *Tower of Shadows* in January of 1971. *Tower of Shadows* was a sister title to *Chamber of Darkness* and shared the horror hosts Headley P. Gravely and Digger. It was another title that Marvel pulled out all of the stops for. It featured the talents of writer/artists Jim Steranko, Neal Adams, Johnny Craig, Wally Wood, and writer-editor Stan Lee. Artwork was provided by John Buscema, Gene Colan, Tom Sutton, Barry Windsor-Smith, and Bernie Wrightson. The title started out strong with Jim Steranko winning a 1969 Alley Award for Best Feature Story for "At the Stroke of Midnight"—the feature story in *Tower of Shadows* #1. Unfortunately, sales for the title were not strong and the title slowly transitioned to a mixture of new stories and "pre-superhero Marvel" reprints. After only nine issues, it was renamed *Creatures On the Loose* and the format was changed to an anthology of science fiction, sword and sorcery, and reprints before eventually being cancelled with issue #37 (September 1975).[19]

While the Comics Code Authority held sway over what could be published in comic books, they had no authority over what could be published in a large-format magazine. Works of horror could still be published, just in a different format. Horror publishers began to explore that option and found a receptive audience.

The first publisher to take advantage of this was Warren Publishing. Previously known for the magazines *Famous Monsters of Filmland* and *Monster World*, Warren Publishing launched the magazines *Creepy* and *Eerie* in 1964. Both magazines were black-and-white horror anthologies, but since they were full-sized magazines instead of comic books, they were not subject to the rules and regulations laid out by the Comics Code Authority. In other words, they could print whatever they wanted. Warren Publishing explained it thusly: "The Comics Code saved the industry from turmoil, but at the same time, it had a cleansing kind of effect on comics, making them 'clean, proper and family-oriented'.... We would overcome this by saying to the Code Authority, the industry, the printers, and the distributors: 'We are not a comic book; we are a magazine. *Creepy* is magazine-sized and will be sold on magazine racks, not comic book racks.' *Creepy's* manifesto was brief and direct: First, it was to be a magazine format, 8½" × 11", going to an older audience not subject to the Code Authority."[20]

Creepy and its sister magazine *Eerie* both hit the newsstands in 1964. Both of them were horror anthologies in the style of the (now classic) EC Comics. Like the classic EC anthology comics, each magazine had its own horror host. Uncle Creepy and Cousin Eerie (for *Creepy* and *Eerie* respectively) would introduce the readers to wonderfully gory tales in the tradition of the pre–Code horror books. *Creepy* and *Eerie* would go on to be successful for Warren Publications, too. *Creepy* would publish 145 issues from November 1964 until February 1983 and *Eerie* would publish 139 issues in the same timeframe. The creative rights to both *Creepy* and *Eerie* have had a bit of a rocky road since that time. Warren Publication declared bankruptcy in 1983 and the company assets were purchased by Harris Publications in an auction in August 1983. In 1998, James Warren (founder of Warren Publications) sued Harris Publications and regained control of the rights for *Creepy* and *Eerie*.[21]

Warren Publications is possibly best known for the third title in their horror magazine trilogy: *Vampirella*. Launched in September of 1969, *Vampirella* would have a publication run of 113 issues and be published regularly until December of 1987. *Vampirella* was a black-and-white horror anthology book hosted by and starring the buxom and scantily-clad "bad girl" heroine of the same name—much to the delight of prepubescent boys everywhere. In her origin story Vampirella was from the planet Drakulon—a world where a vampiric race, the Vampiri, lived and blood literally flowed in rivers. The Vampiri had the innate ability to transform themselves into bats. They had superhuman strength. They could fly by sprouting wings, and naturally they drank blood.

The planet Drakulon orbited twin suns, Satyr and Circe, that were causing planetwide droughts and spelling certain doom for Vampirella and her entire race. Vampirella's story begins when an Earth spaceship (christened the "Arthur C. Clarke") crashes on Drakulon. Vampirella is sent to investigate and she is attacked. She fights back and discovers that the human astronauts have drinkable blood in their veins. To ensure the survival of her race, she pilots the ship back to Earth where her adventures begin. On Earth, Vampirella becomes a "good" vampire and devotes her energy to ridding the world of the evil vampires. Evil vampires on Earth exist as descendants of Dracula, who originally came from Drakulon, but was corrupted by the forces of Chaos.[22] With a setup like that, Vampirella's famous skimpy outfit, and her other "assets," how could you possibly go wrong? It's a small wonder that Vampirella has been published almost consistently from 1969 through today. The original *Vampirella* series was published by Warren Publications until their bankruptcy with the last Warren Publications issue being *Vampirella* #112 (March 1983). After Harris Publications acquired the rights, they published several different Vampirella series and miniseries between 1991 and 2007—even publishing the all-reprint *Vampirella* #113 in December of 1997 as a continuation of the original series. On March 17, 2010, Dynamite Entertainment acquired the rights to Vampirella from Harris Publications and began publishing a new series starting with *Vampirella* #1 (November 2010) and a new monthly series *Vampirella and the Scarlet Legion* in May 2011. *Vampirella and the Scarlet Legion* lasted five issues whereas the Dynamite Entertainment *Vampirella* series ran for a total of 38 issues with the last issue being published in February of 2014. The series was rebooted with a new *Vampirella* #1 in June 2014 with author Nancy Collins. This series ran 13 issues with *Vampirella* #13 being published in August of 2015. In 2016, the series was rebooted again and ran for six issues before being restarted once again in March of 2017. The new ongoing *Vampirella* series is still being published. In this new series, Vampirella has awoken from a thousand-year sleep to find herself in a bizarre, dystopian future.

Eerie Publications (not to be confused with the magazine *Eerie*) also published several black-and-white horror anthology magazines. All of their publications were a mixture of original stories and "pre–Code" horror story reprints. Known for their lurid covers, Eerie Publications typically were not as well known or as well circulated as the magazines from Warren Publications. Eerie Publications' best-known work would be *Weird* which ran 69 issues from January 1966 through November 1981. Eerie Publications also published *Horror Tales* (27 issues, June 1969–February 1979), *Strange Galaxy* (four issues, February 1971–August 1971), *Tales from the Crypt* [NOTE: No, not the EC *Tales From the Crypt*] (one issue, July 1968), *Tales from the Tomb* (33 issues, July 1969–February 1975), *Tales of Voodoo* (36 issues, November 1968–November 1974), *Terror Tales* (46 issues, March 1969–January 1979), *Terrors of Dracula* (nine issues, May 1979–September 1981), *Weird Worlds* (five issues, December 1970–August 1971), and *Witches' Tales* (34 issues, July 1969–February 1975) before finally succumbing to bankruptcy in 1981.

EC Comics took advantage of the lack of Comics Code Authority regulations on magazines as well. After their "New Direction" line flopped, EC cancelled all of their comic book titles. They took their single remaining comic book title, a humor comic book called *Mad*, and converted it into a magazine. The artists and writers who remained at EC, the "usual gang of idiots," made *Mad* into a political and social satire magazine first published in 1952 and still being published today.

The Silver Age of Comics was a very difficult time for horror comics. Restrictions enforced on the comic book industry by the Comics Code Authority changed the direction of comic writing and art design. With horror comics in the decline, the Silver Age of Comics saw a new resurgence in the superhero genre with the introduction of iconic characters like Spider-Man, the Fantastic Four, the X-Men, Daredevil, the Hulk, and the Avengers from Marvel as well as the Justice League of America, the Flash, and Green Lantern from DC. These new heroes, as well as new creative teams, served to introduce a whole new generation to comic books. Horror was relegated to magazines and watered-down "supernatural mystery" titles which tended to be more of an avenue to reprint old material than to break new ground. Fortunately, the tides in the comic book industry as well as in society were beginning to change.

6

Horror Comics in the Bronze Age of Comic Books

The years between 1970 and 1985 are what is known as the Bronze Age of Comic Books. The resurgence of the superhero genre which started in the Silver Age of Comic Books has bolstered the comic book industry into new growth. Even under the severe restrictions of the Comics Code Authority, writers and artists were creating memorable work. A new generation of superheroes had been created and that brought with it a new generation of comic book readers. Inside the comic book industry itself, new writers and artists were entering the industry as older faces either retired or moved into management positions. Editors and creative teams were challenging the Comics Code Authority more and more often. Outside of the comic book industry in the "real world," society as a whole had changed since the Comics Code Authority was established in 1954. McCarthyism and the "Red Scare" had come and gone. No longer were Americans looking for Communists in every shadow. America had become embroiled in an unpopular armed conflict around the world in the small country of Vietnam, which sparked anti-war protests across America. Two investigative reporters for *The Washington Post* broke the Watergate scandal—a scandal so large and all-encompassing that it led to articles of impeachment for, and the resignation of, the President of the United States of America, Richard Nixon. Teenagers, once isolated and misunderstood, now spearheaded a new counterculture movement and had developed a voice of their own like no other generation before them. With all of these changes in society, it goes without saying that the idea of what was socially relevant or even socially acceptable had changed as well. The Comics Code Authority remained strong throughout the Bronze Age of Comic Books; however, there were two pivotal challenges to the very authority of the Comics Code Authority. One challenge was brought about by a writer's name and the other saw the Comics Code Authority practically defying the United States government itself.

In the DC supernatural mystery anthology *House of Secrets* #83 (January 1970), the book's horror host introduces the story "The Stuff Dreams are Made Oof" as being told to him by "a wandering wolfman." The story was written by Marv Wolfman and the "wandering wolfman" quip was a little inside nod to the writer. This caused the Comics Code Authority to reject the story, flagging the "wolfman" reference as a violation. By the 1954 Comics Code, supernatural creatures, like vampires, mummies, zombies, and (of course) the wolfman, were prohibited. The issue arose because text in comic books is written in an all-capital font, so there is no distinction between "wolfman" (the supernatural creature) and "Wolfman" (the name). DC writer Gerry Conway contacted the Comics Code Authority and explained to them that the story's writer was actually named "Wolfman." Conway appealed the decision and asked if it would still be a violation if that fact was clearly stated. The Comics Code Authority agreed that there would be no violation as long as Wolfman received clear writer's credit on the first page of the story. DC did that and the story was approved. This ultimately led to DC beginning to credit all of the writers and artists in their titles.[1]

It was also around this time that the United States Department of Health, Education and Welfare approached Marvel Comics editor-in-chief Stan Lee to do a story about drug abuse. The United States Department of Health, Education and Welfare was concerned about drug use among children and, knowing that Marvel Comics had a great deal of influence with kids, they thought it would be a good idea to have some sort of anti-drug message written into the comic books, Lee agreed and wrote a three-part Spider-Man story in *Amazing Spider-Man* #96–98 (May–July 1971). The story begins with Spider-Man saving a man who is high on drugs and dancing on a rooftop. Spidey says, "I would rather face a hundred super-villains than throw my life away on hard drugs because it is a battle you cannot win!" The main plot of the story involves Harry Osborn, Sr., who had regained his memory and turned back into the Green Goblin. In a subplot, Peter Parker is surprised to find Harry (his roommate and the son of the Green Goblin) taking pills because his love interest, Mary Jane Watson, had dumped him. The story culminates with Spider-Man defeating the Green Goblin by showing him pictures of his sick son, which turns him back into Harry Osborn, Sr. Lee was happy with the story. He felt like he was able to show drug use as being dangerous and unglamorous without coming across as preachy. The Comics Code Authority had a different opinion. While the Comics Code (oddly enough) didn't expressly forbid depictions of drugs, there was a "catchall" phrase of "All elements or techniques not specifically mentioned herein, but which are contrary to the spirit and intent of the code, and are considered violations of good taste or decency...." The story was submitted to the Comics Code Authority and summarily rejected, as they felt that the very mention of drug use was prohibited. Lee felt that he was in the right—especially since it was the government that asked him to do the story in the first place, so Lee appealed to Martin Goodman, Marvel Comics' publisher. In an interview, Lee would recount: "Well, I was very proud of our publisher because I went to him. His name was Martin Goodman. I said, 'Martin you have got to let me send these three issues without the Code.'" He said, 'Gosh, Stan, that's taking a big step. I mean, we're supposed to abide by the Code.' And I said, 'Yeah, but we're supposed to do what the government tells us and I got this letter from Washington. And besides, this is a good thing. It's letting kids know that drugs are harmful.' This time he said, 'OK, Stan, you go ahead and do it and I'll back you up.'" Marvel Comics ran the story in *The Amazing Spider-Man* #96–98 (May–July 1971) without the Comics Code Authority approval.[2] The world didn't end. In fact, the storyline was very well received with Marvel Comics receiving many supportive letters from parents, teachers, and religious organizations. The rejection by the Comics Code Authority was seen to be counterproductive and made the Comics Code Authority seem out of touch with the times.

In response to this, the Comics Code Authority revised the Code in 1971. It wasn't a complete overhaul by any stretch of the imagination and most of the 1954 Code was still in place, but it did allow for "the sometimes sympathetic depiction of criminal behavior ... [and] corruption among public officials as long as it is portrayed as exceptional and the culprit is punished"; "some criminal activities could result in the death of a law enforcement officer"; "and the suggestion (but not the portrayal) of seduction could be shown."

The most relevant change for horror comics was that the Comics Code Authority would now allow the portrayal of "vampires, ghouls, and werewolves ... when handled in the classic tradition such as *Frankenstein*, *Dracula*, and other high caliber literary works written by Edgar Allan Poe, Saki, Conan Doyle and other respected authors whose works are read in schools around the world."

It is worth noting that zombies were still a taboo subject. Not only did they lack any classic literary reference, the Code went as far as to specify "Scenes dealing with, or instruments associated with, walking dead or torture shall not be used."

With the revisions to the Code, comic book publishers began producing horror comics in earnest once again. Marvel was the first on the scene with the introduction of Morbius the Living Vampire—a scientifically created vampire who first appeared in *Amazing Spider-Man* #101 (October 1971). This was quickly followed by *Tomb of Dracula* (April 1972), *Werewolf By Night* (September 1972), *Ghost Rider* (August 1972), and the horror anthology titles *Dead of Night* (December 1973) and *Supernatural Thrillers* (December 1972).

Tomb of Dracula ran for 70 issues from April 1972 until August of 1979. Dracula battled against (and occasionally with) a band of vampire hunters. The title also served to give Marvel a platform to cast Dracula as the supervillain to the X-Men, Spider-Man, Howard the Duck, and Blade. Blade the Vampire Hunter also debuted in the pages of *Tomb of Dracula* #10 (July 1973).[3]

Not wanting to be limited to just vampires, Marvel Comics introduced a werewolf in *Marvel Spotlight* #2 (February 1972). Jacob "Jack" Russell (similarity to the dog breed being purely coincidental) discovers his family curse—he is a lycanthrope. The character was so well received in the "tryout" title *Marvel Spotlight* that he was given his own title. *Werewolf by Night* ran for 43 issues from September 1972 through March 1977. *Werewolf by Night* #32 (August 1975) would feature the first appearance of the caped superhero Moon Knight—rather fitting.[4]

Johnny Blaze would sell his soul to the devil (or Mephisto, the Marvel Comics version of the "devil") in order to save his ailing father in *Marvel Spotlight* #5 (August 1972). Another graduate from the "tryout" titles, *Ghost Rider* would run for a total of 81 issues from September 1973 through June 1983.[5]

Marvel also introduced two new horror anthology comic books. *Dead of Night* ran for 11 issues from April 1974 through August 1975 and printed mostly old horror reprints. *Supernatural Thrillers* ran for 15 issues from December 1972 through October 1975. *Supernatural Thrillers* was started with the intention of doing comic adaptations of literary works, and it did start out that way. Issue #2 (February 1973) adapted the H.G. Wells novella "The Invisible Man." Issue #3 (April 1973) featured Robert E. Howard's "The Valley of the Worm." Issue #4 (June 1973) featured Robert Louis Stevenson's "Strange Case of Dr. Jekyll and Mr. Hyde." Issue #6 (November 1973) featured "The Headless Horseman Rides Again," an original sequel to Washington Irving's "The Legend of Sleepy Hollow." The title took an unusual turn, though, as issue #5 (August 1973) introduced "The Living Mummy"—a standalone story about an African tribal prince who is captured by Egyptians, mummified, and reawakened in modern times. The Living Mummy ended up being the featured story in each issue for the rest of the title's run—so much so that the title itself was renamed *Supernatural Thrillers Featuring the Living Mummy* starting with issue #7 (June 1974).[6]

DC published several horror anthology titles: *Ghosts* which ran 112 issues from September 1971 to October 1982; *The Dark Mansion of Forbidden Love* a horror/suspense/romance anthology which lasted four issues before the romance angle was dropped and the title was renamed *Forbidden Tales of the Dark Mansion* which ran a total of fifteen issues from October 1971 through March 1974; *Secrets of Haunted House* which ran 46 issues from May 1965 through March 1982; *Secrets of Sinister House* (which ran four issues as *The Sinister House of Secret Love*, a Gothic romance/horror title) which ran fourteen issues from November 1971 through July 1974; *Weird Mystery Tales* which ran 24 issues from August 1972 through November 1975; and *Weird War Tales* which ran 124 issues from October 1971 through June 1983. DC also published the short-lived *Tales of Ghost Castle*, a three-issue series (June 1975–September 1975) hosted by Lucian the Librarian (who would become more famous in Neil Gaiman's *Sandman*) and the five-issue *Doorway to Nightmare* (February 1978–October 1978) hosted by Madame Xanadu. DC is probably best known during this time however for *Swamp Thing*. Alec Holland was a scientist with a lab located deep in the bayou. One night a band of criminals breaks in, ransacks his lab, douses him with chemicals, and dumps him into the swap—leaving him for dead. Far from killing him, though, the chemical cocktail interacts with the swamp itself and transforms Alec Holland into the Swamp Thing—a living embodiment of the swamp ecosystem itself. A sensitive, caring monster, Swamp Things fights to protect his swamp as well as all aspects of "the Green"—the very force of living nature that Swamp Thing is a part of. This concept of the spontaneous generation of life from dead matter isn't new. Creatures like the Heap and DC's own Solomon Grundy use this as a creation story. What separates Swamp Thing from all this is the masterful writing of Len Wein coupled with the intricately detailed and ever-so-slightly disturbing art of Bernie Wrightson. *Swamp Thing* ran for 24 issues from November 1972 through September 1976. Len Wein wrote the first 13 issues and was followed in that role by David Michelinie and Gerry Conway. Bernie Wrightson provided the artwork for the first ten issues with Nestor Redondo taking over with issue #11 and Fred Carillo drawing the final issue.[7]

Charlton continued the trend of horror anthology comics that they started in the last few years of the Silver Age of Comic Books. They published *Midnight Tales* for 18 issues from December 1972 through May of 1976. Like any good horror anthology, *Midnight Tales* had its own horror hosts—Professor Coffin (a.k.a. the Midnight Philosopher) and his niece, Arachne. *Midnight Tales* did have one thing that made it distinct from other comics (horror or otherwise). The series was created and drawn by artist Wayne Howard and Charlton Comics gave him creator credit on the cover. Each and every cover had "Created by Wayne Howard" clearly printed on it, making Charlton the first comic book publisher in the industry to credit the creator.[8]

Less distinctive were the remainder of Charlton's offerings. *Haunted Love*, a horror/romance anthology published 11 issues between April 1973 and September 1975, and *Scary Tales* ran 46 issues between August 1975 and October 1984 and was hosted by Countess R.H. Von Bludd.[9]

During the Bronze Age of Comic Books, the black-and-white horror magazine format remained an extremely popular way for horror fans to get their fix. Not subject to the Comics Code Authority rules and regulations, horror magazine publishers could show stronger content including moderate profanity, minor nudity, and more graphic violence. Marvel Comics branched out into this format publishing *Dracula Lives!, Monsters Unleashed, Vampire Tales, Tales of the Zombie, Haunt of Horror,* and *Masters of Terror* under the brand emblem Marvel Monsters Group. *Dracula Lives!* was published for 13 issues between 1973 and 1975. It ran concurrently with Marvel Comics title *Tomb of Dracula* and the stories would occasionally intersect. Most of the time, however, the stories were independent. *Monsters Unleashed* printed mostly reprints. *Vampire Tales* starred Morbius the Living Vampire and published a mixture of new content and reprints all with vampires as the main character (obviously). *Tales of the Zombie* featured the Zombie—Simon William Garth, a character from a standalone tale written by Stan Lee and drawn by Bill Everett, originally published in the pre–Code horror anthology comic book *Menace* #5 (July 1953). *Tales of the Zombie* ran for ten issues between 1973 and 1975 although Simon Garth did not appear in issue #10, having been finally laid to rest in issue #9. All ten issues of *Tales of the Zombie* were written by Steve Gerber and drawn by Pablo Marcos. Each issue featured an incredible cover by Boris Vallejo.

Around this time, a wave of underground cartoonists began publishing books through small independent presses and, following the growing trend, several of them were horror titles as well, including:

- *Skull*—Rip Off Press (1970)
- *Bogeyman*—San Francisco Comic Book Company (1969)
- *Fantagor*—Richard Corben (1970)
- *Insect Fear*—Print Mint (1970)
- *Up From the Deep*—Rip Off Press (1971)
- *Death Rattle*—Kitchen Sink Press (1972)
- *Gory Stories*—Shroud (1972)
- *Deviant Slice*—Print Mint (1972)
- *Two-Fisted Zombies*—Last Gasp (1973)

These underground horror comics were able to publish exceedingly gruesome, graphic, and disturbing artwork and stories simply due to the fact that the books were not sold through normal newsstand outlets. Underground comics were typically sold at alternative bookstores, alternative record stores, head shops and other counterculture establishments, so the publishers never had any incentive to submit their books to the Comics Code Authority for approval.

By the end of the 1970s, the horror comic boom of the Bronze Age of Comic Books had come to an abrupt end. This was due in part to the massive influx of new horror comics in a short period of time. The comic book market was simply glutted with horror books. On top of that, many of the new horror titles were still anthology titles—just like the classic *Tales From the Crypt*, *Haunt of Fear*, and other Golden Age books. It was almost as if the comic industry had simply pressed "pause" in 1954 and then pressed "play" again in 1971. New readers had new expectations and wanted different things than previous generations of comic book readers and they demonstrated it with their purchases. Of the 18 different horror titles that are listed in this chapter that began publication between 1971 and 1975, only five of them were still being published in 1979. Of those five, none were being published by the end of 1984. Marvel's *Ghost Rider* ended in 1983. DC's *Ghosts* and *Secrets of Haunted House* both ended in 1982 while *Weird War Tales* survived only a year longer ending in 1983. Charlton's *Haunted* was the last surviving book, being in publication until issue #75 in September of 1984 with Charlton Comics itself closing their doors for good in 1985.

7

The Modern Resurgence of the Horror Comic

At the end of the Bronze Age of Comic Books, the horror comic genre was once again in a low place. The rapid influx of new horror comics following the 1971 revision of the Comics Code led to a horror comic book glut. Titles were being produced at a rapid rate to meet what was seen to be an almost insatiable demand. Unfortunately, like so many other boom markets, so many new horror comic titles were being churned out in such short order that the overall quality of the products started to slip. Sure, there were some quality titles released during this time, but for every *Swamp Thing* or *Tomb of Dracula* there were a lot of less-than-stellar titles on the shelves. Still, like the masked killer in a good horror movie, down does not mean out. The horror comic genre clung tentatively to life throughout the end of the Bronze Age of Comic Books and even managed to stage a huge resurgence. This was brought on by a combination of several factors, but one of the most important factors was the increasing popularity of the good old-fashioned comic book shop.

Originally, comic books were only sold on newsstands and in places like grocery stores, drug stores, candy stores, and supermarkets—typical outlets where people would purchase magazines and newspapers. During the 1960s and 1970s, people began actively collecting comic books as a hobby. The first comic book conventions were held and, slowly, specialized comic book stores began appearing throughout the country. A specialized comic book store is just what it sounds like. It is a store that primarily sells comic books and comic book related merchandise.

Specialized comic books stores (also known as "direct market" stores) provided many advantages to comic book fans and the newly emerging market of comic book collectors. Typically a comic book shop would be owned and operated by a comic book collector. This means they would be very familiar with their inventory. Where a newsstand has no real input into the types of comic books they are sent from the distributor, a comic shop owner has complete control of the types, titles, and quantities of comic books in their inventory. Comic shop owners would therefore be very knowledgeable about the comic industry as well. Most comic book stores develop a stable of regular customers and the store owner would tend to be familiar with their customers' tastes. Aside from allowing the comic shop owner to tailor the ordering of their inventory, it also would allow them to recommend new titles to their customers that they might not have discovered on their own. The customer would find new and enjoyable books to read and the store would have more sales—so it was mutually beneficial and it was just good business. Most comic stores would even allow a customer to call up the store and request that they hold certain titles for them, so they are ensured the chance to purchase the book before it sells out. This "pull and hold" system is invaluable for comic collectors—especially for popular titles which can sell out quickly.

Inventory at a comic shop is treated differently as well. A comic store's inventory would be exclusively comic books and comic book related merchandise. This means the average comic store would have a larger inventory of available comic book titles for sale than a newsstand would. Before I began purchasing my comics from a comic shop, I had a selection of grocery stores and drug stores that I would visit on a weekly basis in order to find all of the titles I collected, and it was a time consuming process. Comic books sold on newsstands were treated like any other periodical—the distributor would send a selection that would be displayed for sale and any unsold issues would be returned for credit at the end of the month. Comic book stores did not operate under this model. Comic book stores purchased their inventory like a traditional retail store, so there were no returns. This allowed comic book stores to maintain an inventory of "back issues," which made it easy for comic book collectors to find any older issues that they missed in order to complete their collection. This different method of stocking their inventory meant that comic book stores typically received their comics a week before the same books were available on newsstands. The risk of a non-returnable inventory was offset by the fact that comic books purchased this way were available at a cheaper wholesale rate from the distributor. A comic shop couldn't return unsold books, but they made more per sale.

Comic book shops were able to take more risks with the type of comic books that they carried. Newsstand purchases were open to anyone who happened to walk by, whereas a customer would need to make a special trip to a comic shop. That allowed comic shops to carry comic books with material which could have been seen as too offensive (due to graphic violence, nudity, or profanity) to be distributed on a newsstand or even material that specifically catered to a more mature audience.

Since the average customer who frequented a specialized comic shop was interested in comic books as something to be collected, the physical condition of the comic book itself was very important to them. On your average newsstand, comic books would be displayed right alongside magazines and newspapers. They could be displayed in the old familiar wire racks, stacked up in a heap with a rock on top to keep them from being blown away in the wind, or even clothes-pinned to a wire along the top of the newsstand. Since today's newspaper would most likely be used to wrap fish or line the bottom of a birdcage tomorrow, it was of no consequence if the newspaper had a crease or tear or if an errant drop or two of rain hit it. For a customer buying a comic book as a collectible item, the condition of the book is paramount. Like any other collectible, having the item in as close to perfect condition as possible is preferable. Since comic shops were owned and operated by comic collectors, they would be more mindful of the condition of the comic books they had for sale. Comic book stores would display their comic books for sale on full-height shelves in order to minimize the broken spines or dog-eared pages which result from mishandling or improper storage. Many shops would sell new comic books already sealed in a protective Mylar bag with an acid-free backing board as these became available throughout the 1980s.

By 1980, the rise of the direct market was not lost on comic book publishers. Marvel was the first comic book publisher to experiment with an exclusive direct market title. In March of 1981, Marvel published *Dazzler* #1 as a "direct sale" only" book, so it was just available in comic shops. The book quickly sold over 400,000 copies and helped establish the direct market as a viable selling alternative. Other publishers took notice and began tailoring more and more of their offerings towards the direct market as well. Comic book publishers could now target a more specific part of their audience. Publishers could (and did) take chances with titles that might not have seen the necessary circulation numbers on a newsstand, but the "non return" policy of specialty comic stores and their more dedicated readers allowed them to still be profitable. The overall quality of the material in comic books improved as publishers moved away from lower grade or "pulp"-grade paper to higher quality paper for direct sale books.[1]

Another boon for the horror comic genre was another revision of the Comics Code in 1989. One of the more interesting changes in this revision was the fact that homosexuality was no longer prohibited as "aberrant behaviour" and instead it was decreed acceptable stating: "*...recognizable national, social, political, cultural, ethnic, and racial groups, religious institutions, law enforcement authorities will be portrayed in a positive light. These include ... social groups identifiable by lifestyle, such as homosexuals....*"

Another very dramatic change in the Comics Code was the statement that read: "*Healthy, wholesome lifestyles will be presented as desirable. However, the use and abuse of controlled substances, legal and illicit, are facts of modern existence, and may be portrayed when dramatically appropriate.*"[2]

This is a radical departure from the Comics Code Authority's previous stand on the portrayal of drug use in comics. Previously, the Comics Code Authority had been so rigidly anti-drug that they rejected a storyline in *Amazing Spider-Man* #96–98 in which not only was the drug use shown in an utterly negative light, but the story itself was written (by the one and only Stan Lee) on the explicit recommendation of the United States Department of Health, Education, and Welfare. Consequently, this led to one of the first times since the Comics Code Authority was enacted that a major comic book publisher released an issue without the Comics Code Authority Seal. *Amazing Spider-Man* #96–98 were received very favorably by the public and went on to receive critical acclaim for the handling of the subject matter.

By the 1980s, the Comics Code Authority was unquestionably losing its teeth. As direct sales increased, sales at newsstands decreased. The panic and outrage about horror comics was 30 years in the past by this point and comic book publishers began to notice a decline in the importance of the Code. The publication of *Amazing Spider-Man* #96–98 without the Comics Code Authority Seal on the cover didn't go unnoticed. Eventually other publishers would follow in Marvel's footsteps. DC's *Saga of the Swamp Thing* #29 (October 1984) was released without the Comics Code Authority Seal on the cover due to a particularly gruesome two-page spread. The Comics Code Authority Seal was back with issue #30, but it was dropped altogether with issue #31, and the series ran the rest of its 145-issue run without the Comics Code Authority Seal—making it the first ongoing comic series by a major publisher to forgo the Comics Code Authority Seal.

As the decade went on, the Comics Code Authority became relaxed in their rulings. *Moon Knight* #21 (July 1982) featured a story in which Moon Knight encountered some zombies. Although Marvel skirted around the banned word by still referring to them as "zuvembies," they were obviously zombies and were even referred to as "the walking dead" at one point. Despite that, the issue still bore the Comics Code Authority Seal on the cover. Likewise DC's *Elvira's House of Mystery* #2 (April 1986) was Comics Code Authority approved despite having numerous decapitations throughout.[3]

The Comics Code Authority Seal even became the target of lampooning. One example of this is the cover of *Sensational She-Hulk* #40 (June 1992). During John Byrne's successful run of the title, it was known for being one of the first comics to break the fourth wall and have the characters interact directly with the readers. The cover of issue #40 was a blatant swipe at the Comics Code Authority as it featured a nude She-Hulk covering herself up with the Comics Code Authority Seal of Approval. The Comics Code Authority Seal of Approval itself, which used to be large and boldly featured on the covers of comics, was slowly becoming smaller and less prominent on the covers which would certainly seem to parallel the lessening influence of the Comics Code Authority throughout the years. By the 1980s, the Comics Code Authority Seal of Approval appearing on a comic book cover would be smaller than the publisher's logo and even smaller than the cover price of the book. Had he still been alive and commenting on the comic book industry, I can imagine Dr. Fredric Wertham would have had something to say about how the comic book industry clearly placed more value on making a profit by emphasizing price over the appearance of the Comics Code Authority Seal of Approval.

At the same time, a new wave of independent comic books was taking the comic industry by storm. These comic books were being published by smaller publishers and printed almost exclusively in black and white—primarily as a cost saving method. Many of these independent publishers were creator-owned and self-published. Since they were so small, they were able to take risks that major publishers either could not take or were not willing to take.

Dave Sim's *Cerebus the Aardvark* along with Wendy and Richard Pini's *Elfquest* were some of the earliest independent comics to sell in large numbers, but they were quickly followed by Kevin Eastman and Peter Laird's *Teenage Mutant Ninja Turtles* which became a huge seller as a black-and-white independent comic published by Mirage Studios before making the larger leap into cartoons and major motion pictures. Independent publishers were not afraid to take chances on horror books, either. In 1986, FantaCo Enterprises began publishing *Gore Shriek* which is considered to be one of the most iconic and groundbreaking independent horror titles. The year 1986 also saw the first issue of *Deadworld* by Arrow Comics (and then later by Caliber Comics), a graphic black-and-white horror comic book telling the story of how the remnants of humanity try and survive a world devastated by the outbreak of the zombie apocalypse. This is, of course, a very familiar story now but at the time it was a radical departure from typical horror books.[4]

As the decade drew on, major comic book publishers began to experiment with releasing horror books again—although with a different twist. Publishers now knew that the demographic of the average comic book reader had shifted to an older audience with more refined tastes. The boom of self-published independent comics demonstrated that comic readers were interested in the creative teams and what they could do as much as the stories themselves.

DC took the lead this time with Volume 2 of *Saga of the Swamp Thing*. Originally written by Martin Pasko, full creative control was given to Alan Moore starting with issue #20 (January 1984). Moore took the title in more of a horror/fantasy direction, rewriting the origin of the Swamp Thing to make him more of a monster rather than a man simply transformed into a monster. In *Saga of the Swamp Thing* #21 (February 1984), D-List supervillain the Floronic Man performs an autopsy on Swamp Thing's body and discovers the body to be only superficially human with nonfunctional organs made up of vegetable matter, which meant that the Swamp Thing was never human at all. Scientist Alec Holland was in fact killed in the explosion and fire in his laboratory, and the swamp itself had absorbed Holland's mind, his memories, and his skills and fashioned a sentient being which believed itself to be Holland. Moore also introduced the world to the hard-drinking sorcerer/conman John Constantine with his first appearance being in *Saga of the Swamp Thing* #37 (June 1985) [although some purists will argue Constantine's first appearance to be an unnamed cameo in *Saga of the Swamp Thing* #25 (June 1984)]. December of 1988 would see John Constantine get his own title, *Hellblazer*, which would end up running 300 issues—not counting one-shots and spin-offs.[5]

In 1993, DC introduced its Vertigo line. The Vertigo line of comics was a direct-sale line of books which were all clearly labeled on the cover that they were for mature audiences. The titles did not bear the Comics Code Authority Seal as they were never submitted to the Comics Code Authority for approval. Selling only to comic shops and providing their own rating system, the Vertigo line set the standard for what publishers were able to do with a modern horror comic.

The Vertigo line started when DC assistant editor Karen Berger began recruiting new writing talent from the U.K. The writers (Neil Gaiman, Peter Milligan, and Grant Morrison being among the first) were brought in to add a fresh new perspective on the comic industry and to help the medium "grow up."[6] Several existing titles were put under the Vertigo banner including Alan Moore's *Swamp Thing* (starting with issue #129, March 1993), Neil Gaiman's *Sandman* (starting with issue #47, March 1993), Grant Morrison's *Doom Patrol* (starting with issue #64, March 1993), *Animal Man* (starting with issue #57, March 1993), Garth Ennis' *Hellblazer* (starting with issue #63, March 1993), and Peter Milligan and Chris Bachalo's *Shade: the Changing Man* (starting with issue #33, March 1993). New titles started under the Vertigo line included *Deadman*, *iZombie*, a relaunch of *House of Mystery* and *House of Secrets*,

Lucifer, Preacher (another Garth Ennis title), and *Haunted Tank*. Titles like *Kid Eternity* and *Jonah Hex* were relaunched with a horror spin to their writing as well. Vertigo writers took their own style to the classic vampire stories with *Vamps* and *Bite Club*. There was even a good old-fashioned horror anthology book entitled *Flinch*.

Despite using some characters from the established DC Universe, the Vertigo books and the stories therein were considered mostly separate from the DC Universe as a whole from the point of story arcs. They remained this way until the end of the 2011 "Flashpoint" story arc when the Vertigo Universe and all of its characters were merged back into the DC Universe. Although none of the original Vertigo titles are still being published, both *Lucifer* and *Hellblazer* have been relaunched with new creative teams.

In 2000, Marvel began publication of their own line of comics geared toward mature audiences. The Marvel MAX imprint, like DC's Vertigo line, were direct-sale titles with the covers clearly marked for mature readers. This would mark the first time in the history of the company that Marvel would publish explicit, uncensored content. The first title launched under the MAX line was *Alias* written by Brian Michael Bendis, and keeping true to Marvel's new allowed content, the first word on the first page of *Alias* is an "f-bomb." While not strictly a horror title, it did deal with some very unsettling content and was certainly not intended for children. The series centered around Jessica Jones, who was formerly the costumed crimefighter Jewel. Jones has left the superhero business behind her and is now a private investigator. One of the antagonists in the title is a surprisingly reworked Purple Man—previously a D-list villain in the Marvel Universe and now a cold, calculating psychopath. Marvel's risk with an R-rated title paid off, though. Sales were strong and *Alias* went on to win a *Comic Buyer's Guide* award for "Favorite Comic Series" in 2003 and a Harvey Award for "Best New Series" in 2002 as well as being nominated for two Eisner Awards for "Best Continuing Series" and "Best Serialized Story" in 2004. The title was also adapted to TV in the Netflix original series *Jessica Jones*.[7]

For obvious reasons, none of the Marvel MAX line were ever submitted to the Comics Code Authority for approval, but even the mighty Marvel Comics had started to see the lessening relevance of the Comics Code Authority by this time. With most of their sales coming through the direct market, sales of comics on newsstands were becoming less and less consequential. The Marvel MAX line notwithstanding, some of Marvel's other (non-MAX) comics were being published without the Comics Code Authority Seal of Approval on the cover. In 2001, Marvel Comics stopped submitting any of their comic books to the Comics Code Authority for approval, choosing to rely on their own rating system to direct readers towards age-appropriate content. DC followed suit in 2010 implementing its own "in-house" rating system and subsequently withdrawing from the Comics Code Authority.

The rise of the direct market as the place where most people purchased their comic books continued to lead to diminishing influence of the Comics Code Authority. Even before the disbanding of the Comics Code Authority in 2010, nearly all comic book publishers had chosen to broaden their offerings and, like many times before, some of the more popular titles were horror titles. The horror comic book genre has seen not just a resurgence, but more of a renaissance. Unfettered by unnecessary censorship, comic book publishers (both large and small) have embraced the horror comic genre in new ways. Homegrown talent of traditional comic book artists and writers have been allowed to flourish, while at the same time talent from outside the comic book industry has contributed to some amazing work. Gone are the days where the comic book is considered to be the embarrassing stepchild of the industry. Now major authors and screenwriters are contributing to comic books whereas traditional comic book writers have crossed over to become best-selling authors in their own right.

It has been over 30 years since the modern rebirth of the horror comic genre began, and so it would be all but impossible to have an in-depth discussion on each and every horror comic book that has been published since that time. The following lists some of the more groundbreaking, interesting, or just plain unusual titles that have been published during the modern resurgence of the horror comic book genre. While they might not all define modern horror comics, each of these have added to the genre we all know and love in some way.

Marvel Comics

Marvel Comics has always had a rich tradition of producing quality horror comics. This tradition goes all the way back to their early days of Atlas Comics in the 1950s when they published *Adventure Into Terror* and *Menace*. During the horror comic book resurgence of the Bronze Age of Comic Books, Marvel Comics again led the way with popular titles like *Tomb of Dracula*, *Werewolf by Night*, and *Ghost Rider*. It is only natural that Marvel Comics would continue in this tradition and produce new and interesting horror comic books during this most recent increase in the popularity of the genre.

In 2001, after withdrawing from the Comics Code Authority, Marvel Comics introduced the Marvel MAX line of titles aimed specifically at adult readers. The Marvel MAX line was the first time ever that Marvel Comics had produced comic books with uncensored content and each title bore a warning on the cover that the book was intended for mature readers only. Marvel Comics used the Marvel MAX line to release several horror comic titles including:

Blade (2002)—A darker, grittier, and noticeably more violent story arc for Marvel's famous Blade the Vampire Slayer written by screenwriter, television producer, and novelist Marc Guggenheim.

Hellstorm: Son of Satan (2006)—Written by science fiction writer Alexander Irvine, this miniseries sees Daimon Hellstrom in an unusual role—a hero in post–Katrina New Orleans.

War Is Hell: The First Flight of the Phantom Eagle (2008)—Written by Garth Ennis with artwork by Howard Chaykin, this miniseries is a reimagining of the origin of the Marvel Comics Silver Age hero the Phantom Eagle—Lt. Karl Kaufman, the American son of German parents who went on to become a masked World War I flying ace. This particular version of the Phantom Eagle reappears in the Marvel Comics 2015 *Secret Wars* event and is featured in the miniseries *Where Monsters Dwell* (2015)—a title also written by Garth Ennis.

Thor: Vikings (2003)—Another miniseries written by Garth Ennis. In this series, an army of zombie Vikings makes landfall at the South Street Seaport in New York City and proceeds to do what Vikings (zombie or not) do best—that is: rape, pillage, and plunder. This continues until Thor and Doctor Strange show up.

Dead of Night (2008)—This Marvel MAX reboot of the famous Bronze Age horror anthology title includes appearances by Man Thing, the Werewolf by Night, and the Bronze Age supernatural hero and former member of the Defenders, Devil-Slayer (although this particular iteration of the Devil-Slayer is actually Danny Sylva, the great-nephew of Eric Simon Payne—the original Devil-Slayer). This series was written by horror novelist Brian Keene.

Haunt of Horror (2006)—This series featured comic book adaptations of some of the best known works by Edgar Allan Poe and H. P. Lovecraft. As an added bonus, all of the issues are fantastically illustrated by legendary artist Richard Corben.

Zombie (2006)—This title centers on the Zombie (Simon William Garth), who first appeared way back in 1953 in the Atlas title *Menace* and who went on to be more well known as the central character in Marvel's Bronze Age black-and-white magazine *Tales of the Zombie* (1973–1975).[8]

Terror, Inc. (2007)—The antihero Terror first appeared in the Marvel Comics imprint Epic Comics title *St. George* #2 (August 1988). Created by the writers Dan Chichester and Margaret Clark and the artist Klaus Janson, Terror (at that time called Schreck—old Germanic for "fright" or "scare") was an undying assassin with the ability to absorb the talents and memories of others by grafting their dismembered limbs onto his own body. Terror received a revitalization with the Marvel MAX title *Terror, Inc.* in which his origin was retold as being a warlord of Attain who took part in the Sack of Rome. The Pope retaliated against this action by sending a demon (specifically a *mare* or a Germanic entity that sits on a person's chest while they sleep and gives them bad dreams—obviously related to the English word "nightmare" with the entity itself being more closely related to a succubus) to attack him. The being who would be Terror fights the demon and kills it, which inadvertently curses him and changes him into a walking rotting corpse. Shunned by his people, Terror sets out to wander the Earth. He discovers his newfound ability to graft the dismembered limbs of a person (or animal) to his body and the powers that come with it and styles himself as the ultimate enforcer—terrible to look at and all but invulnerable. *Terror, Inc.* lasts just five short issues, but Terror is revisited in the 2009 Marvel MAX miniseries *Terror, Inc.: Apocalypse Soon.*

Druid (1995)—Before Marvel Comics parted ways with the Comics Code Authority and started the Marvel MAX line, they were already experimenting with darker and more edgy storylines. Case in point, *Druid* in which Warren Ellis gives a very dark and creepy take on Doctor Druid (quite possibly one of the worst Avengers ever).

Hellstorm: Prince of Lies (1993)—This is a well-done series centered on Marvel's oft maligned Son of Satan, Damon Hellstrom. The series has a bit of a slow start but improves greatly after issue #12 when Warren Ellis signs on as the writer (consequently, also Warren Ellis' first work for Marvel Comics). Unfortunately sales for the title never improved and the series was cancelled with issue #21 (December 1994). The work Ellis did on attempting to turn this title around did lead to Marvel Comics giving him the aforementioned *Druid* series.

Marvel went on to modern horror notoriety with the *Marvel Zombies* series. Created by Mark Millar, the Marvel Zombies first appearance was in *Ultimate Fantastic Four* #21 (September 2005) when the Reed Richards of the Marvel Ultimate Universe tapped into a parallel universe in which all life has succumbed to a plague which turns everyone into flesh-eating zombies. While the origins of the plague are never revealed, the infection is spread via contact with blood—typically through a bite. Once infected, the victim eventually reaches a state where they appear to be dead (to the point that their flesh starts to decay), they maintain their original intelligence (and super powers where appropriate) while developing a powerful, all-consuming hunger for living flesh. The hunger affects the personality of the victim, causing them to be more and more feral and less rational until their hunger is sated. When the victim is able to feast on living flesh, the hunger subsides and their intelligence and personality returns for a while until they are eventually driven to feed again. All of the major Marvel superheroes are represented in this parallel universe and they have all been zombified—from Captain America and Spider-Man all the way to Wolverine, the Hulk, and even Thor. Robert Kirkman (although more famous for another zombie series) wrote the first *Marvel Zombies* miniseries in 2006 and several more have followed since then including *Marvel Zombies vs. The Army of Darkness* (2007)—a crossover in which the Marvel Zombies encounter Ash Williams from *Evil Dead*.[9]

Hellraiser (1989)—Banking on the success of the 1987 movie, Epic Comics (a Marvel Comics imprint) began publishing comic book spinoffs of the *Hellraiser* franchise. Each comic was an anthology book containing short stories with Clive Barker acting as a consultant on all of them. A total of 20 issues were published between 1989 and 1992. Three special issues (including the *Hellraiser: Summer Special* and *Hellraiser: Holiday Special*) were published between 1992 and 1994 as well as a comic book adaptation of *Hellraiser III: Hell on Earth*. Epic also published *Clive Barker's Book of the Damned: A Hellraiser Companion* (1991–1993) and *Pinhead* (1993–1994) as well as the crossover titles *Hellraiser vs. Nightbreed: Jihad* (1991) and *Pinhead vs. Marshal Law: Law in Hell* (1993).

The Dark Tower—Starting in 2007, Marvel Comics began publishing comic books based on the Stephen King series of novels *The Dark Tower*. These comics are not an adaptation of the novels. Instead they expand on flashbacks or other details more briefly mentioned in the novels themselves. Stephen King serves as the creative and executive director of the project while the comic books are plotted by Robin Furth (Stephen King's personal assistant and author of *The Dark Tower: A Complete Concordance*) and scripted by Peter David. The first chapter, entitled *The Dark Tower*, is made of 30 issues in five volumes. Those are: *The Dark Tower: The Gunslinger Born* (2007), *The Dark Tower: The Long Road Home* (2008), *The Dark Tower: Treachery* (2008), *The Dark Tower: The Sorcerer* (2009), *The Dark Tower: Fall of Gilead* (2009), and *The Dark Tower: Battle of Jericho Hill* (2009). The second chapter, entitled *The Dark Tower: The Gunslinger*, consists of another 30 issues in five volumes: *The Dark Tower: The Journey Begins* (2010), *The Dark Tower: The Little Sisters of Eluria* (2010), *The Dark Tower: The Battle of Tull* (2011), *The Dark Tower: The Way Station* (2011), *The Dark Tower: The Man in Black* (2012), *The Dark

Tower: Sheemie's Tale (2013), *The Dark Tower: Evil Ground* (2013), and *The Dark Tower: So Fell Lord Perth* (2013).

The series was originally supposed to end with the 2013 publication of *The Dark Tower: So Fell Lord Perth*, but on April 24, 2014, a third chapter, *The Dark Tower: The Drawing of the Three*, was announced. This chapter was based primarily on the novel *The Dark Tower II: The Drawing of the Three* and focused on the newly gathered (or "drawn") members of Roland's "ka-tet." This chapter is made up of *The Dark Tower: The Prisoner* (2014), *The Dark Tower: House of Cards* (2015), *The Dark Tower: Lady of Shadows* (2015), *The Dark Tower: Bitter Medicine* (2016), and *The Dark Tower: The Sailor* (2016). The series is also supplemented by *The Dark Tower: The Gunslinger Born Sketchbook* (2006), *Marvel Spotlight: The Dark Tower* (2007), *The Dark Tower: Gunslinger's Guidebook* (2007), *The Dark Tower: End-World Almanac* (2008), and *The Dark Tower: Guide to Gilead* (2009)

The Stand—In 2008, Marvel Comics also began publishing a comic adaptation of the Stephen King novel *The Stand*. Written by Roberto Aguirre-Sacasa with art by Mike Perkins and Laura Martin, the 31-issue series is based on the 1990 *Complete & Uncut* version of the book. The comic book series is divided into six story arcs: *The Stand: Captain Trips* (September 2008–January 2009), *The Stand: American Nightmares* (March 2009–August 2009), *The Stand: Soul Survivors* (October 2009–March 2010), *The Stand: Hardcases* (June 2010–November 2010), *The Stand: No Man's Land* (February 2011–May 2011), and *The Stand: The Night Has Come* (August 2011–January 2012). The series was also supplemented by *The Stand: Sketchbook* (2008). A complete collection of the story arcs was published in 2012 as *The Stand Omnibus* which included bonus material not published in the original comic books.

Stephen King's N (2010)—As you can probably tell, I am a big Stephen King fan so any comic adaptation of his work is most likely going to show up on a list of mine. This four-issue series published in 2010 is a comic book adaptation of *N*, a short story originally published in the collection *Just After Sundown*.

Darkhold: Pages from the Book of Sins (1992)—The Darkhold is Marvel Comics' version of the Necronomicon. Crafted by an Elder God, the Darkhold has been responsible for the creation of vampires and werewolves and providing access to terrible dark magic to anyone powerful (or foolish) enough to read from its pages. Created by writer Gerry Conway and artist Mike Ploog way back in *Marvel Spotlight* #3 (May 1972), the Darkhold has bounced its way throughout the Marvel Universe ever since then. The 1992 series *Darkhold: Pages from the Book of Sins* unfortunately does not feature art by Mike Ploog, but it does tell the tale of Victoria Montisi and the Darkhold Redeemers—a group of people dedicated to stopping the carnage caused by people using lost pages of the Darkhold to their own nefarious means. With the Darkhold making an appearance in everything from *Werewolf By Night* to *Marvel Chillers* to *Marvel Zombies* with stopovers in the "Secret Empire" crossover and even the *Marvel's Agents of S.H.I.E.L.D.* television show, this series gives some interesting background as to what all of the fuss is about with this book.

Franken-Castle (2010)—At a glance, this storyline would seem to be over-the-top enough to have been published in the Silver Age of Comic Books. It was written and published in 2010, however. Not only that, but Rick Reminder (the writer of the story) takes a classic trope of inserting a monster into a traditional title and polishes it into a very interesting and well-written story. During the events of Marvel's 2010 Dark Reign storyline Norman Osborn tries to establish himself up as the savior of humanity—even ascending to become the director of S.H.I.E.L.D., which he promptly disbands and renames H.A.M.M.E.R. Frank Castle (a.k.a. the Punisher) wants no part of this and decides to take care of the Norman Osborn problem in typical Punisher fashion and assassinate him. Osborn takes the assassination attempt in typical Norman Osborn fashion and throws all of H.A.M.M.E.R.'s resources into finding the Punisher and killing him. This culminates in *Dark Reign: The List–Punisher* #1 (December 2009) when Dark Wolverine (a.k.a. Daken, Wolverine's son) finally catches up with the Punisher. A brawl ensues and the Punisher holds his own against Daken for a while. Daken has his father's mutant healing factor whereas Frank Castle does not, so Daken eventually gets the upper hand. He slices off both of the Punisher's arms before finally decapitating him. Frank Castle's body is picked up by Morbius the Living Vampire and he and the Legion of Monsters (Werewolf by Night, Manphibian, Man-Thing, Satana, and N'Kantu the Living Mummy) reanimate Castle's body into Franken-Castle in the hopes that Franken-Castle would maintain enough of his military experience to help the Legion of Monsters defend themselves against a group of marauders who have been hunting them down. The Franken-Castle storyline continues in *The Punisher* #11 (January 2010) through *The Punisher* #16 (June 2010) then the series is renamed *Franken-Castle* for issues #16 (August 2010) through the final issue of #21 (November 2010). Without revealing too much, the story's climax includes a three-way showdown between Franken-Castle (with the Legion of Monsters as backup), Daken, and Wolverine himself.

Doctor Voodoo: Avenger of the Supernatural (2009)—From his first appearance back in the Bronze Age title *Strange Tales* #165 (September 1973), Brother Voodoo has battled the forces of evil and the supernatural alongside Spider-Man, Moon Knight, and Black Panther. In *New Avengers* #53 (July

2009), Brother Voodoo embraces a mantle of more than just a Voodoo houngan when he is chosen to replace Stephen Strange as the new Sorcerer Supreme (and has a name change to Doctor Voodoo). This also led to the short-lived *Doctor Voodoo: Avenger of the Supernatural* title which ran five issues from December 2009 through April 2010. Brother Voodoo also made an appearance in the one-shot *Marvel Zombies: Dead Days* (July 2007) as one of the last few heroes of the world to survive the zombie virus. Brother Voodoo from an alternate Earth (Earth-666 to be precise) appears in *Secret Avengers* #33 (October 2012) as the leader of the Avengers of the Undead. Earth-666 is an alternate Earth where the world was populated with various monsters (vampires, werewolves, mummies, etc.). The Avengers of the Undead serve as the protectors of that dystopian world. Aside from Brother Voodoo, the Avengers of the Undead are made up of Black Widow (who is now part human and part spider), Captain America (a werewolf—drawing from the famous "Cap Wolf" story arc of *Captain America* #405–#408, August 1992–October 1992), Daredevil (now an actual horned demon), Franken-Castle (based on the *Franken-Castle* title), Hawkeye (part human and part hawk), Thor (now an undead mummy), and Wolverine (a vampire). At the time of this writing Brother Voodoo could possibly be crossing over into a more mainstream role as the character is being hinted to appear in the movie sequel *Doctor Strange 2*.

Man Thing (2018)—With his first appearance in the Bronze Age title *Savage Tales* #1 (May 1971) and regular appearances in *Adventure Into Fear*, Man Thing has had a long background in horror. After nearly 13 years without a title of his own, Man Thing is back in a big way—this time with *Fear Street* and *Goosebumps* author R. L. Stine doing the writing. As an added bonus, each issue of *Man Thing* features a short horror story written by R. L. Stine and drawn by a guest artist.

DC/Vertigo

American Vampire (2010)—Vampires as a race are capable of evolution and a new species of vampire native to America has developed. This series spans the decades and shows the influence the new American Vampire has had on American history.

Preacher (1995)—Jesse Custer, a preacher in a small backwater Texas town, is having a crisis of faith. On top of that, he just became possessed by a supernatural entity known as Genesis. Genesis is the spawn of the coupling of an angel and a demon. Being made up of pure goodness and pure evil, but no sense of individuality, makes Genesis immensely powerful, but the unnatural circumstances of its birth makes Genesis alone and directionless in the universe. Now Jesse/Genesis sets out to do what anyone would in this case: to go find God for some answers! He is accompanied in this quest by his old girlfriend and an Irish vampire. It only gets stranger from there!

Arkham Asylum: A Serious House on Serious Earth (1989)—Sometimes shortened to *Batman: Arkham Asylum*, this graphic novel is Grant Morrison's first work on a Batman title. In it, he weaves a dark and twisted tale of psychological horror which is only made more creepy and disturbing by Dave McKean's shadowy artwork. A technique that would become more prevalent in Vertigo books, the fonts change from character to character. Batman speaks in a bold black-and-white font. Maxie Zeus has blue with a Greek font. The Joker doesn't even get word balloons. His words are scrawled in red directly on the black background like bloody scratches—sometimes making his dialog as hard to read as his character's motives are to determine. In the story, the inmates have risen up and taken control of Arkham Asylum (on April Fool's Day, of course) and are threatening to start killing hostages unless Batman agrees to come inside and meet with them. The Dark Knight makes his way through the dim Gothic hallways and secret passages while encountering disturbingly twisted versions of his normal staple of villains in a very different deconstruction of the Batman mythos.

Batman: Red Rain (1991)—This graphic novel is the first volume in what would eventually become known as the Batman and Dracula Trilogy. All of them are part of the DC Comics Elseworlds line—an imprint used to tell stories which happened outside of the normal DC Comics Universe (and so not subject to more than 80 years of continuity). In the first volume, *Batman: Red Rain*, Batman investigates a series of murders of homeless people only to find they have been killed by vampires under the leadership of Dracula himself. In the subsequent battles, Batman is bitten and begins to transform into a vampire. Batman struggles to maintain his humanity while knowing that his new vampiric powers are the only thing that would allow him to defeat Dracula. Batman and Dracula battle to the death (or "death") and the ensuing struggle pushes Batman over the edge into a full-blown, mindless vampire. Bruce Wayne is gone and Gotham City now has a new Dark Knight to contend with. The trilogy continues in *Batman: Bloodstorm* (1994). Dracula is defeated, but his minions still continue to terrorize Gotham City—now under the control of the Joker. Alfred, Commissioner Gordon, and many of the Gotham PD have become vampire hunters and fight to quell this new invasion of the undead. The vampiric Batman attacks the Joker, draining him of his blood and killing him. In a flash of humanity, Batman recognizes what he has done and stakes the Joker, preventing him from rising up as a new vampire. He then convinces Commissioner Gordon and Alfred to do the same to him in order to put an end to his reign of terror. The trilogy concludes with *Batman: Crimson Mist* (1999). Gotham City is in the grips of a new crime wave and needs a savior again. Regretfully, Alfred removed the stake from the vampire Batman's body, which allows him to reanimate. Being staked down for so long has caused both Batman's body and mind to rot. Driven mad from not feeding on blood for so long, Batman flies into an uncontrollable rage and, still keeping an inkling of Batman's thoughts, heads directly for Arkham Asylum where carnage ensues. Batman kills and drains the blood from nearly every Arkham Asylum inmate—from Penguin, the Riddler and Scarecrow all the way down to Black Mask, Victor Zsasz, and Amygdala. Only Killer Croc and Two-Face manage to escape. The two villains strike a deal with Alfred and Commissioner Gordon to end the vampire Batman problem once and for all. In a final showdown in the ruins of the Batcave, Batman wins the battle but realizes in the process he has lost everything that means anything to him. In a last act of humanity, he walks out into the first rays of the morning sun in the hopes that he will finally be able to find the peace he has so long sought.

This trilogy is one of the most memorable works for both the Batman comic books and the horror comic genre. This is due in no small part to the creative team behind it. Doug Moench (whose early works included writing for *Eerie, Vampirella,* and *Werewolf by Night*) does an incredible job of scripting the story. Moench's story is perfectly complemented by the artwork of Kelley Jones. Jones' unique art style couldn't fit this version of Batman any better. Batman himself is towering and imposing with a huge flowing cape that appears to be part of the overall darkness of Gotham City itself that Batman merely wraps himself in. Batman's gloves practically end in fiendish claws and the over-styled "ears" on his cowl should be humorous in their exaggeration, but instead they lend an otherworldly, demonic look to the character. Kelley Jones' Batman is a Dark Knight indeed—a vision that you can understand why strikes fear into the hearts of criminals. In this author's opinion, the creative team of Doug Moench and Kelley Jones is the best thing to happen to comic books in a long time.

Batman: Haunted Gotham (1999)—Of course, I had to recommend another Elseworlds Batman story by the creative team of Doug Moench and Kelley Jones. *Batman: Haunted Gotham* provides a little bit of a different spin. In this story, Batman is fighting the forces of the supernatural instead of becoming one of them. Gotham City has been cut off from the rest of the world by an army of dark forces including werewolves, ghosts, demons, zombies, and (of course) the Joker has to get involved. Bruce Wayne has been trained from birth to fight these creatures by Thomas and Martha Wayne who are very much still alive in this Elseworlds Universe—at least at the beginning of the story. I mean, the Batman always needs an origin story, right?

DC House of Horror (2017)—I will admit that I have a soft spot for Halloween specials, so I couldn't have been happier to see that DC decided to continue the tradition of releasing a Halloween special comic right around that most spectacular time of the year. Starting in 2007 with the *DC Universe: Infinite Halloween Special* and continuing through 2010 after being renamed the *DC Universe Halloween Special*, DC had published an annual comic book full of good old-fashioned ghost stories every October. After 2010, they took a break but released *DC House of Horror* in October 2017 which I hope is the beginning of a new tradition. This book takes some of the most traditional DC superheroes and gives them a spectacular horror twist by turning the scripting over to traditional horror writers like Brian Keene, Weston Ochse, Edward Lee, Mary SanGiovanni, Wrath James White, Nick Cutter, Ronald Malfi, and Bryan Smith—a lineup which includes several Bram Stoker nominations and awards and dozens and dozens of novels between them. Edward Lee writes the first story in the anthology "Bump in the Night" in which the quiet town of Smallville, Kansas, is shocked awake by the crash of a spaceship. Jonathan Kent goes outside for a closer look only to be killed by the shrieking alien entity from within the capsule. Martha Wayne hears the commotion and goes outside to find her husband dead and the tiny humanoid with its sights set on her now. This creepiness just sets the stage for the rest of the stories of twisted horrific versions of Batman, Wonder Woman, Green Lantern, Shazam, and other DC staples.

Clean Room (2015)—Written by Gail Simone (notable for her runs on *Birds of Prey, Wonder Woman*, and *Deadpool*) and drawn by Jon Davis-Hunt (now doing his first major U.S. work after long stretches on U.K. comic books *2000 AD* and *Judge Dredd Megazine*), *Clean Room* is a wonderful piece of horror. Gail Simone has perfected the "slow burn" in her storytelling. This book doesn't rely on horrifying imagery or the more "in your face" style of some books. No, this book tells a story that just creeps around the dark shadows in your head and lies in wait—just like good horror should. I mean, a jump scare is one thing—someone pops out from behind a door and yells "Boo!" and you are startled, then everyone laughs it off. Good horror is something you see (or read) and while it may not be unsettling at first, the idea just kind of sticks in your head and you find you can't stop thinking about it—especially when you're all alone and walking to your car in the dark. *Clean Room* centers on journalist Chloe Pierce. Her fiancé recently joined a cult-like group led by billionaire self-help guru Astrid Mueller, and a few months later he kills himself. Mueller blames Pierce and begins investigating her organization to get to the bottom of what happened. Mueller find her answers only to wish she hadn't. There are demonic creatures tearing into our reality. People have told stories about them for generations, but most people can't see them. Astrid Mueller can. Not only that, but she is recruiting an army to fight them back to wherever they came from—provided it's not too late.

The Dark and Bloody (2016)—Iris Gentry is a veteran recently returned from a tour of duty in Iraq. He goes back to his home in rural Kentucky only to find he has few options for providing for his family. He resorts to running moonshine for his former ranking officer, which links him to a past that he has been trying to forget. During their combat days, Iris' regiment was involved in something that they should have left alone and now those chickens are coming home to roost as well. What sacrifices is a man willing to make for his country? For his family? How much of your past is out of your control and how much of your present do you really control? This is another wonderful "slow burn" horror title. Don't expect wall-to-wall gore. Definitely expect to have elements of this book pop up in your head when you least expect (or want) them to.

Gotham by Midnight (2015)—Gotham City has the Gotham PD to handle regular crime and Batman for supervillains, but what about the *really* weird stuff? To tackle all things supernatural, Jim Gordon assembles a special task force of paranormal specialists headed by Jim Corrigan (part-time policeman and part-time Spirit of Vengeance as the Spectre). Written by Ray Fawkes and drawn by Ben Templesmith, this "New 52" title is an interesting spin on the Batman Universe and the things that go bump in the Gotham night. Of course, you can't have a comic book set in Gotham City that doesn't have an appearance or two from Batman, but cameos by the Cowled One are few and far between.

The Wake (2013)—Marine biologist Lee Archer is approached by someone claiming to be from the Department of Homeland Security. She is "asked" to accompany him to a top secret location to offer her opinion on a creature. The top secret location turns out to be a hidden underwater oil rig deep in the Arctic Circle. She arrives to find out she is not alone—also there are an expert in folklore, a deep-sea hunter, and another scientist who Archer knows from her past. The creature turns out to be something she has never seen before. To make matters worse, it has friends and its friends aren't particularly happy about one of their own being held in captivity. Written by Scott Snyder and drawn by Sean Murphy, this title has all of the makings of a great horror tale: mysterious government agents, unknown menacing creatures, and the helpless feeling of being trapped and isolated away from anyone you know (more importantly, anyone who could help you). This is all just in Part One of the story. Part Two picks up with *The Wake* #6 (April 2014) and takes place 200 years in the future. The whole mysterious creature issue has been solved by then, but that's not a good thing.

Hellblazer (1988)—It is impossible to make a list of standout horror comics of the modern era and not mention *Hellblazer*. One of the first, and the longest running Vertigo title, *Hellblazer* ran for a total of 300 issues from 1998 through 2013. *Hellblazer* was centered on John Constantine—a street-savvy conman/magician/occult detective. John Constantine is a hard-drinking chain-smoker who saved the world more than once (and parts of London many more times than that), but he usually accomplished this through the use of trickery, guile, deception, or even outright lies and you never really knew if his motivation was out of a sense of duty or just to save his own skin. John Constantine tangled with all sorts of demons, devils, ghosts, and things that go bump in the night and proved that he is a good guy to have on your side in a fight; however, he's definitely a bad guy to have as one of your friends. Constantine would typically make it out of a fight without any lasting damage, but his close friends were rarely so lucky. Being as closely aligned with the spirit world as Constantine was, his dead friends would quite literally haunt him nearly everywhere he went.

In a series that ran for 25 years, you can imagine the creative teams behind it changed hands a few times. The series started out written by Jamie Delano with Garth Ennis taking over in 1991 and having the longest tenure as writer on the series with his eight-year run. Warren Ellis took over in 1999 with the intention of becoming the next long-term writer for the title, but creative differences led Ellis to quit the title with issue #143 (December 1999). Ellis had written a story for *Hellblazer* called "Shoot" in which a female researcher searches for the causes of school shootings only to discover that John Constantine was present for several of them. Eventually John Constantine himself pays a visit to the reporter telling her (in typical Constantine fashion) she did not have the "faintest fucking idea" as to what she saw in the incidents and the shooters and their victims were products of their society. The story was unfortunately scheduled to be printed shortly after the tragic shooting at Columbine High School in April of 1999. Top brass at DC were not happy with the story or the timing and insisted Ellis change it. Ellis refused to budge and the story was not printed, prompting Ellis to quit. "Shoot" would eventually see the light of day, though. It was printed in its entirety in October 2010 as part of the special *Vertigo Resurrected* #1 and received very positive reviews. Ellis was eventually praised for his use of the character of John Constantine as someone who was unabashedly unafraid to confront the hard truths of modern society.

After the unexpected departure of Warren Ellis, Darko Macan took over as writer for the series until Brian Azzarello took over with *Hellblazer* #146 (March 2000). Azzarello came to *Hellraiser* after his run on Vertigo title *100 Bullets*. Azzarello's writing tenure encompassed one long story arc with John Constantine in America. Azzarello's time on *Hellblazer* lasted until issue #174 (August 2002) when Mike Carey took over. Mike Carey had previously written for the Vertigo title *Lucifer*—a spinoff title from popular Neil Gaiman Vertigo title *Sandman*. Carey returns John Constantine to his roots, moving him back to London. Carey, a native of Liverpool, also has the distinction of being the only Liverpool native to have written for John Constantine—a Liverpudlian himself. Carey's tenure lasted until issue *Hellblazer* #215 (February 2006) when crime novelist Denise Mina took over and wrote until *Hellblazer* #228 (March 2007). Andy Diggle picked up the writing mantle with *Hellblazer* #230 (May 2007). Diggle, a veteran writer of Vertigo titles *The Losers* and *Swamp Thing* wrote until *Hellblazer* #249 (December 2009) at which point Diggle left the title and DC Comics to accept an exclusive contract with Marvel Comics. Peter Milligan, another Vertigo veteran having written both *Shade, the Changing Man* and *Animal Man*, took over writing with *Hellblazer* #250 (February 2009) and wrote the series until its final issue, #300 (April 2013).

In 2011, it was announced that a younger John Constantine would be making an appearance in the standard DC Universe after the New 52 reboot. John Constantine was part of the new Justice League Dark with Shade the Changing Man, Deadman, and Madame Xanadu. *Justice League Dark* was also written by Peter Milligan. Following the end of *Hellblazer* in 2012, DC relaunched the title as *Constantine* featuring the New 52 John Constantine. In *Constantine*, John Constantine was a younger man whereas the character aged rather realistically in *Hellblazer* so by the time the series came to an end, John Constantine was pictured to be in his late 50s. *Constantine* ran for 23 issues ending in May of 2015 only to be launched again as *Constantine: The Hellblazer*. This series, written by Ming Doyle and drawn by Riley Rossmo, enjoyed a brief 19-issue run before ending as part of the 2016 DC Rebirth event. The DC Rebirth event essentially undid all of the New 52 continuity in an effort to revert major storylines (and their respective continuities) back to before the New 52 event. In September 2016, the one-shot *Hellblazer: Rebirth* reestablished John Constantine back into the standard DC Universe. John is back in London and *Hellblazer* characters like Chas Chandler and Mercury are back in the story as well. Following up on the one-shot, the new *Hellblazer* ongoing series was launched in October of 2016 and is still being published at the time of this writing.

Scooby Apocalypse—Not wanting to miss out on the trend of taking a familiar property and relaunching it in a post-apocalypse setting, DC Comics launched *Scooby Apocalypse* in May of 2016 to generally favorable reviews. The good, old-fashioned gang of meddling kids is back, but this time there's no more creepy old guys in bedsheets and rubber masks. Set in the post-apocalyptic future, this reimagining of the familiar old characters certainly has some potential. Velma Dinkley was a leading scientist at the Nevada Complex where she coordinated the "Smart Dog" project—a program which modified dogs and gave them the ability to talk. Norville "Shaggy" Rogers was a dog handler at the Nevada Complex where he was responsible for the treatment and training of the "smart dog" prototypes. On his first day at work, he saves the runt of the litter from being torn to pieces by the other prototypes. Scoobert "Scooby" Doo was the runt of the "smart dog" program that Shaggy saved. Scooby has been modified with a chip in his cerebral cortex which allows him to communicate with others—either through talking or through a pair of "emoji-goggles." Daphne Blake was a budding journalist whose career took a nosedive when she failed to expose a story she had been working on for over a year. After that, she took the only work she could find as the host of *Daphne Blake's Mysterious Mysteries*. Fred Jones was a long-time friend of Daphne Blake and the cameraman for *Daphne Blake's Mysterious Mysteries*. After the apocalypse, the gang finds plenty to do when, all of a sudden, ghosts, ghouls, and vampires are real and not just old men in cheap masks. On top of all this, the gang must keep one step ahead of Scrappy-Doo, another one of the "smart dog" project test subjects with a single-minded purpose to kill Scooby-Doo, who he sees as soft-hearted and weak.

Dark Horse Comics

Dark Horse Comics was founded in 1986 by Mike Richardson in Milwaukie, Oregon. Richardson started by opening a comic book store called Pegasus Books in Bend, Oregon, in 1980 and used the funds from the store to start his own publishing company. Dark Horse Comics was founded with the idea to provide a more open playing field for creative professionals and it has definitely lived up to that promise. Dark Horse Comics also had the distinction of never submitting any of their comic books to the Comics Code Authority for approval—which was a bold move at the time. Even in 1980, the Comics Code Authority still had some pull in the industry. Since Richardson was a former comic shop owner himself, he probably saw the importance of selling directly to the direct market and the lessening impact of newsstand sales. This would not be the last of Dark Horse Comics' bold moves, though. They have established themselves as a company willing to take risks and not compromising when it comes to the quality of their work or their artists. Through the years, a veritable Who's Who of the comic book industry has done work for Dark Horse Comics including: Mike Mignola (*Hellboy*), Frank Miller (*Sin City*), Eric Powell (*The Goon*), Joss Whedon (*Buffy The Vampire Slayer*), Mike Allred (*Madman*), Stan Sakai (*Usagi Yojimbo*), Mike Richardson (*The Mask*), and Rob Reger (*Emily the Strange*). Naturally, Dark Horse Comics has published some quality horror comic books as well.

Rat God—In early 1900s New England, a white settler falls for a Native American woman. When she disappears, he goes looking for her in the deep woods. Eisner Award Hall of Fame inductee Richard Corben writes and draws this truly unsettling tale that would do H.P. Lovecraft proud.

Freaks of the Heartland—Trevor lives on a farm in a very rural area with his abusive father, his meek mother, and his little brother. Despite being just six years old, Trevor's little brother is a huge hulk of a person and quite strong. He is also kept chained up in the barn. One day, Trevor decides to free his little brother and run away—only to find his brother isn't the only dirty little secret their town is hiding.

Harrow County—Emmy always thought that there were ghosts, goblins, and things that go bump in the night living in the woods around her house. On her 18th birthday, she finds out that they are all real—and that's just the beginning of the secrets!

Creepy Comics—Yep, Dark Horse Comics has resurrected the old-school anthology and brought it back to its full glory. New writers and new artists (plus some of your old favorites), but the same old *Creepy*.

Hellboy: Seed of Destruction—Created and written by Mike Mignola with first appearance in *San Diego Comic-Con Comic* #2 (August 1993), Hellboy and his companions in the Bureau for Paranormal Research and Defense (BPRD) have appeared in several miniseries, crossovers, and one-shots, but all of the stories are interconnected and tell the story of Hellboy and the BPRD protecting the world as we know it from the forces of evil like Baba Yaga, Grigori Rasputin, and the Lovecraftian Ogdru Jahad—godlike beings who wish nothing more than to use Hellboy's "Right Hand of Doom" and his demonic heritage to usher in an apocalyptic end to humanity.[10]

With two motion pictures and literally hundreds of books, Hellboy doesn't need much of an introduction. *Seed of Destruction* collects the first

Hellboy comics. Personally, I would recommend them all, but if you only read one, it should be this one.

Beasts of Burden (2009)—Created by writer Evan Dorkin and artist Jill Thompson, *Beasts of Burden* centers on a team of intelligent animals that investigate paranormal events occurring in their neighborhood of Burden Hill. The characters first appeared in a story called "Stray" in *The Dark Horse Book of Hauntings* (2003) and have since appeared in *The Dark Horse Book of Witchcraft* (2004), *The Dark Horse Book of The Dead* (2005), and *The Dark Horse Book of Monsters* (2006) before appearing in their own four-issue miniseries in 2009. In 2011, the characters appeared alongside Hellboy in *Hellboy/Beasts of Burden: Sacrifice* and have since had several one-shots including: *Beasts of Burden: Neighborhood Watch* (2012), *Beasts of Burden: Hunters & Gatherers* (2014), *Beasts of Burden: What the Cat Dragged In* (2016), and *Beasts of Burden: Animal Rites* (2018). The group is made up of five dogs (Ace, Rex, Jack, Whitey, and Pugsley) and two cats (Orphan and Dymphna—a former witch's familiar). This series is a refreshing take on the traditional horror/detective story. The series has won multiple Eisner Awards as well as the 2011 National Cartoonist Society Award for Best Comic Book Artist (for Jill Thompson). Not bad considering the story idea originally came about because Evan Dorkin wanted to write a non-traditional haunted house story and decided on writing about a haunted doghouse.

Criminal Macabre: A Cal McDonald Mystery (2003)—Steve Niles created Cal McDonald in 1990. The first Cal McDonald story, "Big Head," was published in the anthology comic book *Fly in My Eye: Daughters of Fly In My Eye* by Arcane Comix. In a similar vein to John Constantine, Cal McDonald is a hard-drinking, drug-using detective with a network of ghouls as his assistants. He takes cases involving the horrific or paranormal and typically works without police interference—mainly because the police don't want to be involved with him. In 1996, Dark Horse published its first Cal McDonald story, "Hairball," which was serialized in *Dark Horse Presents* #102–105 and later collected as a one-shot. Steve Niles next published two Cal McDonald novels, *Savage Membrane* and *Guns, Drugs, and Monsters* in which Cal is in pursuit of a living severed head searching for its body. Cal returned to the comic book medium with the 2003 miniseries *Criminal Macabre: A Cal McDonald Mystery*. During that time, Cal's adventures have been published in a series of one-shots and miniseries including *Criminal Macabre: Two Red Eyes* (2006), *Criminal Macabre: My Demon Baby* (2007), *Criminal Macabre: Cell Block 666* (2008), *Criminal Macabre: Die, Die, My Darling* (2012), and *Criminal Macabre: The Eyes of Frankenstein* (2013) in which Cal McDonald encounters the severed head (again) and even the vampire Nosferatu. Along the way, artwork for the comic books has been provided by Jim Whiting, Kyle Hotz, Nick Stakal, Ben Templesmith, and the horror art staple Kelley Jones. All of the Cal McDonald stories have been collected in a three-volume Omnibus, with volumes one and two published in 2011 and volume three published in 2015.

Colder (2012)—Declan Thomas was a catatonic patient whom a young nurse took it upon herself to take into her home. For five years she cared for Thomas, watching as his body temperature got lower and lower. Even with a body temperature in the 50s, the man remained alive. One day, Thomas stands up and tells the nurse that they need to talk. Declan Thomas was committed to an asylum and experimented on over 50 years ago (despite him only looking to be about 25) before the asylum burned down. Now Declan is being pursued by an entity calling itself Nimble Jack. Nimble Jack feeds on madness and, unfortunately, Declan has madness to spare. On top of that, his body temperature continues to drop each day. Declan now has to get away from Nimble Jack while still figuring out what is going to happen when his temperature finally reaches zero. A second chapter in this series, *Colder: The Bad Seed*, was published in 2014 followed by *Colder: Toss the Bones* in 2015. Paul Tobin writes this story and it is perfectly complemented with creepy-bordering-on-insane art by Juan E. Ferreyra.

House of Penance (2016)—The Winchester House was built by Sarah Winchester, the wife of William Wirt Winchester, heir to the Winchester Repeating Arms Company. In the late 1880s both William Winchester and the couple's infant daughter died suddenly, leaving Sarah Winchester with a substantial inheritance. Sarah Winchester came to believe that the ghosts of people killed by Winchester rifles were haunting her and so she had construction started on a house. Work on the house continued around the clock for over 30 years until Sarah Winchester's death. The final product was a seven-story mansion filled with every manner of haphazard construction. There were stairways that led to nowhere, doors that opened into walls, windows that opened into other interior rooms, and other peculiar elements. Legend has it that Sarah Winchester did this to confuse the vengeful spirits that came to the house seeking vengeance. *House of Penance* is a brilliant work of Gothic horror set during the construction of the Winchester House. Sarah Winchester, either terribly frightened or seriously deranged, is supervising the chaotic work on the Winchester House when a visitor arrives. The mysterious visitor could be there to rid Sarah Winchester of her demons or he could just as easily be one himself. Peter Tomasi spins an amazing tale of suspense while Ian Bertram's hyper-detailed artwork helps solidify the eerie visual elements. This series was released to great praise by the likes of Scott Snyder and Garth Ennis and it is easy to see why.

Shadows on the Grave (2017)—Richard Corben, horror art legend and Eisner Hall of Fame award winner, is still working well into his late 70s. Not only that, but his mind is just as sharp and his hands are just as steady as they have always been, as this eight-issue series demonstrates. Each issue of this anthology title is masterfully scripted and intricately drawn. The series is done in black and white—a point that Corben says is an artistic choice and not a cost-savings measure (as if there was ever really any doubt). There's really not much else that needs to be said. If you are a fan of Richard Corben, well-written horror, or fantastic art, then you need to pick up this series.

Edgar Allan Poe's Spirits of the Dead (2014)—Edgar Allan Poe's writing with Richard Corben's illustrations—does anything else need to be added? In case you do need more clarification: Richard Corben (whose art appeared in *Skull, Creepy, Eerie, Fantagor,* and even the cover for the Meat Loaf album *Bat Out of Hell*) drew a series of comic book adaptations of some of Edgar Allan Poe's best-known stories. These stories were originally published in the pages of *Dark Horse Presents*. They are all collected in this one single volume: "The Conqueror Worm," "The Fall of the House of Usher," "The Raven," "The Red Death," and "Murders in the Rue Morgue."

Aliens: Dead Orbit (2017)—Dark Horse Comics has had the exclusive license to publish comic books based on the *Alien* movie franchise since 1988 and they have used it well. Dark Horse Comics has explored this sci-fi/horror universe with a series of one-shots and limited series over the past 30 years. The most recent offering, *Aliens: Dead Orbit,* is a wonderfully suspenseful and claustrophobic story. A terrible accident has struck a space station, leaving an engineering officer alone with a timer, a utility kit and (of course) one of nature's deadliest creatures. Written and drawn by James Stokoe, this series is definitely worth a read—just remember to breathe while you're reading!

Image Comics

The Walking Dead—It goes without saying that Robert Kirkman's most famous work should be listed. In case you need a plot summary, the zombie apocalypse has happened and lawman Rick Grimes leads a ragtag band of people (including his wife, son, and former deputy) who are trying to survive the perils of the undead and the living. Honestly, the pacing can be a little slow at times, but this title is one of the few books that I have ever had to stop reading, sit the book down, and go for a walk in the sunshine before I could finish.

Nameless—This six-issue miniseries by Grant Morrison will take you on a ride. An asteroid is headed for Earth and it is wreaking havoc with the folks on the planet as well as the astronauts sent to explore it. The story is presented in a non-linear, disjointed format, and even you as the reader are never sure what is real and what is a nightmare.

Nailbiter—A small Oregon town has produced 16 of the nation's most notorious serial killers. The most recent one (known for chewing off his victim's fingernails and the ends of their fingers) has just recently been apprehended; however, the agent who arrested him is missing. His friend takes up the search and also tries to find out what is going on in this town.

Revival—A "rural noir" series by Tim Seeley and set in central Wisconsin. This series follows the struggles of police officer Dana Cypress in a world where the dead have returned to life. A familiar story, but different than *The Walking Dead* in that the dead are rising only in an area around a small town while the rest of the world remains untouched.

Outcast—Robert Kirkman tackles demons instead of zombies in this series. Kyle Barnes is a man who grew up watching his friends and family battling with demonic possession. Now an adult, he and a pastor revisit people from his past to try to find why Kyle is so "special."

The Beauty (2015)—There is a new sexually transmitted disease going around and nobody seems to mind. This is probably because one of the side effects of the STD is that an infected person becomes more and more beautiful every day. Of course, just like the pharmaceutical commercials on television, there are some side effects that should be listed. Infected people have a tendency to run a slight fever. An infected person may be slightly hungrier and tend to eat a little more—don't worry, though the "beauty" part of the side effects will take care of any extra weight gain. Detectives Vaughn and Foster discover there is one more little side effect that nobody is mentioning—the infection will kill you in a spectacular manner. Why isn't anyone talking about this little caveat? Detectives Vaughn and Foster are working to uncover the mystery behind that.

The Black Monday Murders (2016)—Do you ever get the feeling that those hot-shot stockbrokers have made some type of deal with the devil to get the money and power that they have? Well, in this series written by Jonathan Hickman and drawn by Tomm Coker, that is basically what has happened. A group of elite financiers have made a blood pact with an elder god in exchange for power and money. Theodore Dumas is an NYC detective who is trying to uncover all of the secrets. This story has everything: magic-controlled banking cartels, vampiric Russian oligarchs, Black Popes, and plenty of other elements right out of a conspiracy theorist's dream—all conspiring to keep the "little people" under control while they worship at the feet of God Money.

Fatale (2012)—While working on a story, a reporter discovers a woman named Josephine, or "Jo," a classic *femme fatale* travelling through life with men eating out of her hand. What's unusual is that Jo, while appearing quite young, seems to have been around since the 1930s and is now being chased by a violent cult. This horror/noir comic book series created by Ed Brubaker and Sean Phillips was initially announced to be a 12-issue series but was later expanded to 24 issues. The first issue of the series went to press four times. Brubaker and Phillips received multiple Eisner Award nominations for it including "Best Continuing Series" (Brubaker and Phillips), "Best New Series" (Brubaker and Phillips), "Best Writer" (Brubaker), "Best Penciler/Inker" (Phillips), and "Best Cover Artist" (Phillips).

Severed (2011)—In 1916, 12-year-old Jack Garron runs away from his adopted home to try and find his birth family. Little does Jack know that also on the road is something that looks like a man, but with a mouth full of sharp teeth and a hunger for human flesh. Written by the team of Scott Snyder and Scott Tuft with haunting art by Attila Futaki, this relentless, atmospheric tale is absolutely one of those with elements that will keep you up at night. The seven-issue series was published in 2011, but a hardcover collecting all seven issues plus never-before-seen bonus material was published in 2012.

Underwinter (2017)—A group of four struggling musicians land a gig for a mysterious client. They are told that they will have to play blindfolded in what they assume is going to be something like an *Eyes Wide Shut* party put on by some bored rich folks. They arrive to find there is definitely something more nefarious going on, but by then it's too late to get away. It's both written and drawn by Ray Fawkes, which means there is no buffer between the creator's vision and the artwork on the page. Fawkes' otherworldly art style adds to the overall feeling of isolation and disconnectedness of the story. *Underwinter* ran for six issues in 2017 followed by the five-issue *Underwinter: A Field of Feathers*.

Witch Doctor (2011)—Dr. Vincent Morrow is a different kind of specialist. He is a doctor who specializes in "supernatural medicine" and his patients range from vampires to fairies. Dr. Morrow is just as comfortable dealing with a patient possessed by demons as he is conversing with the Lovecraftian Deep Ones. Dr. Morrow is assisted in his practice by Penny Dreadful, a college student who herself is possessed by some ancient entity, and Eric Gast, a paramedic who is quite new to the field of supernatural medicine. *Witch Doctor* is written by Brandon Seifert and drawn by Lukas Ketner. As of the time of this writing, the title consists of the four-issue miniseries *Witch Doctor* (2011), an issue #0 printed as a flipbook in *The Walking Dead* #85 (May 2011), the one-shot *Witch Doctor: Resuscitation* (2011), and a second six-issue miniseries *Witch Doctor: Mal Practice* (2012). The first miniseries and issue #0 have been collected into the trade paperback *Witch Doctor Vol. 1: Under the Knife* (2011), and the second miniseries as well as the one-shot *Witch Doctor: Resuscitation* have been collected into the trade paperback *Witch Doctor Vol. 2: Mal Practice* (2013).

Wytches (2014)—Throughout the course of human history, men and women have been burned at the stake, drowned, tortured, and persecuted for practicing witchcraft and all of them were innocent. They all died to protect the horrible, centuries-old secret that real witches do exist. Ancient, powerful, and elusive—real witches have existed for centuries on end and the only thing worse than knowing that they exist is being unfortunate enough to actually encounter one.

Charlie and Lucy Rook are having a problem with their daughter, Sailor. Sailor was being bullied by a girl at her school, Anne, and one day Anne disappeared. Rumors begin to spread that Sailor killed Anne and hid her body somewhere. The rumors spread like they do in small towns to the point that Charlie and Lucy decide it is best if they move away—hoping to make a fresh start in Litchfield, New Hampshire, the next town over. Unfortunately, the rumors followed them, and Sailor is once again shunned at her new school. To make matters worse, the quiet town of Litchfield harbors its own dirty little secrets. Deep in the nearby woods lives a coven of wytches, and they have a long-standing tradition where a person can "pledge" someone to the wytches in order to gain a favor from them. Sailor is pledged to the wytches and kidnapped. Meanwhile, Charlie meets a hunter who tells him what happened to his daughter and what he needs to do to fight the wytches and get her back.

This six-issue miniseries was published in 2014 with creator Scott Snyder promising to deliver the second volume soon, although Snyder is currently involved in several projects for DC Comics, so it is unknown when volume two of *Wytches* will see the light of day. On a more positive note, a film adaptation of *Wytches* is currently in production by Plan B Entertainment with Brad Pitt producing and Scott Snyder with artist Jock serving as executive producers.

Fortunately for horror comic book fans, it's not just the "big four" that have the monopoly on horror comics. There have been plenty of very creative works come out of smaller presses in the past few years.

AfterShock Comics

AfterShock Comics was founded in 2016 by Joe Pruett (editor of the *Negative Burn* anthology), Mike Marts (former executive editor for the Marvel

Comics X-Men franchise), Lee Kramer, Jon Kramer, and Michael Richter. Since its inception, AfterShock Comics has been able to attract some of the industry's best talent and won the New Publisher of the Year Diamond Gem Award in 2017. Their vision has paid off as they have a top-notch lineup of talent and a deep catalog of titles including some excellent horror titles.

Babyteeth (2017)—Sadie Ritter is 16 years old and pregnant. That's hard enough on its own, but Sadie's new little bundle of joy is going to be the antichrist. Is there such a thing as an appropriate baby shower gift when the baby in question is destined to rain down hellfire and brimstone and bring about the apocalyptic end of life as we know it?

A Walk Through Hell (2018)—FBI Special Agents Shaw and MacGregor are called to a new investigation. There is a warehouse in Long Beach that people seem to go into and never come back out of. The last two people to go in were two other FBI agents and now Special Agents Shaw and MacGregor need to find out why. Garth Ennis returns to writing horror for the first time since *Preacher* and *Crossed* and (surprise) he hasn't lost his touch.

Black-Eyed Kids (2016)—Urban legends are a fascinating thing. They are constantly changing and evolving with the times and new ones are occasionally invented. Joe Pruett writes his own take on one of the newer urban legends to come down the pipe—the Black-Eyed Kids. In case you haven't heard of them or read on the Internet about them, picture this: you are alone late one night in your comfortable suburban home when you are startled by a knocking at the door. You answer the door to find two children on your doorstep—alone and afraid. They ask if they can come inside and use your phone to call for a ride. You start to feel a little uneasy and this feeling quickly grows to an all-encompassing feeling of dread. You look more closely at the children only to discover that their eyes are two pools of solid black. You quickly try to close the door, but the black-eyed kids are already in your house. Super creepy stuff here! This is one series you'll want to read in broad daylight. Even if you do, though, there will be that one night when you're at home and there is a light knock at your door…

Dark Ark (2017)—If you remember your Sunday school lessons, then you probably remember the story of Noah. The world had fallen into wickedness and the only way God knew to deal with it was to wipe out all creation with a great flood. Noah and his family were always faithful to God, so Noah was instructed by God to build an ark. He was to bring on board the ark two of every creature so that the world could be repopulated after the devastating flood had receded. *Dark Ark* tells a story that I certainly never heard in Sunday school. The evil sorcerer Shrae was also commanded by more sinister forces to build an ark. Shrae was instructed to populate his ark with all of the dark and unnatural creatures (vampires, dragons, naga, manticore, etc.) so that they would survive the great flood as well. A sinister tale of biblical proportions.

Pestilence (2017)—History tells us of the Black Plague that swept Europe in the 14th Century killing over 100 million people, but what if recorded history is a huge cover-up? What if, instead of an outbreak of the bubonic plague, the Black Plague was history's first unrecorded zombie outbreak? Former Crusader Roderick Helms and his fellow secret agents of the Church, Fiat Lux, are instructed to seek out the cause of this undead plague and vanquish it before all of mankind falls beneath its snapping jaws. The first chapter of the story is this six-issue miniseries. Chapter 2 is now being published with the first issue of *Pestilence: The Story of Satan* hitting the stores in May of 2018.

Unholy Grail (2017)—Arthur Pendragon. Merlin. The Lady of the Lake. Excalibur. Camelot. The Knights of the Round Table. These are all shining examples of heroic legends. *Unholy Grail* takes the standard Arthurian legend and flips it on its ear. Arthur's rise of power in this series is bloody, savage, and ruthless. Merlin is a demon. Camelot is a haunted place. Think H. P. Lovecraft meets *Le Morte d'Arthur*.

Drawn and Quarterly

Twenty-three-year-old Chris Oliveros started *Drawn and Quarterly* in 1990 with a $2,000 loan from his father. His original intention was to publish *Drawn and Quarterly*, an anthology comic book published four times a year (obviously). It didn't take long before Oliveros found he was attracting more talent than four comic books a year could contain, so *Drawn and Quarterly* branched out to publish other comic books as well as traditional books. *Drawn and Quarterly* has accumulated a staple of some of the best talent around including Joe Sacco, Joe Matt, Daniel Clowes, Chester Brown, Kate Beaton, Guy Delisle, Julie Doucet, and Rutu Modan. *Drawn and Quarterly* has developed the reputation of publishing consistently excellent work with many Harvey Award winners. A publisher with this type of pedigree isn't the first place I would have looked for a horror comic book. They do publish one rather delightful work, though.

Beautiful Darkness (2014)—Prince Hector and Princess Aurora are having tea after the ball when suddenly part of the roof of their house collapses in on them and they have to leave. Once outside, you discover their "house" was actually the decaying skull of the body of a dead young girl who died deep in the forest. Now the prince and princess must find a new place to live and keep all of their subjects safe along the journey. This "anti-fairy tale" is exquisitely drawn and colored. The bold sweeping lines and bright, friendly colors would look at home in a children's book. Even the characters themselves are drawn to look wide-eyed and whimsical. The story is anything but whimsical, though. Their journey is grueling, and the tiny creatures experience a wide range of all-too-human emotions and reactions. The juxtaposition of the beautiful, friendly artwork with the ugly, savage actions of the characters really leaves an uneasiness in your stomach. The end of the story (obviously not what you would call "happily ever after") will leave you unsure as to whether to laugh or cry. Overall, the story seems to parallel the fact that nature can be very kind and beautiful while nature can just as easily be savage and cruel. This is a great story to read, but not so great as a bedtime story for the little ones.

Fantagraphics Books

Fantagraphics was founded in 1976 by Gary Groth and Mike Catron. One of their first publications was the comic book industry news magazine *The Comics Journal* (which is still being published today although only twice per year). Fantagraphics started publishing comic books in 1979. They began by publishing "fringe" or "alternative" comic books, but by the 1990s Fantagraphics had published several critically acclaimed and award-winning comic books including the Hernandez brothers' *Love and Rockets*, Daniel Clowes' *Eightball*, and Peter Bagge's *Hate*. Fantagraphics has published a wide variety of genres of comic books, classic comic strip anthologies, magazines, graphic novels, and even the adult Eros Comix line. Naturally, with this kind of storied past, Fantagraphics has produced some memorable horror comic books throughout the years.

Ghosts and Ruins (2013)—A beautiful graphic novel that could easily compliment your decor as a coffee table book. This book is a collection of good old-fashioned haunted houses with the stories to accompany them about the ghost who haunts each house. Some of the stories are creepy while some tend towards the humorous. Each story is coupled with wonderful drawings of each house done by the book's writer and artist, Ben Catmull, in scratchboard on masonite. This book is worth a look just for the drawings alone. The art plus Catmull's exquisite writing make this a perfect reading companion for a dark and stormy night.

Delphine (2006)—Richard Sala originally serialized this tale in Fantagraphics' *Ignatz Collection*; it has now been collected into a series of four trade paperbacks. In *Delphine*, Sala retells a loose adaptation of Snow White from the point of view of Prince Charming. A man disembarks from a train in a small village surrounded by a thick, evil-looking forest. That man is searching for his lost love from college, Delphine, and all he has to go on is an address written on a sheet of paper. The village is strange, its denizens are stranger, and the woods? Nobody wants to venture too far into their thick darkness. Drawn in sepia tones with only the occasional flash of color, the art itself is as dark and brooding as the story which unravels like a spider spinning a web. Disney this ain't!

Evil Eye (1998)—Another Richard Sala work—his first comic book work, as a matter of fact. *Evil Eye* introduces Judy Drood the girl detective and Peculia, a mysterious black-haired waif whose adventures seem to always end up with her encountering some type of supernatural creature. Granted, this series is more light-hearted and fun instead of gory or shocking, but Sala's writing and art (think Edward Gorey meets Charles Addams) make for a delightful read.

Four Color Fear (2010)—One of Fantagraphics Books' specialties is publishing collected reprints of old comic strips. This extends to old comic books as well. *Four Color Fear* collects some of the best comic books from the pre-Comics Code Authority age of the 1950s—the dawn of the horror comic genre. Many different publishers are represented in this volume, from Ace to Ziff-Davis (most of which have been already written about in this book), and the artwork represents a "Who's Who" of the Golden Age horror comic book genre. You'll find fantastic artwork by Jack Cole, Reed Crandall, Frank Frazetta, Al Williamson, Basil Wolverton, and Wally Wood among others. This 304-page hardcover is a great (and, let's face it, inexpensive) way to be able to experience some of the great classic horror comic books.

Doctor of Horror (2018)—While we're on the subject of classic horror book reprints, I have to mention *Doctor of Horror*. At the time of this writing, this book has not yet been released, but it is one that your fearless author is very excited to get his greedy hands on. *Doctor of Horror* collects and reprints the earliest EC Comics work of "Ghastly" Graham Ingels. Ingels was synonymous with EC Comics with his unforgettable artwork. Nobody could draw a rotted, shambling corpse like Ghastly! This book collects Ghastly's earliest EC Comics work from *Tales From the Crypt, Haunt of Fear, Crime Suspen-Stories,* and *War On Crime,* including his very first EC Comics story, two adaptations of stories by Edgar Allan Poe (with a wonderfully twisted take on "The Cask of Amontillado"), and EC Comics' first adaptation of a Ray Bradbury story. On top of that, this book (like all Fantagraphics Books collections) is chock full of commentary and historical information from EC Comics experts to enhance the experience.

IDW Publishing

IDW Publishing was founded in 1999 as the publishing arm of Idea and Design Works, LLC. IDW Publishing was created initially to publish licensed comic book adaptations of video games, movies, and television shows. By the early 2000s IDW Publishing was producing its own original comic books and is now the fifth largest comic book publishing company in America (behind Marvel Comics, DC, Image Comics, and Dark Horse Comics). IDW Publishing has released several comic book series based on licensed horror movie franchises, but they have also produced many high-quality original horror comic book titles.

30 Days of Night (2002)—Obviously vampires can only come out at night. So what would happen if a group of vampires suddenly wised up and decided to go somewhere that had a month of darkness at a stretch—like Barrow, Alaska, for example? This title was IDW's first original comic book title and it set the stage for them to become a major player in the comic book industry. Written by Steve Niles and featuring Ben Templesmith's eerie black-and-white work, this book is prime reading for those long winter nights.

Following the breakout success of the first *30 Days of Night*, Steve Niles teamed up with Sam Kieth (*The Maxx, Zero Girl*) for a second series which ran for 12 issues in 2011. *30 Days of Night* volume two introduced all-new characters into the story as well as expanded the vampiric activity to Los Angeles. Niles brought the action back to Barrow, Alaska, in the third volume of *30 Days of Night* which was released in December of 2017 and is still being published at the time of this writing. The series has also spawned several miniseries and one-shots taking the vampires to far-flung locations like Russia in *30 Days of Night: Red Snow* (2007) and even deep space in *30 Days of Night: Dead Space* (2006). The series has been collected in the two-volume *30 Days of Night Omnibus* (2011) and the more recent *30 Days of Night: 15th Anniversary Edition* (2017).

Locke & Key (2008)—This comic book series is written by Joe Hill—the pen name for Joseph Hillstrom King. You would be correct in assuming that he is the son of Stephen King and you would also be correct in assuming he is just as masterful at the art of horror writing. The story opens with the Locke family (Tyler, Kinsey, and Bode Locke with their mother) relocating after the violent murder of Mr. Locke. The family moves back home to the old family estate in Lovecraft, Massachusetts. Once in the house, Bode Locke discovers the Ghost Door—a doorway that by going through it will separate his spirit from his body. Bode uses his newfound power to spy on his family and get into mischief. He also discovers a well with a little girl living in it— at least she *looks* like a little girl. The overall story of *Locke & Key* is told in three acts with each act being made up of two six-issue storylines. The first storyline, "Welcome to Lovecraft," was published in *Locke & Key* (2008) and was followed by *Locke & Key: Head Games* (2009), *Locke & Key: Crown of Shadows* (2009), *Locke & Key: Keys to the Kingdom* (2010), *Locke & Key: Clockworks* (2011), *Locke & Key: Omega* (2012), and concludes in *Locke & Key: Alpha* (2013). The story is told in a non-chronological order and bounces from the present day to the late 1980s to the Revolutionary War period with a brief stop off in the Lovecraftian Plains of Leng along the way.

Welcome to Hoxford (2008)—Deranged murderer Ray Delgado, along with a handful of other extremely dangerous inmates, are transferred from the state-run prison that they had been in to the Hoxford, a privately-run institution owned by the Russian-based Usmanov Corporation. Delgado's psychiatrist, Dr. Jessica Ainley, arrives at the Hoxford to check on her patient. After an "incident" in one of the prison showers, the facility is put on lockdown. Dr. Ainley is forced to stay locked inside the warden's office until nightfall when the dark truth about the Hoxford comes out. With the first light of the moon, the prison's staff transform into werewolves and begin hunting the prisoners. Delgado takes it on himself to lead some of the prisoners to the armory so they can equip themselves to fight back. This series was created, written, and drawn by Ben Templesmith.

Wire Hangers (2010)—Alan Robert is the bassist for the New York-based band Life of Agony. He also has artistic influence other than music, though. He graduated with a Bachelor of Fine Arts from New York's School of Visual Arts where he studied cartooning under Walter Simonson. In 2010 he created the *Wire Hangers* miniseries doing both the story and interior artwork. In it, reporter Anna Davis goes deep undercover to get the exclusive story on who or what is behind a series of abductions that has been plaguing New York City. The truth that she uncovers is not at all what she was looking for, though.

Crawl To Me (2011)—This four-issue series is another stunning work by Alan Robert. Ryan Shelby just moved into a new house with his wife Jess and their infant daughter Grace. It doesn't take too long for Ryan to discover that their house has a dark and creepy basement crawlspace and, what's worse than that, there's something living in it. The living situation in the house gets weirder and weirder until Ryan has no choice but to get down on his hands and knees and crawl directly into the crawlspace. What he finds down there is completely unexpected!

We Will Bury You (2010)—Written by the brother and sister team of Brea Grant and Zane Grant, *We Will Bury You* is the story of Miyah and Fanya—two lesbian lovers who are struggling to make a life together in 1920s America. Aside from the regular societal problems you can imagine they would face, there's also the zombie apocalypse happening as well.

Wormwood: Gentleman Corpse (2006)—Created, written, and drawn by Ben Templesmith, *Wormwood: Gentleman Corpse* is the story of Wormwood—a dimension-hopping demigod worm who fights against supernatural threats. Wormwood can take full control of a dead body by burrowing into its head. Wormwood can do this with any kind of body, but he typically prefers well-dressed human men—hence the name. The seven-issue *Wormwood: Gentleman Corpse* has been collected into a trade paperback—the hardback edition of this even spent some time on the New York Times Bestseller List. A unique mix of horror and humor, Wormwood's adventures have continued in *Wormwood: Gentleman Corpse–Segue to Destruction* (2007), *Wormwood: Gentleman Corpse–Calamari Rising* (2008), *Wormwood: Gentleman Corpse–Down the Pub* (2008), *Wormwood: Gentleman Corpse–Mr. Wormwood Goes to Washington* (2017), and *Wormwood: Gentleman Corpse–Christmas Special* (2017) as well as being collected in *Wormwood: Gentleman Corpse–First Few Pints* (2015) and *Wormwood: Gentleman Corpse Omnibus* (2016).

Sword of Dracula (2005)—Veronica Van Helsing (descendant of the famous Abraham Van Helsing) is the leader of the multinational commando unit the Polidorum. Their mission, as you could imagine, is to hunt down and kill vampires. They get a tip on the location of the most dangerous war criminal of all time—Dracula himself. The Polidorum have been searching for Dracula for decades and so they jump at the chance to finally apprehend him. They storm his hideout and find him there, but a much greater danger to mankind presents itself. Biblical fallen angels Azazel and Samyaza have escaped their ancient prison and are preparing to spread havoc across the Earth. Now Van Helsing has to choose between bringing her greatest enemy to justice or try to forge an alliance with him against an even greater evil. This series was originally published as a six-issue miniseries by Image Comics in 2003 and IDW Publishing collected them into a graphic novel in 2005. Throughout the course of the story, several artists rotate through and their styles are all visually quite different. This can be a rather jarring perspective—especially when all of the issues are collected together like this. Overall, though, this is one of the more unique takes on the tried-and-true Dracula legend.

Night Mary (2005)—Seventeen-year-old Mary Specter's father owns and operates a sleep disorder clinic. Over the years, he has trained Mary to use her lucid dreaming talent to enter his patients' dreams in order to help them.

Unfortunately one of his newest patients is a serial killer and when Mary enters his dreams, her life starts to change.

Zombies! Feast (2006)—A prison transport bus is in the process of transferring a group of dangerous killers to a different facility when the bus breaks down near a small town. The prisoners escape, but their freedom is short-lived since the dead have all of a sudden returned to life and are now feasting on the living. The prisoners make their way to the town and run into a small group of survivors holed up there. The town's residents are now caught in a hellish triangle—violent killers on one side and the living dead on the other.

Zombies vs Robots (2006)—The title of the comic book series sounds like one of those old 1950s drive-in classics and, quite honestly, the storyline could just as easily be the plot for one of those movies, too. It sounds campy, but it ends up quite well done—so bear with me. A group of scientists invent a portal that will let them time-travel into the future. They send one of their colleagues through to test it out, which doesn't pan out as the best idea afterwards when he comes back quite spectacularly dead. The scientists then decide to send one of their robots through the portal. They had a bunch of robots around because apparently they had a huge excess of grant money or something, but hey, what says "science" more than "robots," right? The robot comes back through the portal intact and functioning but unfortunately also brings back some type of mutant future germ which ends up killing all human life on the planet and resurrecting them as zombies—all human life, that is, except for one single baby. The robotic army now finds itself in charge of the last remaining human life on Earth. They then decide to care for the child and ultimately clone it in order to restore human life to the planet. I'm sure this contingency plan was in their programming due to some little-known subset of Asimov's Laws of Robotics. This title is written by Chris Ryall (who also happens to be the Chief Creative Officer and Editor-In-Chief of IDW Publishing) and it ends up being a very solid story. More action and tongue-in-cheek humor than dark and foreboding horror, but what it does—it does well. The story continues in *Zombies vs Robots vs Amazons* (2007) in which you discover that *all* life wasn't wiped out by the mutant future germ. In fact, a whole island of Amazons survived untouched and they throw themselves into the fight as well. *Zombies vs Robots: Adventure* (2010) is a four-issue miniseries which tells the serialized tales of the growing human resistance in "Masques," a zombie war story, "Kampf" and a tribute to the old Marvel Comics "it's a zombie but we can't call it a zombie" days with "Zuvembies vs Robots." The survivors head underground for protection in *Zombies vs Robots: Undercity* (2011) and the story concludes in volume 2 of *Zombies vs Robots* (2015). The entirety of the series is collected in *Zombies vs Robots: Warbook Omnibus* (2015). This is a zombie apocalypse story like you've never seen before!

In The Dark—A throwback to the good-old EC Comics days, this book is an anthology title with 20 original horror stories from some of the best talent in the comic book industry today including Scott Snyder (*American Vampire*), Steve Niles (*30 Days of Night*), Paul Tobin (*Colder*), Brian Keene (*Doom Patrol*), Matthew Dow Smith (*Sandman Mystery Theatre*), Sean E. Williams (*Fairest*), Jody Leheup (*Uncanny X-Force*), and Valerie D'Orazio (*Punisher MAX*) doing the writing. They are backed up by an amazing group of artists including Declan Shalvey (*Deadpool*), Andy Belanger (*Swamp Thing*), Dalibor Talajic (*Tomb of Dracula*), Jonathan Brandon Sawyer (*Fubar*), and David James Cole (*Birds of Prey*). The book features an introduction by Scott Snyder and an essay on the rise and decline of horror comic books by Mike Howlett (although by now you have hopefully read a pretty good book on the subject). In an interesting mix of the past and the present, this Golden Age of Comic Books-inspired horror anthology was funded by the thoroughly modern concept of crowdsourcing. All of the funding for *In the Dark* was raised by a successful Kickstarter campaign.

IDW Publishing also continues to publish comic books based on popular horror movie franchises. This has included *The Devil's Rejects* (2005), *George A. Romero's: Dawn of the Dead* (2004), *George A Romero's: Land of the Dead* (2005), *Shaun of the Dead* (2004), *Saw: Rebirth* (2005), *Masters of Horror* (2006) (adapted from the short-lived Showtime television series which aired for two seasons in 2005–2007), *True Blood* (2010), *True Blood: Tainted Love* (2011), *True Blood: The French Quarter* (2011), *Underworld* (2003), *Underworld: Red in Tooth and Claw* (2004), *Underworld: Evolution* (2006), *Underworld: Rise of the Lycans* (2008), *Silent Hill: Dying Inside* (2004), *Silent Hill: Among the Damned* (2004), *Silent Hill: Dead/Alive* (2004), *Silent Hill: Paint it Black* (2005), *Silent Hill: The Grinning Man* (2005), *Silent Hill: Sinner's Reward* (2008), *Silent Hill: Past Life* (2010), and *Silent Hill: Downpour: Anne's Story* (2014). All of the Silent Hill miniseries and one-shots available at the time have been collected into the 432-page *Silent Hill Omnibus* (2008). In addition to movie and television licensed products, IDW Publishing have also released very well done comic book adaptations of horror master Richard Matheson's novels *I Am Legend* (2007) and *Hell House* (2004).

FantaCo

It is impossible to talk about influential comic book publishers in relation to the modern resurgence of the horror comic genre without mentioning

FantaCo. FantaCo was founded in 1978 by Thomas Skulan and it was originally a traditional brick-and-mortar comic book store and comic book mail order company located in Albany, New York. It wasn't long before FantaCo expanded into publishing their own comic books, magazines, and books. FantaCo was a victim of the Speculator Crash of the comic book industry in the late 1990s, closing their store and ceasing publication of all of their comic book lines in 1998. In the 20 years that FantaCo was publishing comic books, they released some of the most memorable horror comic titles and also helped launch the careers of some of the comic book industry's most well-known artists and writers.

Gore Shriek (1986)—FantaCo's flagship horror comic title and easily one of the major influences on the rebirth of the horror comic genre, *Gore Shriek* was only published for three years and only had six issues (not counting *Gore Shriek* #6.5 which was only available for sale directly from the artists or at the FantaCo store). This black-and-white horror anthology comic book, edited by Stephen R. Bissette (*Saga of the Swamp Thing*), was among the first comic books to make an attempt to break free from the restraints of the Comics Code Authority. Each issue was only sold in comic book shops, so FantaCo was never under any pressure to submit the books to the Comics Code Authority for approval. This is probably for the best since the eerie stories and gruesome artwork would have never been approved and each cover proudly bore a label stating "Not Intended for Children." Greg Capullo (*X-Force*, *Spawn*) was among those who launched their career at FantaCo, with his first professional work appearing in *Gore Shriek* #1 (1986).

Gore Shriek had its six-issue run with one annual and the all-reprint special *Gore Shriek: Delectus*. In 1990, FantaCo published *Gore Shriek* volume 2 which ran for a total of three issues with a very small overall print run. *Gore Shriek* #3 (1991) has an estimated print run of only 3,000 copies. In 2016, small-press comic book publisher Rough House Publishing announced *Gore Shriek: Resurrectus* which, in cooperation with Tom Skulan, was a 48-page black-and-white comic book publishing new stories and art. The issue is touted as a "new ongoing series," but as of the time of this writing, only one issue has been published. In 2017, FantaCo brought the *Gore Shriek* title back under their banner by publishing *Gore Shriek: Chronicles*. *Gore Shriek: Chronicles* is still a 48-page black-and-white horror anthology comic book with new content. It also contains a complete index to every back issue of *Gore Shriek* as well as full-color reproductions of every *Gore Shriek* cover. *Gore Shriek: Chronicles* was published as a result of a successful Kickstarter campaign.

Night of the Living Dead (1991)—FantaCo was the first comic book publisher to acquire the publication rights for the George Romero classic zombie movie. *Night of the Living Dead* was a four-issue comic adaptation of the movie. This was followed up with *Night of the Living Dead: Aftermath* (1991), which was written by George Romero, and *Night of the Living Dead: London* (1993), which was written by horror master Clive Barker. After FantaCo closed their doors, the rights for the *Night of the Living Dead* comics were picked up by Avatar Press.

Tales of Screaming Horror (1992)—This one-shot is a black-and-white horror anthology comic book very reminiscent to *Gore Shriek* with the exception that this book was both written and drawn by Gurchain Singh. Singh would do the same thing in 1993 with the release of the one-shot *Vault of Screaming Horror*.

Blood & Kisses (1993)—Created by Leif Jones, this is a tale of Gothic romance wrapped up with obsession. The artwork consists of large areas of black with the occasional splash of contrast to pull your eye to details—very reminiscent to Frank Miller's *Sin City*. *Blood & Kisses* is a new twist on the classic vampire tale.

Zombie War (1992)—In a new twist on the classic zombie story, the dead are once again rising from the grave, but this time they maintain a semblance of their memories and talents. This scenario is complicated by the fact that the dead from the world's military cemeteries have started a full-fledged assault on the living. This comic series and its follow-up *Zombie War: Earth Must Be Destroyed* (1993) as well as two other titles, *No Guts No Glory* (1991) and *Infectious* (1994), were published as a partnership between FantaCo and Tundra Press—a creator-owned comic book publisher owned by Kevin Eastman of *Teenage Mutant Ninja Turtles* fame. All of the FantaCo/Tundra titles folded after Tundra went out of business in 1993. *Zombie War* was picked up by IDW Publishing and relaunched in 2013 with the title still being drawn by Kevin Eastman and written by Kevin Eastman and Tom Skulan.

There is no doubt FantaCo was a driving force in the modern resurgence of the horror comic genre. Those simple black-and-white pages helped launch the careers of many of the comic industry powerhouses. They also helped revitalize the comic book industry as a whole by showing them that they didn't need to be subject to the Comics Code Authority if they didn't want to and that there was a thriving market for publishers willing to take risks. Unfortunately, with FantaCo being out of business for 20 years, back issues are difficult to come by with the exception of those few titles which have been reprinted or relaunched by other publishers.

Top Shelf Productions

From Hell—Alan Moore writes this tale speculating on the identity and motivation of Jack the Ripper. Originally published as a serial story in *Taboo* and now available in a trade paperback, this series has won multiple Eisner and Comic Buyer's Guide Fan awards, as well as an International Horror Guild Award. Set aside some time for this one, though. The trade paperback is nearly 600 pages!

Chaos! Comics

Chaos! Comics was founded in 1994 in Scottsdale, Arizona, with Brian Pulido as president and a writer for some titles. Chaos! Comics primarily published "bad girl" comics which had a spike in popularity in the 1990s. Chaos! Comics is best known for *Purgatori, Chastity, Jade, Jade Death, Lady Demon,* and *Bad Kitty*. Outside of the "bad girl" titles, Chaos! Comics is also known for *Evil Ernie*. Chaos! Comics published titles for licensed properties including the bands Megadeth, The Insane Clown Posse, and Static-X as well as several WWE characters. From the horror comic front, Chaos! Comics is best remembered for comic book titles based on horror movie licensed characters including *Halloween* (2000), *Halloween II: The Blackest Eyes* (2001), and *Halloween III: The Devil's Eyes* for the *Halloween* movies and *The Mummy: Valley of the Gods* (2001) for the *Mummy* movies. Chaos! Comics filed for bankruptcy in 2002 with their non-licensed characters being sold off to comic retailer Tales of Wonder who, in turn, sold them to Devil's Due Publishing. The Lady Death character was sold to CrossGen Entertainment and eventually sold again to Avatar Press.

Devil's Due Publishing

Devil's Due Publishing was founded in 1998 by Joshua Blaylock as both a commercial art studio and a small press comic book publisher. Devil's Due is best known for publishing comic book titles based on licensed properties with their most popular property being G. I. Joe, based on the Hasbro toy (and movie) line. They also published *Army of Darkness: Ashes 2 Ashes* (2004) and *Army of Darkness: Shop 'Til You Drop Dead* (2005), based on the *Army of Darkness* movies, and two volumes of *Chucky* (a four-issue series in 2007 and a one-shot in 2009), based on the *Child's Play* films. Devil's Due Publishing acquired the rights to the *Halloween* movie licensing and published the four-issue miniseries *Halloween: Nightdance* in 2008. On June 16, 2015, Devil's Due Publishing announced plans to merge with First Comics—publisher of *American Flagg, Grimjack, Badger,* and *Dreadstar*.

Avatar Press

Avatar Press was founded in 1996 by William A. Christensen in Rantoul, Illinois. Like many other comic book publishers in the 1990s, Avatar Press got their start by publishing "bad girl" comics including *Pandora, Helline, The Ravenine,* and *Lady Death* (after Chaos! Comics went out of business). Since that time, Avatar Press has concentrated on expanding their offerings. They made a point to offer an opportunity for comic book creators to work for a publisher that allowed them to publish creator-owned books with absolutely no restrictions on the content. This has allowed Avatar Press to attract some of the most notable names in the comic book industry—including Frank Miller, Warren Ellis, Alan Moore, and Garth Ennis. Needless to say, this "blank slate" approach has allowed Avatar Press to produce some very memorable horror comic titles.

Crossed (2008)—Garth Ennis lends his twisted hand to this story of a different kind of apocalypse. A pandemic has broken out and anyone infected will develop an unstoppable urge to carry out their most carnal, violent thoughts. Infected people are known as the "Crossed" due to the manifestation of a large cross-shaped rash on their face. The Crossed differ from other zombie plagues in the fact that they still retain a basic, human level of intelligence. This means they can use weapons, drive vehicles, and set complex traps. The infection is spread through contact with bodily fluid and the Crossed use this to their advantage by treating their weapons with their own bodily fluids (I will leave that to your imagination). The infection is also spread by direct bodily fluid contact such as bites or rape (no shortage of either as you can imagine)—assuming, of course, the victim survives the initial attack. The contagion has spread throughout the entire world with the Crossed running amok killing, raping, maiming, engaging in cannibalism— literally anything that enters their mind. Governments and militaries are overrun. Major cities have become abattoirs. Most of the Middle East has been destroyed, with Israel deploying their nuclear weapons in an attempt to stop the outbreak. One of the last organized acts by the United States government was to shut down as many nuclear power plants as possible and then kill the nuclear scientists and technicians to prevent them from reactivating the plants. They didn't get them all, as the Crossed overran Wolf Creek in Kansas and Browns Ferry in Alabama and detonated them by physically removing the control rods. Human civilization is all but gone and the survivors are left in a hellish landscape. Very few times have I ever stopped reading a book and flipped back thinking, "Wait, did I just see *that*?." This is by no means a book for the faint of heart.

Crossed ran for nine issues and has been followed by *Crossed: Family Values* (2010), *Crossed: 3D* (2011) (Yes, it is really in 3D), *Crossed: Psychopath* (2011), and the currently ongoing *Crossed: Badlands* (2012). There have also been some one-shots along the way including the *Crossed: 2013 Special* (2013), *Crossed: 2014 Special* (2014), and *Crossed: Plus One Hundred* (2014), which shows a bleak glimpse of the world 100 years post–Crossed infection.

Alan Moore's The Courtyard (2003)—This two-issue series is an adaptation of a short story Moore wrote for *The Starry Wisdom: A Tribute to H. P. Lovecraft*. It is the first part of a trilogy, with the remainder being the four-issue *Neonomicon* (2010) and the 12-issue *Providence* (2015). In the trilogy, Moore delves deep into the H. P. Lovecraft Cthulhu Mythos centering around FBI agent Aldo Sax—a specialist in "anomaly theory" who attempts to correlate seemingly unrelated data into a cohesive whole. Aldo Sax is investigating a series of seemingly unrelated ritual murders scattered across the United States. In typical Lovecraftian manner, Sax uncovers a truth that he wishes he had left alone. The story travels between Red Hook, Brooklyn, and Salem, Massachusetts, and even spans time between modern day and the 1920s. Alan Moore, H. P. Lovecraft. The Esoteric Order of Dagon. Nyarlathotep. What else do you need?

Chronicles of Wormwood (2007)—Garth Ennis writes this irreverent (no surprise) tale of Danny Wormwood, TV Executive and all-around nice guy— despite the fact that he is the antichrist. Danny has the power to bring about Armageddon, but he just chooses not to. The story centers on Danny, his best friend (a reincarnated Jesus Christ), and Jimmy (a talking rabbit that Danny created just for fun). Danny's dad (a.k.a. Satan) and his best friend's dad (a.k.a. God Almighty) both try to convince Danny to start up the apocalypse, but he'd prefer to leave humanity to its own devices. The best thing to do in that situation? A road trip. The series runs for six issues and is then continued in the one-shot *Chronicles of Wormwood: Last Enemy* and concluded in the six-issue *Chronicles of Wormwood: The Last Battle* (2009). Obviously this is not a suggested read for the super religious.

Night of the Living Dead: Beginning (2006)—After FantaCo closed their doors, Avatar Press picked up the rights to produce comic books based on the George Romero classic zombie film *Night of the Living Dead*. Their first foray into this is a very well done three-issue series. The series serves as a prequel to the movie and provides some background on events that took place leading up to the first scene of the movie. What happened at the farmhouse before everyone from the movie got there? Who was the famous Cemetery Zombie? What happened to bring Ben to where he was? All of these questions are delved into and the answers are on good authority since this series is written by John Russo—the original creator and co-writer of *Night of the Living Dead*. Russo also played a part in *Night of the Living Dead* as one of the zombies stabbed in the head when assaulting the farmhouse. This series was followed up by two one-shots with John Russo once again filling in some backstory on the previous lives (pre-undead lives?) of some of the zombies in *Night of the Living Dead*. *Night of the Living Dead: Hunger* (2007) is the story of what happens to drive-in theater employee Laura Crampton, who is just trying to make it through her shift while sticking to her diet (spoiler: it doesn't go as planned for her). *Night of the Living Dead: Just A Girl* (2007) finally reveals the story of Karen—the creepy little zombie girl. *Night of the Living Dead: New York* (2009) expands the reach of the movie beyond a rural area outside Pittsburgh to tell what happens when the dead rise and begin to feast on the flesh of the living in crowded New York City. *Night of the Living Dead: Death Valley* (2011) is set in Death Valley, California, in the year 1969. It has been a year since the zombie outbreak on the East Coast. Surely it is safe for some teenagers to have some fun deep in the California desert. The zombie outbreak never reached this far out, did it?

Escape of the Living Dead: (2005)—This five-issue series is also written by *Night of the Living Dead* creator and co-writer John Russo. While technically a sequel to the movie, it doesn't take place in the continuity of the movies *Night of the Living Dead* or *Return of the Living Dead*. This series is set in the year 1971—three years after the zombie outbreak of the movies. A scientist in a secret lab has been experimenting on some of the last remaining zombies and he runs afoul of a group of outlaw bikers. The facility is breached and, well, you can probably guess what happens from here. This series is followed by *Escape of the Living Dead: Fearbook* (2006) and the three-issue series *Escape of the Living Dead: Airborne* (2006).

Avatar Press also has several other horror-related licenses that they produce comic book adaptations for including *Species* (2005), *Friday the 13th* (2005), *Friday the 13th: Bloodbath* (2006), *Friday the 13th: Fearbook* (2006), *Friday the 13th: Jason vs Jason X* (2006), *A Nightmare On Elm Street* (2005), *Texas Chainsaw Massacre* (2005).

Archie Comics/Archie Horror

While you may never have expected anyone to mention Archie Comics in a book about horror comics, the Archie Horror line has come about and impressed a lot of people—me included. In 2013, Archie Comics announced the horror title *Afterlife with Archie* to be written by Roberto Aguirre-Sacasa and drawn by Francesco Francavilla. *Afterlife with Archie* was to be Archie Comics' first ever horror title and their first ever series to be rated "TEEN+." The series was partially inspired by a zombie-themed variant cover Francavilla drew for *Life with Archie: The Married Life* #23 (January 2000). *Afterlife with Archie* launched in 2013 and was a runaway hit. The first eight issues sold out, prompting multiple printings and it received rave reviews—some calling it the best horror comic series to come out in a long time. It won three awards at the 2013 Ghastly Awards for Best New Series, Best Ongoing Title, and Best Colorist for Francesco Francavilla. When *Afterlife with Archie* #6 was released in October of 2014, it revealed the whereabouts of Sabrina Spellman (Sabrina the Teenage Witch) who hasn't been seen since the events of *Afterlife with Archie* #1. The success of this issue prompted Archie Comics to announce a solo series starring Sabrina. In March of 2015, Archie Comics announced that, due to the success of *Afterlife with Archie* and *Chilling Adventures of Sabrina*, their horror titles would be published under the Archie Horror imprint. *Chilling Adventures of Sabrina* #2 (June 2015) was the first issue released under the Archie Horror imprint followed by *Afterlife with Archie* #8 (July 2015). Further titles have been released more recently under the Archie Horror banner and they are all worth checking out.

Afterlife with Archie—The zombie apocalypse starts in Riverdale. 'Nuff Said! This series is definitely worth a look. On its face, you'd think this is just another *Archie Meets the Punisher* or *Archie vs Predator*, but this book is very well written and even touching in places. Without giving too much away: Reggie runs over Hot Dog (Jughead's dog) with his car and kills it. Distraught, Jughead takes Hot Dog's body to Sabrina the Teenage Witch and begs her to do something. Sabrina's aunts remind her of the dark forces that could get stirred up by meddling with the natural order of things like this, but Sabrina is so touched by Jughead's situation that she helps out anyway. Just like *Pet Cemetery* or "The Monkey's Paw," what is brought back isn't quite Jughead's buddy, Hot Dog. The reanimated Hot Dog bites Jughead and he falls deathly ill, dies, and reanimates as a zombie. Zombie Jughead shambles his way to the Riverdale High School gym where (as luck would have it) there is a Halloween dance happening. Things proceed from there exactly how you would expect.

Chilling Adventures of Sabrina—Set in the 1960s, Sabrina Spellman lives with her witch aunts Hilda and Zelda, her warlock cousin Ambrose, and her familiar, the black cat Salem. Sabrina is getting close to her 16th birthday, which means she will be forced to choose between becoming a full-fledged witch or settling down to a normal, mortal life with her boyfriend Harvey Kinkle. To complicate matters, a former ex-girlfriend of Sabrina's estranged father (named Madam Satan, naturally) has returned from Hell looking for revenge on the whole Spellman family.

Jughead: The Hunger—Riverdale is terrorized by a serial killer known as the "Riverdale Ripper," and Jughead Jones discovers that not only is he the killer, but he is also a werewolf—which, let's face it, goes a long way to explain why he could pack away the hamburgers like he did! Archie Andrews catches Jughead in the act but resolves to help him. Betty Cooper, the youngest in a long line of werewolf hunters, also wants to help Jughead, but she vows to put him down if necessary. Archie and Betty find what they think is a cure—having Jughead eat wolfsbane—and it works for a while. After an uneventful several months, though, Archie and Betty discover the mauled body of Reggie Mantle, and Jughead is nowhere to be found. Archie and Betty leave Riverdale to track down Jughead, vowing to help him if they can but to do what is necessary if it comes to it.

Vampironica—The newest Archie Horror title and taking place in its own continuity, *Vampironica* centers on Riverdale's resident rich girl, Veronica Long. In this story, Veronica is turned into a vampire and now must come to grips with this radical transformation of her life plus the fact that she might actually need to feed on her small group of friends.

So there you have it—dozens and dozens of titles to prove that the horror comic genre is still very much alive and even thriving today. Overtly creepy? Stomach-turning? Something to keep you awake at night? Tongue-in-cheek humor? Good old-fashioned ghost stories? Straight-up blood and gore? Nearly something for every taste can be found being published somewhere today. This is truly a great time to be a horror comic fan.

8

Crossover Hits

The popularity of horror comics has led some to be adapted into major motion pictures or TV shows. Here are some of the more popular crossover hits.

The Walking Dead—Obviously one of the more popular comic-to-TV crossovers. Robert Kirkman's Image Comics series has been adapted to a TV series on the AMC Network. While the comic series has published since 2003, the TV series debuted in 2010 and has drawn strong ratings. At the time of this writing, Season 8 has just ended and Season 9 has been announced with the writers having been very public that they have plans for stories all the way through Season 12. The show's popularity has prompted a sister show, *Fear The Walking Dead,* which also airs on AMC. *Fear* is not based on a comic, but it does take place in the same "universe" that *The Walking Dead* does. *Fear* is set on the West Coast, whereas *The Walking Dead* (both the comic and the TV show) takes place on the East Coast—specifically around Atlanta, Georgia, Washington, D.C., and Alexandria, Virginia.

Hellboy—From his first appearance in the comic in 1993, over a decade passed before Professor Bruttenholm's adopted son appeared in a feature film. The long wait was definitely worth it, though. The 2004 *Hellboy* movie, directed by Guillermo Del Toro, grossed nearly $100 Million worldwide and spawned a sequel *Hellboy 2: The Golden Army* in 2008. While the original film borrowed heavily from the comics, the sequel had an original non-comic related story. Originally there were plans for a third film, but in 2017 it was announced that the sequel had been cancelled. Hellboy creator Mike Mignola stated that the *Hellboy* movie franchise would undergo a reboot instead with *Hellboy: Rise of the Blood Queen* to be released on January 11, 2019. *Hellboy: Rise of the Blood Queen* is expected to have an "R" rating and to be a darker and more gruesome version of *Hellboy*.

From Hell—Released in 2001, this film starring Johnny Depp is (admittedly loosely) based on the Alan Moore graphic novel. Originally published serially and collected in 1999 into a nearly 600-page graphic novel, *From Hell* is Moore's take on the famous Jack the Ripper murders in Whitechapel, England, in the late 1800s, including Moore's ideas on the identity and motivations of the Ripper.

30 Days of Night—In a strange twist of fate, *30 Days of Night* was originally intended to be a movie. Steve Niles pitched his idea about a group of vampires invading Barrow, Alaska, but no movie studios were interested. In 2002, IDW published the story as a three-issue comic miniseries. Ben Templesmith added his unique and creepy art style to Niles' writing and came up with a fresh take on a vampire story. Once the miniseries was published, Niles then approached movie studios again and found a more receptive audience. In 2007, *30 Days of Night* was released to mixed reviews and moderate success. The sequel *30 Days of Night: Dark Days* adapted the comic miniseries of the same name and was released direct to DVD in 2010.

In 2007, the FEARNet cable network released a seven-episode TV miniseries *30 Days of Night: Blood Trails* as a prequel to the movie. The storyline is based on a subplot of the comic that was never touched on in the movie and takes place two days before the events of *30 Days of Night*. FEARNet also released *30 Days of Night: Dust to Dust*, a six-episode miniseries set one month after the events of *30 Days of Night*. *Dust to Dust* was an original script written by Steve Niles and not based on any of the comics.

Preacher—The DC/Vertigo comic written by Garth Ennis and drawn by Steve Dillon was adapted to TV by AMC. Season 1 premiered in 2016 to positive reviews and good ratings and the show was renewed for a second season.

Outcast—Written by Robert Kirkman of *The Walking Dead* fame, this Image Comics series was developed into a TV series for Cinemax. Series 1 premiered on June 3, 2016, and the show was renewed for a second season even before the first episode aired. The third season is set to premiere on June 24, 2018.

Spawn—While technically a superhero comic, Al Simmons does get his powers from an Infernal source, which makes it classify as a horror book to me—at least tangentially! That being said, the 1997 HBO animated series does stick a lot closer to the comic than the movie, which was released the same year. In July 2017, Todd McFarlane announced he had written a script for, and was planning on directing, a new Spawn movie.

Constantine—Based on the DC/Vertigo *Hellblazer* comic, this 2005 movie starred Keanu Reeves as John Constantine. Personally, I doubt that the studio could have cast someone who looked (or acted) less like John Constantine, but that's a complaint for another time. The movie itself is a relatively close adaptation of the "Dangerous Habits" storyline from *Hellblazer* #41–

46—which was originally written by Garth Ennis. Overall, the movie is solid, but some casting changes would have made it more like the Hellblazer we all know and love. This, in my opinion, was rectified in the 2014 NBC series *Constantine*. Matt Ryan's John Constantine could have been lifted directly from the pages of the comic. The series was very well written and enjoyable but suffered from low ratings and was cancelled after only one season. Ryan reprised the role for a guest appearance in an episode of the CW's *Arrow*, thus bringing John Constantine into the "Arrowverse." The CW has announced plans for an upcoming Constantine web series on the CW Seed where all episodes of Season 1 of *Constantine* are available for viewing at the time of this writing.

Ghost Rider—So it's hardly a secret that the *Ghost Rider* films were based on the Marvel Bronze Age *Ghost Rider* comic. It's also hardly a secret that the two Nic Cage films were less than inspired. Marvel Mythology has moved on and declared that the actual Spirit of Vengeance can move from person to person. The newest incarnation of the Ghost Rider is a young Hispanic man by the name of Roberto "Robbie" Reyes. This Ghost Rider appears in the ABC TV Show *Agents of S.H.I.E.L.D.* and is played by Gabriel Luna.

Blade—Eric Brooks (better known as Blade the Vampire Slayer) made his first appearance in Marvel's *Tomb of Dracula* #10 (July 1973). The character has gone on to inspire three films: *Blade* (1998), *Blade II* (2002), and *Blade: Trinity* (2004) with the titular character being played by Wesley Snipes. There was also a short lived *Blade the Series* TV show, starring Kirk "Sticky Fingaz" Jones, which ran on Spike for one season in 2006.

Swamp Thing—*The Swamp Thing* comics took a definite turn towards the horror genre when Alan Moore took over writing *The Saga of the Swamp Thing* in 1984. This 1983 movie predates that turn, but with undisputed master of horror Wes Craven directing and providing the screenplay, this ends up being a very solid film. The effects are dated, but overall this is a very watchable movie. The same cannot be said for the 1989 sequel *The Return of the Swamp Thing*. In a strange twist of fate, Peter David wrote the novelization of the film. He was so disappointed with the screenplay that he rewrote large swaths of the story and, surprisingly enough, his publisher allowed the book to be published with his "improvements" intact. It just goes to show that sometimes the book can be better than the movie—even when the movie comes first!

The Crow—This 1994 film is best known for being Brandon Lee's final film, and tragedy seems to surround it. The movie was adapted from a 1989 Caliber Comics miniseries written by James O'Barr. O'Barr came up with the idea as a means of dealing with the sudden death of his fiancée in an accident with a drunk driver. It hardly ended up being the cathartic experience that O'Barr had hoped for. In a 1994 interview, he said "as I drew each page, it made me more self-destructive, if anything.... There is pure anger on each page." O'Barr's pain is almost visceral on each panel of the story. Published in black and white, the darkness of the art only adds to the darkness of the story. Haunting would be the best way to describe it.

The success of the movie inspired a series of sequels which were generally forgettable. *The Crow: City of Angels* was released in 1996. It debuted at #1 at the box office that weekend, and then fell off sharply receiving poor reviews. Later sequels [*The Crow: Salvation* (2000) and *The Crow: Wicked Prayer* (2005)] were released directly to video. There have been a few attempts at a reboot of *The Crow*—including some with the direct involvement of James O'Barr. At the time of this writing, the reboot appears to be stuck in development hell, having lost the director and primary star.

iZombie—Olivia "Liv" Moore is a medical resident who was turned into a zombie after being attacked by a group of people who had taken a new designer drug. She discovers that she can maintain her "normal" human mind by eating a brain every now and again. She takes a job as a coroner's assistant, which gives her access to all the brains she could ever want. There is a catch, though. Eating a brain gives her temporary access to the dead person's memories and personality. Passing herself off as a psychic, she begins assisting the police by providing them with clues to find the killers of murder victims. This TV series on the CW has just been renewed for its fourth season. It is loosely based on a comic series of the same name. *iZombie* was written by Chris Robertson and drawn by Michael Allred. The series ran a total of 28 issues from 2010 until 2012, providing a fresh new take on the zombie tale.

I, Frankenstein—Adam (the name given to Dr. Frankenstein's creation) discovers he is the only being capable of protecting the world from an army of demons. This 2014 movie is based on a Darkstorm Studios graphic novel written by Kevin Grevioux. Grevioux helped create and also went on to have a role in *Underworld*. In a "reverse crossover," Grevioux wrote the comic adaptation of *Underworld: Rise of the Lycans* and is currently working on more *Underworld* comics.

Virus—This is another film that started out as a comic that was originally intended to be a film. Chuck Pfarrer wrote this sci-fi horror story as a script in the early 1990s, but the special effects weren't advanced enough at the time for him to bring his vision to reality. Instead, he sold the script to Dark Horse Comics where it was published as a miniseries in 1992. *Virus* the film was eventually made in 1999 and developed a strong cult following despite poor reviews and being an overall box office flop.

Dylan Dog: Dead of Night—This 2011 film was based on Tiziano Sclavi's long-running Italian comic series *Dylan Dog*. The series began in 1986 and is still being published today. Dark Horse Comics publishes the English version of *Dylan Dog*. While *Dylan Dog: Dead of Night* did poorly at the box office and received mediocre reviews (at best), the 1984 film *Cemetery Man* or *Dellamorte Dellamore* was better received despite being more loosely based on the comic series.

Faust: Love of the Damned—This Spanish film released in 2000 is based on the Avatar Press comic series of the same name. David Quinn took his sweet time when it came to actually putting out issues of *Faust*, though. *Faust: Love of the Damned* #1 was published in 1987 and was (very) sporadically released. It wasn't uncommon for years to pass between the release of issues. Finally, the story was concluded with the publication of issue #15 in 2012—a full 25 years after the first issue hit the shelves!

Tales From the Crypt—This 1972 British film was directed by Freddie Francis. Just like the comic of the same name, it is an anthology of five separate stories. Interestingly enough, only two of the stories actually came from a *Tales From the Crypt* comic. Rumor has it this is because the movie's producer, Milton Subotsky, did not have access to the original EC *Tales From the Crypt* comics. Instead, he used two paperback reprints given to him by *Creepy* editor Russ Jones. The remaining stories are from EC's *Vault of Horror* and *Haunt of Fear*. The screenplay inspired a novel tie-in written by Jack Oleck. The movie inspired a sequel, which brings us to…

The Vault of Horror—Also known as *Further Tales From the Crypt* or *Tales From the Crypt II*, this 1973 film was another anthology movie. None of the stories in the film are actually from *Vault of Horror*, though. One story was from EC's *Shock SuspenStories* and the remainder were actually from *Tales From the Crypt*. Also missing from the film is the Vault Keeper, the horror host of the *Vault of Horror* comic.

Crawl To Me—Another unfortunate denizen of development hell, the movie adaptation of Alan Robert's 2011 IDW Publishing comic miniseries was announced in 2012. The director dropped out of the production in 2013. Since then, *Crawl To Me* has been lurking around in the depths—not unlike something scratching around in a dark, creepy crawlspace.

Dr. Giggles—This fairly predictable horror film about a crazed slasher who happens to be a dentist was based on a 1992 two-issue comic book series from Dark Horse Comics.

Afterword: Whatever Happened to…?

Whatever Happened to EC Comics?

Best known for their infamous trio of horror comics *Tales from the Crypt, The Vault of Horror,* and *The Haunt of Fear,* EC Comics had a full range of comic book titles that spanned the popular genres of the time. Between 1950 and 1954, EC Comics published the science fiction titles *Weird Fantasy, Weird Science* and *Weird Science-Fantasy*; the crime title *Crime SuspenStories*; the war titles *Two-Fisted Tales* and *Frontline Combat*; the suspense title *Shock SuspenStories*; the fantasy title *Piracy*; and the comedy titles *Mad* and *Panic*. After the formation of the Comics Code Authority, EC Comics was one of the few comic book publishers that never submitted any of their books to the Comics Code Authority for approval. This is partially because EC's William Gaines was vehemently against the Comics Code Authority and partially because very few of EC Comics' titles would pass the scrutiny of the Comics Code Authority.

EC Comics held on for a short time without submitting their books to the Comics Code Authority, but nearly every retailer at the time refused to carry any comic books without the Comics Code Authority Seal of Approval on the cover. Low sales and a lack of any real distribution prompted EC Comics to toe the line. In 1955, EC Comics announced the cancellation of all of their horror, science fiction, and crime comics and the launch of their "New Direction" line which would carry the Comics Code Authority Seal of Approval. The New Direction titles (*Impact, Valor, Extra!, Aces High, Incredible Science Fiction,* and *Psychoanalysis, M.D.*) did not sell well, though. EC Comics' problems were not over, either. On top of low sales for the New Direction line of titles, EC Comics' major national distributor went bankrupt in 1955. This proved too much for EC Comics to deal with. In 1955, EC Comics announced the cancellation of all of their comic book titles.[1] Their humor comic book *Mad* had always sold well, so EC Comics changed the format of the title. *Mad* was to be published as a magazine instead of a comic book. This allowed EC Comics to publish content without having to be concerned with the Comics Code Authority since the Comics Code applied only to comic books—not magazines. Originally edited by Harvey Kurtzman, Al Feldstein took over as editor in 1956 and held the position until 1984 when he retired. Feldstein brought on many of the names that have become associated with *Mad* such as Don Martin, Frank Jacobs, Mort Drucker, Dave Berg, and Sergio Aragonés. William Gaines sold EC in the early 1960s to the Kinney Parking Company, which also acquired National Periodicals (DC Comics) and Warner Bros. Gaines was named as a Kinney board member and was generally permitted to run *Mad* as he saw fit without corporate interference. After Gaines' death in 1992, *Mad* slowly became more ingrained with the Time Warner corporate structure. Now owned solely by DC Comics (under the parent company of Time Warner), *Mad* is still being published today—over 60 years after its first issue.[2]

Despite there not being a (non–*Mad*) EC publication since 1956, EC Comics have remained very popular due in no small part to having their material reprinted. Ballantine Books, Nostalgia Press, East Coast Comix, Russ Cochran, Dark Horse, and Fantagraphics Books have all published reprints of EC Comics titles throughout the subsequent years. The legacy of EC Comics horror titles has inspired works in other media including the 1972 movie *Tales from the Crypt*, the 1973 movie *The Vault of Horror*, as well as inspiring *Creepshow* and *Creepshow 2*. In 1989, cable-TV network HBO began airing *Tales from the Crypt* which ran through 1996 with seven seasons and 93 episodes and also spawned three *Tales from the Crypt*-branded movies, *Demon Knight*, *Bordello of Blood*, and *Ritual* in 1997.

The EC Comics brand is now back in the hands of the Gaines family. They sell merchandise including T-shirts and collected hardback reprints of all of the old EC Comics classics from their website (www.eccomics.com).

Whatever Happened to Dr. Wertham?

Dr. Fredric Wertham was born as Friedrich Ignatz Wertheimer on March 20, 1985, in Munich, Germany. He legally changed his name to Fredric Wertham in 1927. He studied at King's College London and at the Universities of Munich and Erlangen, graduating with an M.D. degree from the University of Würzburg in 1921. He was influenced by Dr. Emil Kraepelin, a professor of clinical psychiatry at the University of Munich who emphasized the effects of environment and social background on psychological development. He also had regular correspondence with Sigmund Freud. It was actually Freud who influenced Wertham to specialize in psychiatry.

In 1922, Dr. Wertham moved to the United States to work under Adolf Meyer at the Phipps Psychiatric Clinic at Johns Hopkins Hospital in Baltimore, Maryland. He became a United States citizen and married Florence Hesketh in 1927. In 1932, Dr. Wertham moved to New York City in order to accept a senior staff position at the Bellevue Mental Hygiene Clinic. Bellevue was the psychiatric clinic connected with the New York Court of General Sessions in which all convicted felons received a psychiatric examination that was used in their court proceedings. In 1935, Dr. Wertham testified for the defense in the trial of the cannibalistic serial killer Albert Fish, declaring Fish insane. In 1946, Dr. Wertham opened the LaFargue Clinic in the basement of St. Philip's Church in Harlem. The clinic was a low-cost psychiatric clinic funded by voluntary contributions and specializing in African American teenagers.

Dr. Wertham is best known for his book, *Seduction of the Innocent*, in which he describes depictions of violence, sex, and drug use in "crime comics" (Dr. Wertham referred to the comic books in question as "crime comics," but his writing was clear that he was not just referring to the True Crime comic genre, but horror comics and superhero comics as well). Dr. Wertham suggested that reading this type of material would encourage similar behavior in children. In *Seduction of the Innocent*, Dr. Wertham printed panels from various comic books of the time and pointed out what he determined to be inappropriate material. He went into detail on what he found to be recurring themes in the comic books. Dr. Wertham seemed particularly adamant about calling out "injury to eye" panels (panels depicting some type of damage being done to an eye—usually by a sharp object), "bondage" panels (panels showing a person, typically a woman, tied up and helpless), and "headlight" panels (panels showing a woman whose breasts are prominently featured in an apparently salacious manner). This is not to say that horror and crime comics of the time didn't have gruesome imagery—because they certainly did. Dr. Wertham, however, went above the obvious drawn images and went so far as to claim comic books had subliminal hidden images (naked female forms concealed in the drawings of muscles and tree bark), covert homosexual stories (Dr. Wertham claimed Batman and Robin were a closeted gay couple and that Wonder Woman's power and strength came from the fact that she was a lesbian), and even anti-American propaganda (Superman, the paragon of Truth, Justice, and the American Way was described by Wertham as promoting fascist ideals). *Seduction of the Innocent* sold well and even spent some time in the Book of the Month Club. First printings contained a bibliography listing all of the comic books published that Dr. Wertham cited in the book. Fears about possible lawsuits prompted the publisher to physically tear the bibliography page from any available copy they could get their hands on—making true first prints with the bibliography intact a collector's item for both book collectors and comic collectors. The success of *Seduction of the Innocent* led to Dr. Wertham being asked to testify as an expert witness before the Senate Subcommittee on Juvenile Delinquency which, in turn, was the impetus for the creation of the Comics Code Authority.

Dr. Wertham continued to be active on social issues throughout his career. His writings about the effects of racial segregation were used as evidence in the landmark Supreme Court case Brown v. Board of Education. His 1966 book, *A Sign for Cain*, dealt with the involvement of medical professionals in the Holocaust. In 1959, he attempted to sell a book which would have been titled *The War on Children*. This follow-up to *Seduction of the Innocent* was intended to detail the deleterious effects of television on young children, but no publishers were interested and the book was never published, much to Dr. Wertham's frustration.

Despite his apparent crusade against comic books, Dr. Wertham often denied that he was in favor of censorship or that he had some vendetta against comic books in general. By the 1970s Dr. Wertham had revisited the comic book culture in his writings. In 1973, he published *World of Fanzines* in which he wrote very positively about the fanzine culture. Fanzines are non-professional, non-official publications produced by enthusiasts of a particular cultural phenomenon such as a literary genre or musical genre. The term "fanzine" is a portmanteau of "fan" and "magazine." Fanzines run the gamut of comic books, horror films, music, and even role-playing games. Many professional writers were first published in fanzines and some continue to contribute to them after establishing a professional reputation. Dr. Wertham wrote that fanzines were "a constructive and healthy exercise of creative drives." This led to an invitation to speak at the 1973 New York Comic Art Convention—one of the first comic book conventions. Dr. Wertham's reputation preceded him and his address did not go well. He was treated with suspicion and outright heckled during his speech. After this disastrous appearance, Dr. Wertham neither spoke at conventions nor wrote about the comic book industry again.[3]

Before his retirement, Dr. Wertham became a professor of psychiatry at New York University, a senior psychiatrist in the New York City Department of Hospitals, and the director of the Mental Hygiene Clinic at the Bellevue Hospital Center. Dr. Fredric Wertham died on November 18, 1981, at the age of 86.

After his death, Dr. Wertham's papers were donated to the Library of Congress and are held by the Manuscript Division. They were made available for use by scholars for research on May 20, 2010. In 2013, Carol Tilley, assistant professor at the Graduate School of Library and Information Science at the University of Illinois, examined Dr. Wertham's research. She found his conclusions linking comic books to juvenile delinquency to be almost totally baseless. Tilley found that Dr. Wertham "played fast and loose with the data he gathered on comics" to make them appear more harmful than they actually were. Wertham "manipulated, overstated, compromised, and fabricated evidence—especially that evidence he attributed to personal clinical research with young people—for rhetorical gain." Wertham was found to have used a non-representative sample of young people who were already mentally troubled in order to skew his findings. He misrepresented stories from colleagues as being his own and furthermore manipulated statements from the children he interviewed by deliberately neglecting some passages while rephrasing others so they better suited his thesis.[4]

Whatever Happened to All of Those Comic Companies?

Throughout this book, I mentioned several comic book publishers that were influential on the horror comic book genre. While some of the major comic book publishers are still around today (namely Marvel Comics, DC, Image, etc.), there have been many others who have fallen by the wayside. Here is the ultimate fate for those publishers:

Ace Magazines—Founded in 1940 by Aaron A. Wyn and his wife Rose Wyn, Ace Magazines was a publisher of both comic books and pulp magazines. Its most successful superhero title was *Super-Mystery Comics* featuring Magno the Magnetic Man and his sidekick Davey. Ace Magazines also published the horror comics *Baffling Mysteries, Hand of Fate,* and *Web of Mystery* as well as the crime comic book *Crime Must Pay the Penalty.* Ace Magazines had the most success with romance comics. *Glamorous Romances, Love At First Sight, Love Experiences,* and *Real Love* were all published from 1940 until Ace Magazines ceased publication of comic books in 1956.

Excerpts from Ace Magazines titles *Challenge of the Unknown, Crime Must Pay the Penalty, Web of Mystery,* and *Western Adventures Comics* were used by Dr. Fredric Wertham in his book *Seduction of the Innocent* as examples of violent and gruesome imagery present in comic books at the time.

Although Ace Magazines went out of business in 1956, two of their superhero characters, Lash Lightning and Lightning Girl, were revived in Dynamite Entertainment's title *Project Superpowers* in 2008.

American Comics Group—Best known in the context of this book as the publisher of the first ongoing horror comic title *Adventures Into the Unknown*, American Comics Group was founded in 1943 by Benjamin Sangor. American Comics Group originally started publishing comic supplements for newspapers and transitioned into comic books by the mid-1940s publishing horror, crime, mystery, romance, and funny animal comics—all staples for the time. *Adventures Into the Unknown* was the first of a trilogy of horror/suspense titles including *Forbidden Worlds* and *Unknown Worlds*—all of which were published continually well into the 1960s. Romance titles were also quite successful for American Comics Group with both *Romantic Adventures* (later renamed *My Romantic Adventures*) and *Lovelorn* (later renamed *Confessions of the Lovelorn*) launching in 1949 and continually published into the late 1960s.

Adventures Into the Unknown not only has the distinction of being the first ongoing horror comic title, it also managed to survive the backlash against horror comics in the 1950s which culminated in the formation of the Comics Code Authority and their draconian censorship rules. Granted, *Adventures Into the Unknown* was not known for the types of artwork and storylines that were present in many other horror comics, but the fact that the title was able to weather that storm and still continue publishing was a testament to American Comics Group. *Adventures Into the Unknown* was published until 1967 when American Comics Group ceased publication on all of its comic lines with the exception of the commercial comics division, Custom Comics. Custom Comics published books for a wide variety of clients including the A.C. Gilbert toy company, Montgomery Ward, Tupperware, and the United States Air Force until they finally stopped producing comics in the early 1980s.

Atlas Comics—Atlas Comics was born from the death of another comic book company. In 1939, pulp magazine publisher Martin Goodman founded Timely Publications. Timely Publications was created to capitalize on the emerging comic book industry. Timely Publications' *Marvel Comics* #1 (October 1939) featured the first appearances of the Human Torch (the android, not Johnny Storm of Fantastic Four fame) and Namor the Sub-Mariner. Timely Publications would also introduce the world to Captain America and the timing couldn't have been any better. With the onset of World War II, superhero comics (especially patriotic superhero comics) were extremely popular. Captain America and other patriotic superheroes would fight the Nazis and Axis forces in the pages of Timely Publications comic books throughout the war. After the end of the war, though, the popularity of superheroes would wane as readers looked for entertainment in different ways. The last Timely Publications comic book, *Captain America Comics* #75, was published in October of 1950.

Martin Goodman was a shrewd businessman and quickly changed focus. He ceased all publication under the Timely Publications banner and began publishing comic books in other genres under the Atlas Comics banner. Atlas ran the gamut on what they produced. They released comics in basically every genre except the superhero genre—Western, humor, funny animal, crime, war, jungle, romance, espionage, medieval adventures, Bible stories, sports, and of course horror. During the 1950s Atlas produced the horror titles *Adventures Into Terror, Journey Into Mystery, Menace, Strange Tales, Tales of Suspense,* and *Tales to Astonish* among several others. Atlas published a wealth of titles in nearly every comic genre possible. As you can imagine, it was difficult to produce this much volume and produce quality work. Simply put, Atlas Comics survived through the 1950s primarily because they had a stable of young talent who could generate an impressive volume of work for cheap. Luckily for them, some of the young talent they had at their disposal was Stan Lee, Steve Ditko, Bill Everett, and Jack Kirby. In the late 1960s, Martin Goodman asked Stan Lee to come up with a new approach to the superhero. Lee and his team went on to create some of the most famous superheroes and revolutionized the superhero genre. Their new characters (Spider-Man, the Fantastic Four, Thor, Hulk, Iron Man, Daredevil, the X-Men, and Doctor Strange to name a few) would all have their exploits told in new titles under a new banner as Martin Goodman again renamed and refocused the company as Atlas Comics became Marvel Comics. Marvel Comics, of course, is one of the most successful comic book publishers today, having made the transition from comic books to television and major motion pictures.

Arrow Comics—Ralph Griffith and Stuart Kerr founded Arrow Comics in 1985 with the intent of publishing a local comic fanzine. When Griffith and Kerr saw the success of *Teenage Mutant Ninja Turtles* and other black-and-white self-published comic books, they started working on gathering up local comic talent in order to publish their own comic books. This was no mean feat considering Arrow Comics was based in Ypsilanti, Michigan—not exactly the center of the comic book universe. The black-and-white comic book boom of the mid-1980s did prove that quality books could be produced by relatively unknown artists and on a shoestring budget—and that worked in Arrow Comics' favor. They recruited local Michigan artists Randy Zimmerman, Guy Davis, Vincent Locke, Susan Van Camp, Mark Bloodworth, and Tim Dzon and suddenly Arrow Comics had their "bullpen" of talent. Later in 1985, Arrow Comics began publishing *Deadworld*. *Deadworld* told the story of a small group of people trying to find their way through a world ravaged by the outbreak of the zombie apocalypse.

Arrow Comics found some moderate success with *Deadworld, The Realm, Tales from the Aniverse,* and *Oz*, but they soon fell victim to forces outside of their control. As quickly as the black-and-white comic book boom started, the bottom fell out. The ripples caused from the collapse of the black-and-white comic book boom reverberated throughout the industry resulting in the bankruptcy of some of the distributors. Unfortunately for Arrow Comics, revenues from their largest selling titles were held up in the bankruptcy hearings and, in 1989, Arrow Comics sold the licensing for *Oz, The Realm,* and *Deadworld* to Caliber Comics. This is why *Deadworld* issues #1-9 (January 1986-May 1988) were published by Arrow Comics and issues #10-26 (November 1988-January 1993) were published by Caliber Comics.

Arrow Comics saw a brief revival in 1993 with *The Dead*—a new horror title that continued to push the envelope of gore even farther than *Deadworld* did. Sadly, *The Dead* only published two issues, due in no small part to the fact that the envelope of gore was pushed so far that many retailers were hesitant to carry the book. In 2008, Randy Zimmerman and Scott R. Moore revitalized Arrow Comics once again this time with a concentration on publishing webcomics. *Spank the Monkey* and *Rebel Nun*, both Randy Zimmerman's creations, are webcomic strips featured on the Arrow Comics website. There are also promises to bring back some of the best Arrow Comics from the 1980s, but the official Arrow Comics website hasn't been updated in several years at the time of this writing, so there remains the possibility that Arrow Comics is gone again—or at least on a long hiatus.

Avon Publications—Founded in 1941 as a paperback book publisher, Avon Publications is best known in the context of this book as being the publisher of the first horror comic book—the 1947 one-shot *Eerie*. Avon Publications also revised *Eerie* into a series in 1951 and that series ran 17 issues. Throughout the 1950s, Avon Publications published comic books in the horror genre as well as other popular genres of the time including science fiction, Western, romance, war, and funny animal. Most of Avon Publications' comic series only lasted a few issues. Other than *Eerie*, the longest lasting Avon Publications titles were the Westerns *Jesse James* and *Wild Bill Hickok*; the science fiction *Strange Worlds*; funny animal title *Peter Rabbit*; and the spy thriller *The Saint*. *Jesse James* ran 29 issues from 1950 through 1956. *Wild Bill Hickok* ran 28 issues from 1949 through 1956. *Strange Worlds* ran nine issues from 1950 through 1952. After *Eerie* #17, the title became *Strange Worlds* and kept up with the numbering scheme, with issue #18 being released in October of 1954 and the final issue, #22, released in September 1955. *Peter Rabbit* ran

37 issues from 1947 through 1956. *The Saint* ran for 12 issues from 1947 through 1952.

By 1959, Avon Publications had stopped publishing comic books. Avon was purchased by the Hearst Corporation in 1959 and published only books. In 1972, Avon started publishing romance books and saw success with this venture. In 1999, the News Corporation bought out Hearst's book division and Avon's hardcover and non-romance paperback lines were moved to a sister company, leaving Avon solely as a publisher of romance paperbacks.

Caliber Comics—Caliber Comics was founded in 1989 when bookstore owner Gary Reed purchased the rights for *Deadworld* and *The Realm* from financially struggling Arrow Comics. Caliber Comics picked up publication of *Deadworld* and *The Realm* as well as adding their own comic titles to the mix. *Caliber Presents* was one of the first new titles from Caliber Comics. *Caliber Presents* featured work by Vince Locke, Mark Bloodworth, Tim Vigil, James O'Barr, and Guy Davis. *Caliber Presents* #1 (January 1989) also features the first appearance of James O'Barr's *The Crow*.

Caliber Comics continued to grow throughout the 1990s, merging with Stabur Corporation in 1993 with Gary Reed being named president of Stabur. Stabur was also involved in starting up the new toy company McFarlane Toys with *Spawn* creator Todd McFarlane, and Gary Reed was also named vice president of McFarlane Toys.

Unfortunately, the downturn of the comic book industry brought on by the mid-1990s crash of the speculator market had dire effects on Caliber Comics. Due to the shrinking market, Caliber was forced to reduce the number of comic titles they published. On top of that, another element of bad timing eventually spelled doom for Caliber Comics. Caliber Comics had been heavily invested in an upcoming collectible card game based on the *Spawn* comic book series. Production on the game was running behind and the printer outsourced the collation of the cards to another company. The outsourced company apparently didn't understand that cards in a collectible card game were supposed to be randomly distributed in the packs. The game was released with improper collation and initial purchase orders exceeding $2 million were cancelled. Caliber Comics filed a lawsuit and did eventually win, but by that time the printer had already declared bankruptcy and Caliber was just left with useless product and debt. Caliber Comics closed their doors in 2000 and Gary Reed went on to freelance writing and teaching college biology.

In 2015, Gary Reed relaunched Caliber Comics and solicited orders for several new and reprint titles. Reed died suddenly in October 2016, but Caliber Comics does live on. Caliber Comics' zombie epic *Deadworld* continues to be printed, although now by Desperado Publishing, an imprint of IDW.

Charlton Comics—Founded in 1945, Charlton Comics was a division of Charlton Publications—a publisher of song-lyric magazines and puzzle books. Charlton Comics published comic books in a wide variety of genres including crime, science fiction, Western, war, romance, funny animal, superhero, and horror. Charlton Comics was unique in that it controlled all areas of publishing—from editorial to printing to distribution, whereas nearly all other publishers had to outsource printing and distribution. Charlton also had the less enviable reputation of being a "bargain basement" publishing house. Charlton would regularly supplement their inventory by buying up material from defunct publishers. They also had the reputation of paying their creative teams the lowest rates in the industry.

During the height of the horror comic boom in the Golden Age of Comic Books, Charlton already had *The Thing!* with artwork by Steve Ditko. In order to expand their horror comic titles, Charlton Comics purchased properties from the defunct Superior Comics, Mainline Publications, St. John Publications, and Fawcett Publications. Charlton continued the publication of two of Fawcett's horror titles—*This Magazine Is Haunted* and *Strange Suspense Stories*—using unpublished material from Fawcett's inventory. Charlton published *This Magazine Is Haunted* bi-monthly until May of 1958. *Strange Suspense Stories* was published all the way up until 1965.

Comic Media—Comic Media, publisher of the horror titles *Horrific* and *Weird Terror*, was founded in 1952 by Allen Hardy. Comic Media published a handful of action, Western, romance, and horror titles in its short lifespan—the longest running of which (a romance title called *All True Romance*) ran only 20 issues. Comic Media closed their doors for good in 1954 and sold all of their titles and characters to Charlton Comics. Comic Media's primary artist, Don Heck, was recruited by Stan Lee to come work for Atlas Comics (which would become Marvel Comics). While there, he co-created the characters of Iron Man, Hawkeye, and Black Widow.

Dell Comics—Dell Comics was the comic book publishing division of Dell Publishing. Founded in 1929, Dell Publishing got its start by publishing pulp magazines. In 1936, Dell collaborated with Eastern Color Printing to publish *Famous Funnies: A Carnival of Comics*—the first true comic book. In 1938, Dell entered into a partnership with Western Publishing in which Dell would finance and distribute publications that Western produced. Many of these would be licensed material from movies and television properties and this would prove very beneficial for Dell. At their peak, Dell Comics reported selling 26 million copies per month.

Dell's reliance on licensed properties gave them the reputation as a harmless and wholesome comic book publisher. This allowed them to stay out from the fracas that plagued the comic book industry in the mid–1950s when Dr. Fredric Wertham published his book *Seduction of the Innocent* and testified before the Senate Subcommittee on Juvenile Delinquency, claiming that reading comic books caused children to become juvenile delinquents. Dell Comics was one of the few comic book publishers to never submit their comic books to the Comics Code Authority, relying on their wholesome reputation. They bolstered this reputation with their "Pledge to Parents" that promised that their strict editorial process eliminated rather than regulated any objectionable material. "Dell Comics Are Good Comics" was Dell's motto and it carried them through one of the most troubling times in the comic book industry unscathed by controversy.

In 1962, the Dell Comics partnership with Western Publishing came to an end. Western Publishing took nearly all of their licensed properties (and several members of Dell Comics' creative team) and created their own comic book company, Gold Key Comics. Dell Comics struggled on for a little over a decade with its remaining licensed properties as well as some attempts at original material, but their sales continued a steady decline until Dell Comics ceased publication in 1974.

Detective Comics—Yes, Detective Comics was a company before it was a comic book. Detective Comics, Inc. was founded in 1937 by Major Malcolm Wheeler-Nicholson and Jack S. Liebowitz. In 1938, Wheeler-Nicholson was forced out and Detective Comics, Inc. purchased National Allied Publications—a company founded in 1934 (oddly enough) by Major Malcolm Wheeler-Nicholson. National Allied Publications and Detective Comics, Inc. merged to become National Comics Publications, Inc. on September 30, 1946. National Comics Publications would also absorb All-American Publications—the act of which prompted Max Gaines to start his own company, Educational Comics or EC.

National Comics Publications was renamed National Periodical Publications, Inc. in 1961. Despite this fact, the company had been branding itself "Superman-DC" since the early 1940s and was colloquially known as DC Comics long before the official adoption of the name—which didn't happen until 1977.

Eerie Publications—Founded in 1966 by Myron Fass and Stanley Harris, Eerie Publications was a publisher of black-and-white horror anthology magazines. Despite the name, Eerie Publications had nothing to do with the magazine *Eerie* which was published by Warren Publishing. Eerie Publications spent its entire 15 years of existence playing second fiddle to Warren Publications and was never able to match their success and continually fought their reputation as a "cut-rate" version of Warren Publishing.

Eerie Publications' longest running titles were *Horror Tales, Tales From the Tomb, Tales of Voodoo, Terror Tales, Witches' Tales*, and their longest running magazine—*Weird*. *Weird* ran a total of 69 issues from January 1966 through November 1981. All of Eerie Publications' magazines printed a mixture of new material and pre-Code horror comic reprints. Writers and artists were seldomly credited, but did include Dick Ayers, Chic Stone, and even Myron Fass himself. Stanley Harris left Eerie Publications in 1976 after a disagreement with Myron Fass. Harris went on to form Harris Publications, the publisher of *Vampirella*. Eerie Publications held on for a few more years before going out of business in 1981.

Fawcett Comics—Fawcett Comics was the comic book publishing division of Fawcett Publications. Fawcett Comics was one of the most successful comic book publishers during the Golden Age of Comic Books and is best known for publishing *Whiz Comics* and the creation of Captain Marvel (a.k.a. Shazam). Fawcett Comics also published the horror comic titles *This Magazine Is Haunted, Beware! Terror Tales, Worlds of Fear, Strange Suspense Stories*, and *Unknown World*.

By 1953, declining comic books sales coupled with a copyright infringement lawsuit leveled against Fawcett Comics by National Comics (a.k.a. DC) made it no longer feasible for Fawcett Comics to continue publication. Fawcett Comics ceased publication and sold many of their titles and characters to Charlton Comics, who resumed publication of the horror titles *This Magazine Is Haunted* and *Strange Suspense Stories*.

FantaCo Enterprises—FantaCo was founded in 1978 by Thomas Skulan originally as a mail order company and comic book store before expanding into the publication of books, magazines, and comic books. It also hosted FantaCon, a comic book and horror convention in Albany, New York. FantaCo is best known (at least in this author's opinion) for the black-and-white horror anthology title *Gore Shriek*. Published sporadically over the course of three years, *Gore Shriek* had a run of six issues (technically six and a half as there was a special promotional *Gore Shriek* #6.5 which was only available directly from FantaCo Enterprises or the artists themselves) from 1986 through 1989. Edited by Thomas Skulan himself initially, then later by Stephen R. Bissette, *Gore Shriek* drew on the talents of creators like Greg Capullo, Bruce Spaulding Fuller, Eric Stanway, Gurchain Singh, and even Stephen R. Bissette and brought forth one of the most groundbreaking horror comic titles to ever see press during the 1980s. The one-shot *Gore Shriek Delectus* released in 1989 reprinted the best material from the first series. In 1990, FantaCo revived *Gore Shriek* for a three-issue run as well as launching several new horror titles including *Night of the Living Dead, Night's Children, Vault* of *Screaming Horror, Uptown Zombies,* and *Night of the Living Dead: London.* These titles also served to kickstart the careers of Chynna Clugston, Steve Niles, and Jim Whiting.

FantaCo also published many books on the subjects of horror films; splatter films; exploitation films; an early guide to horror, science fiction, and fantasy films on videocassette; and even a full-blown horror novel, *Ninth and Hell Street.* They also published the *FantaCo Horror Yearbook and Price Guide* every year from 1978 until 1996. On top of all that, they hosted the horror convention FantaCon every year from 1979 until 1990, missing only 1982 and 1984–1987.

The mid-1990s speculation bubble crash, the decline of comic books sales, and issues with a distributor caused Skulan to close the doors on the storefront and FantaCo Enterprises in 1998.

After a 23-year hiatus, Skulan revived FantaCon on September 14 and 15, 2013, at the Marriott Hotel in Albany, New York, and FantaCon has been an annual event ever since—much to the delight of horror fans.

Gold Key Comics—For many years Western Publishing and Dell Comics had a mutually beneficial business relationship. Western Publishing would secure all of the licensing and create the comic books whereas Dell Comics would handle all of the publication and distribution. This all changed in 1962 when Western Publishing made the decision to make their entire publishing process in-house, forming Gold Key Comics as the imprint for this. When Gold Key Comics was founded, they took over many of the licensed properties that had belonged to Dell Comics. Gold Key Comics had the exclusive rights to publish several licensed properties from popular television series of the time as well as licensed properties based on Walt Disney Studios and Warner Bros. works. Gold Key Comics acquired the license for the television show *The Twilight Zone* and they were the first comic book company to publish comic books based on *Star Trek. Star Trek* and *The Twilight Zone* were long running titles for Gold Key Comics. *Star Trek* ran 61 issues from July 1967 through March of 1979 and *The Twilight Zone* ran a total of 92 issues from November of 1962 through May of 1982. These titles plus the other licensed properties helped Gold Key Comics to maintain strong sales throughout the 1960s. Aside from *The Twilight Zone*, Gold Key Comics also published the horror/supernatural series *Ripley's Believe it or Not, Boris Karloff Tales of Mystery,* and *Grimm's Ghost Stories.*

As time went on, Gold Key Comics slowly began to lose their licensed titles. In 1966, Gold Key Comics lost all of the King Features Syndicate characters (Popeye, Flash Gordon, The Phantom, etc.) to Charlton Comics. In 1970, Gold Key Comics lost nearly all of the Hanna-Barbera characters to

Charlton Comics and ultimately lost *Star Trek* to Marvel Comics in 1979. The timing on this was particularly poor for Gold Key Comics since this was right before the release of *Star Trek: The Motion Picture* and the subsequent revival of the franchise. By 1977, many of the company's titles had been cancelled and the remaining surviving titles reprinted material instead of producing new original content.

While Gold Key Comics were still being sold individually on the newsstands and the ubiquitous wire comic spinner racks in stores, Western Publishing began experimenting with a new type of distribution. Western Publishing started packaging typically three comics in a plastic bag. These bagged comics were sold at toy stores, department stores, newsagents at airports, bus stations, and other types of outlets where the standard comic rack wasn't a feasible retail fixture. Western published these comics under the Whitman logo—an imprint previously used to publish coloring books. Being a publishing house allowed Western to be able to leverage some unique distribution opportunities to the point that they even distributed bagged comics from rival publisher DC under the Whitman logo and did so quite successfully. At their peak in the 1970s Whitman was distributing over 50,000 copies of select DC titles a month in their comic bags.

The comic industry slowdown of the 1970s eventually spelled the end for Gold Key Comics and Whitman, though. In 1981, Western Publications stopped all distribution to newsstands and only released their comics in bags while discontinuing the use of both the Gold Key Comics and Whitman Comics logos. The comics arm of Western Publications struggled on for a little while longer, but Western Publishing ultimately stopped publishing comic books altogether in 1984.

Gilberton—Albert Lewis Kanter started what would become Gilberton in 1941. Kanter had the vision of using the fledgling comic book medium as a way to introduce young readers and more reluctant readers to works of literature. He created *Classic Comics* for the Eliot Publishing Company in October of 1941. *Classic Comics* debuted with *The Three Musketeers* and followed up with *Ivanhoe* and *The Count of Monte Cristo*. These literary adaptations were a huge hit and Kanter found that he quickly outgrew his publisher. In 1942, Kanter moved his operation to a new office location and changed the company name to Gilberton Company, Inc. Gilberton Company began publication of *Classics Illustrated* with issue #4.

Classics Illustrated would go on to publish 169 issues over the course of nearly 30 years of business. Literary works including *Moby Dick, Robin Hood, The Hunchback of Notre-Dame, Oliver Twist,* and *Call of the Wild* would be adapted—including the horror-related titles *Frankenstein: or, The Modern*

Prometheus and *Dr. Jekyll and Mr. Hyde*. Gilberton would also launch the spin-off title *Classics Illustrated Junior* which would adapt fairy tales and folktales.

Between 1942 and 1962 Gilberton would see sales totaling 200 million books. By 1962, however, Gilberton was beginning to struggle. The company had lost their second-class mailing permit, which drove up the cost of shipping. On top of that, the rise of television, cheap paperback books, and the introduction of Cliff's Notes led to an overall decline in their circulation. In 1967, Kanter sold Gilberton to the Catholic publication Twin Circle—a division of the publisher Frawley Corporation. Twin Circle published two issues of *Classics Illustrated* but primarily concentrated on foreign sales and reprinting older titles, and by 1971 both *Classics Illustrated* and *Classics Illustrated Junior* were cancelled due to poor circulation. Since the demise of Gilberton, the *Classics Illustrated* line of comic books have been reprinted throughout the years by different companies.

Harvey Comics—Founded in 1941 by the brothers Leon, Robert, and Alfred Harvey, Harvey Comics is best known for their publication of comics based on licensed characters. During the horror comics boom of the Golden Age of Comic Books, Harvey Comics did have a foray into the horror comics realm publishing *Black Cat Mystery* and *Witches Western Tales* under their Harvey Thriller line; however, the vast majority of their books came from their line of characters licensed from Famous Studios. Harvey Comics focused on publishing more "kid friendly" books for the duration of their business life including *Richie Rich, Little Dot, Little Lotta, Casper the Friendly Ghost, Hot Stuff the Little Devil,* and *Wendy the Good Little Witch*.

In the early 1980s, Harvey Comics was in negotiations with Marvel Comics to have Marvel Comics assume the publication of some of the Harvey Comics characters. Unfortunately the deal fell through when the Harvey brothers could not reach an agreement on the terms, and Harvey Comics stopped publication of comic books in 1982. In 1986, Alan Harvey (Alfred Harvey's oldest son) resumed publication of Harvey Comics, publishing mainly digests and reprints. The reborn Harvey Comics was sold to HMH Communications in 1989 and subsequently rebranded Harvey Comics Entertainment or HCE. HCE published the reprint titles until HCE ceased publication of comic books in 1994.

Key Publications—Key Publications was founded in 1951 and folded in 1956. During the horror comics boom of the 1950s, Key Publications published *Mister Mystery, Weird Mysteries, Climax, Weird Tales of the Future,* and *Weird Chills*. None of the titles were produced for any real length of time. *Mister Mystery* ran 19 issues from September 1951 through October 1954, and

Weird Mysteries ran 12 issues from October 1952 through September 1954. While being known for producing some of the most vile horror comics of the time, the founder, Stanley P. Morse, was almost totally disconnected from the process. When asked about the content of his horror comics, Morse once said, "You did what you had to do—what moved 'em off the racks.... I don't know what the hell I published. I never knew. I never read the things. I never cared."

Steve Ditko, co-creator of Spider-Man, had his first professional comic book work at Key Publications. Ditko illustrated Bruce Hamilton's science fiction story "Stretching Things" for Stanmor Publications—a division of Key Publications. The story was eventually sold to Farrell Publications and published in *Fantastic Fears* #5 (February 1954). Ditko's first published work was a six-page story, "Paper Romance," in Key's *Daring Love* #1 (October 1953).

Quality Comics—Founded in 1937, Quality Comics would quickly become a major force in the Golden Age of Comic Books. This is not difficult to believe considering Quality Comics was able to draw on the talents of comic book legends like Jack Cole, Reed Crandall, Will Eisner, Lou Fine, Gil Fox, Paul Gustavson, Bob Powell, and Wally Wood. Quality Comics published the books that introduced the world to superheroes like Captain Triumph, Doll Man, the Human Bomb, Kid Eternity, Phantom Lady, and Plastic Man. During World War II, Quality Comics published the exploits of patriotic heroes like Blackhawk, Miss America, Red Torpedo, and Uncle Sam. Quality Comics also published the Will Eisner creation *The Spirit*.

By the mid-1950s, sales of superhero comic books (which were the majority of Quality Comics' titles) were on the decline. Quality branched out into different comic genres including war, romance, and humor. During this time they published the horror comic title *Web of Evil* for 21 issues from 1952 through 1954. Unfortunately, none of the new ventures met with much success and Quality Comics ceased publication with comic books cover-dated December 1956. Many of Quality Comics' characters and titles were sold to National Periodical Publications (which would become DC Comics), who continued publication of the titles *Blackhawk* and *G.I. Combat*. Over the decades, DC has revived some Quality Comics characters such as Plastic Man as well as creating updated versions of others (namely Black Condor and The Ray).

St. John Publications—Founded in 1947, St. John Publications published comic books for just over a decade. In that time they had some rather impressive industry firsts. In October 1953, St. John Publications published the world's first 3-D comic book, *Three Dimension Comics* #1 featuring Mighty Mouse. *Three Dimension Comics* #1 was published in September 1953 in an oversize format and then reprinted in a standard comic book size in October 1953. It sold 1.2 million copies, which is even more impressive given that it had a 25-cent cover price, whereas other comics cost ten cents. St. John published the first movie-comedian tie-in series, *Abbott and Costello Comics*, and one of the earliest predecessors to the modern graphics novel, the "picture novel" *It Rhymes with Lust* (1950). St. John saw the introduction of Joe Kubert's prehistoric hero Tor. They also had the distinction of employing Matt Baker, the first African American comic book artist in mainstream media. Baker provided artwork for the true crime title *Authentic Police Cases*, the humor title *Canteen Kate*, as well as the romance books *Cinderella Love* and *Teen-Age Romances* to name just a few.

Before leaving the comic book industry in 1958, St. John Publications published *Strange Terrors, Weird Horrors, Nightmare, Amazing Ghost Stories*, and the 3-D comic *The House of Terror*.

Star Publications—In 1949, comic book publisher Novelty Press sold off its catalog of characters and artwork to L.B. Cole. Cole initially worked for Novelty Press as the cover artist for their superhero comic *Blue Bolt*. Cole formed a partnership with Gerhard Kramer and founded Star Publications. Using their newfound assets, they started out by continuing publication of *Blue Bolt*—even continuing the numbering of the title so that Star Publications' first issue of *Blue Bolt* was issue #102. By 1951, the horror comic boom was in full swing and Star Publications was quick to cash in on the trend. *Blue Bolt* was renamed *Blue Bolt Weird Tales of Terror* and converted to a horror comic. It would eventually change names again to *Ghostly Weird Stories*. Star Publications also published the horror titles *The Horrors* and *Startling Terror Tales* with stories and artwork so grisly that they were singled out by Dr. Fredric Wertham in his book *Seduction of the Innocent*. This negative attention coupled with the public outcry against horror comics brought on by Dr. Wertham's testimony before the Senate Subcommittee on Juvenile Delinquency as well as the untimely death of Gerhard Kramer culminated in Star Publications going out of business in 1954.

Warren Publications—James Warren founded Warren Publications in 1957 and started publishing *Famous Monsters of Filmland* and *Monster World*. These two offerings were quickly followed up by the science fiction magazine *Spaceman* and the satire magazine *Help!* In 1964, Warren began publishing the black-and-white horror magazines *Creepy* and *Eerie*. Since both *Creepy* and *Eerie* were standard magazine format with a cover price of 35 cents (instead of the standard 12 cents that comic books were priced), the publications were not subject to the restrictions placed on comic book content by the Comics Code Authority and so they were able to print more graphic content than would ever be allowed in a comic book at the time. Both *Creepy* and *Eerie* helped propel the horror comic/magazine genre along during the mid-1960s. They also paved the way for other boundary-pushing magazines like *Heavy Metal*, Marvel Comics' *Epic Illustrated*, and Skywald Publications' *Psycho*. The horror comic book genre survived the Silver Age of Comic Books almost exclusively due to the publication of magazines like *Creepy* and *Eerie*.

Things weren't all sunshine and roses for Warren Publications, though. In 1967 Archie Goodwin, longtime editor of both *Creepy* and *Eerie*, left the company. Warren Publications moved their operations from Philadelphia to New York City and changed distributors. This came right as a downturn in the industry happened, so Warren Publications quickly developed a cashflow problem. Many of the artists and writers left the company and both *Creepy* and *Eerie* were relegated to printing reprints of earlier material just to keep the magazines in circulation. For over two years, *Creepy* and *Eerie* struggled on as a revolving door of editors made their way through. In 1969, Warren Publications turned everything around with the premiere of *Vampirella*. *Vampirella* was a runaway hit for Warren Publications to the point that artists and writers who had previously left began to return to the company.

Warren Publications continued to be relevant and successful throughout the 1970s, but the early 1980s brought significant change. A combination of lower circulation numbers, internal business strife, and James Warren's failing health all led to Warren Publications stopping publication of all of their magazines in 1981 and inevitably declaring bankruptcy in 1983. In August of 1983, Harris Publications purchased the Warren Publications company assets at auction and resumed publication of both *Creepy* and *Vampirella* with both titles containing a mixture of both new and reprinted material. James Warren sued Harris Publications in 1998 and reacquired the rights to *Creepy* and *Eerie*. *Creepy* and *Eerie* are currently being published by Dark Horse Comics.

Throughout the years that Warren Publications was active, their alumni of artists and writers reads like a "Who's Who" of the comic industry. Their pages were graced with the artwork of Neal Adams, Gene Colan, Frank Frazetta, Angelo Torres, Al Williamson, Johnny Craig, Reed Crandall, John Severin, Russ Heath, Wally Wood, Dave Cockrum, Richard Corben, Al Hewetson, Ken Kelly, Tom Sutton, and Berni Wrightson. As if all-star artwork wasn't enough, Warren Publications also had the writing talent of Bruce Jones, Doug Moench, Don McGregor, Steve Skeates, and T. Casey Brennan to name just a few.

Ziff-Davis—Even magazine publishing powerhouse Ziff-Davis couldn't resist the lure of producing comic books during the Golden Age of Comic Books. Founded in 1927 by William B. Ziff, Sr., and Bernard G. Davis, Ziff-Davis has long been a publisher of hobbyist magazines—namely cars, photography, and electronics. Starting in the late 1940s, Ziff-Davis published pulp magazines as well as some digest-sized fiction magazines. In the early 1950s, Ziff-Davis started publishing comic books under their own name as well as the banner Approved Comics. Ziff-Davis took a different approach than many other comic book publishers and did not publish any superhero comic books. Instead they focused on crime, sports, Western, romance, and horror comics with *Weird Thrillers* being their best-known horror comic. None of their titles lasted more than just a few issues, but it was hardly because of the talent they had on board. Jerry Siegel (co-creator of Superman) was the art director for the comic book line. Ziff-Davis also employed John Buscema, Sid Greene, Sam Kweskin, Rudy Lapick, Mike Sekowsky, Ernie Schroeder, and Ogden Whitney.

In 1953, Ziff-Davis abandoned the comic book publishing line and sold their most popular titles to St. John Publications. Ziff-Davis did continue to publish the comic book *G.I. Joe* until 1957 where it ran a total of 57 issues, making it their longest running comic book title.

After leaving the comic book publishing business behind, Ziff-Davis continued to publish hobby magazines, branching out into the newly emerging personal computer hobbyist field in the early 1980s. Today Ziff-Davis is a large magazine publisher with significant Internet holdings including Mashable, Geek.com, Humble Bundle, *PC Magazine*, and Ookla.

Whatever Happened to the Comics Code Authority?

The Comics Code Authority was established in 1954 by the Comics Magazine Association of America as a means for comic book publishers to self regulate the types of content published in comic books. Dr. Fredric Wertham's book, *Seduction of the Innocent*, and his testimony before the Senate Subcommittee on Juvenile Delinquency, where he attempted to link juvenile delinquency with children reading comic books, led to increased public outcry about the content published in comic books. Comic book publishers banded together to create the Comics Magazine Association of America and to set up the Comics Code Authority in an attempt to avoid having the Federal government step in with their own regulation. It was successful in that the federal government never put into place any type of regulation on what comic book publishers were allowed to print. Parents, teachers, and other concerned groups were reassured by the presence of the Comics Code Authority as it made them feel like Code-approved comic books (which by the late 1950s were essentially all of them) were once again safe for their children.

The Comics Code Authority established the procedure by which comic books would be approved. A comic book publisher would submit their proofs (a proof being the last stage in a comic book's creation before it actually goes to print—typically a finished product just awaiting the final editorial approval) to the Comics Code Authority. The submitted book would be reviewed by a team of reviewers who were trained to pick out any material in the book which was not up to the Comics Code Authority's standards. The reviewers would make notes about any changes to the art, plot, or dialog that needed to be made and return the annotated proof to the publisher. The publisher would then make the requested changes and resubmit the proof. Eventually the Comics Code Authority's reviewers would be satisfied and the publisher would be notified that their comic book could be published and bear the Comics Code Authority Seal of Approval on the cover.

In the late 1950s through the 1960s, having the Comics Code Authority Seal of Approval on the cover of a comic book was very important if a book was ever going to be made available for sale. Due to the amount of attention that comic books were getting at the time, most retailers and distributors refused to carry, display, or sell any comic book without the Comics Code Authority Seal of Approval on the cover. This meant that any comic book publisher who refused to submit to the rules and regulations put forth by the Comics Code Authority would quickly find themselves with books they could not sell—obviously not an enviable position for a business to be in. There were a few exceptions to this, however. Comic book publishers Dell Comics and Gold Key Comics never published any horror or true crime comic books. Nearly all of their titles were based around licensed characters from movies, television shows, or cartoons and so the content they presented in their comic books had to adhere to the standards put forth by the licensors of the products. In other words, Dell Comics and Gold Key Comics already practiced a rigid form of self-censorship. Both publishers used this to build their reputation for publishing "wholesome," "safe," and "kid-friendly" comic books and thus never participated in submitting their comic books to the Comics Code Authority. The same could not be said for the rest of the comic book industry. By the mid-1950s it was clear that the Comics Code Authority was not going anywhere and even though comic book publishers were technically not required to submit their books to the Comics Code Authority for approval, they understood it made the best business sense to do so.

By the beginning of the Silver Age of Comic Books in the 1960s, comic book publishers had come to grips with what was going to be required of them in order to continue producing comic books under the new rules. Many publishers either went out of business or stopped publishing comic books altogether while others adapted and survived. The rules and regulations set forth by the Comics Code Authority were unquestionably tough and comic book publishers had to make some drastic changes in order to follow. Within the span of a few short years, the comic book industry went from being able to publish essentially any type of content to having to adhere to a ruleset so strict that even the script of a "Rated G" movie at the time couldn't pass the Comics Code Authority's scrutiny without making adjustments. During the Silver Age of Comic Books, stories became lighter and much less serious to the point of over-the-top campiness. As a result of this, the average age of a comic book reader fell dramatically during this time. During the Golden Age of Comic Books, teenagers and adults made up the majority of the readership of comic books. During the Silver Age of Comic Books, the average comic book reader was a pre-teen child. These factors helped contribute to the overall reputation of comic books as children's entertainment as opposed to any type of significant media.

By the beginning of the Bronze Age of Comic Books in the 1970s, things had begun to change. The Comics Code Authority revised the Comics Code in 1971, relaxing the standards a bit and making elements of the Comics Code less "black and white." A criminal did not always have to be portrayed as a bumbling, brainless thug. A politician could be shown to be corrupt instead of always being portrayed as a spotless paragon of virtue. Horror elements could be shown in comic books once again—although still not to the same degree as in the pre–Code days. This relaxation of the Comics Code was brought on partially by a new generation of comic book artists and writers entering the industry and partially because of the changing views of society. It just stands to reason that elements of everyday life that were anathema in the 1950s were better able to be discussed in the 1970s. Society as a whole had changed and the Comics Code Authority had to change with it. The Bronze Age of Comic Books saw comic book readership among teenagers and college-aged people increase during this time—due in no small part to the writing that was allowed once again after the revision of the Comics Code.[5]

By the 1980s, the Comics Code Authority had lost a significant amount of its relevance. During the Golden Age of Comic Books and the Silver Age of Comic Books, comic books were sold on newsstands. By the 1980s the rise of the specialty comic book shop had changed the way readers shopped for comic books. Sales of comic books at specialty comic book shops were increasing whereas sales of comic books on newsstands were decreasing. Comic book publishers found they were able to target their audience in a more specific manner, and the blessing of the Comics Code Authority had less and less to do with whether or not a comic book would be sold. Comic book publishers began to ignore the Comics Code Authority altogether. Dark Horse Comics, founded in 1986, never submitted a single one of their books to the Comics Code Authority. Dark Horse sold their comic books strictly through the "direct-sale" route of specialty comic book shops and became one of the largest comic book publishers in the industry. Publishers like Marvel Comics and DC still submitted their books to the Comics Code Authority, but they were less concerned about whether or not the Comics Code Authority Seal of Approval was allowed to be present on the cover or not. The books would be submitted through the normal process. If the Comics Code Authority approved the book, then the Comics Code Seal of Approval would appear on the cover. If the Comics Code Authority rejected the book, then the publisher would simply run the issue without the Seal of Approval on the cover and life (and more importantly—sales) would go on. This change did not go unnoticed to the other significant contributor to the comic book industry— the advertisers. In the Golden Age of Comic Books, not only would a retailer not sell a comic book without the Comics Code Seal of Approval on the cover, but advertisers would not pay to have their advertisements run in a non-Code approved comic book. As the Comics Code Authority Seal of Approval began to have less of an effect on the sales of a comic book, it also had less of an impact on whether a particular advertiser would purchase ad space in a comic book.

In 1989, the Comics Code would be revised one final time in response to the growing "direct-sale" market. The 1989 revisions to the Comics Code make provisions that comic book publishers could publish and distribute content suitable for mature readers provided that the comic books in question were only available for sale in a specialized comic book store and not on the newsstand. In that case, the books could be published without having to submit them to the Comics Code Authority.

In 2001, Marvel Comics instituted the Marvel Rating System wherein each comic book has a rating on the cover showing the age-appropriateness of the book. The Marvel Rating System ranges were: "All Ages," "T" (appropriate for most readers but parents are advised to read with or before young children), "T+ Teens and Up" (appropriate for ages 13 and above), "Parental Advisory" (recommended to teen and adult readers—with more mature themes and more graphic imagery), and "Max: Explicit Content" (mature readers only, not sold on newsstands and not sold to anyone under 18). With their own rating system in place, Marvel Comics withdrew from the Comics Code Authority and stopped submitting their books for approval. In January of 2011, DC Comics implemented their own rating system which ranged from "E—Everyone," to "T—Teen" (12 and older), to "T+—Teen plus" (15 and older), to "M—Mature." They also withdrew from the Comics Code Authority. By the time DC had left the Comics Code Authority, the only publisher left still submitting their books was Archie Comics. Seeing that they were the last holdout, Archie Comics withdrew from the Comics Code Authority the day after DC did. At this point, there were no publishers left contributing to the Comics Code Authority and so it was rendered defunct. The intellectual property of the (now former) Comics Code Authority, as well as the famous Comics Code Seal of Approval, currently belongs to the Comic Book Legal Defense Fund—a nonprofit organization formed in 1986 to protect the First Amendment rights of comic book creators, publishers, and retailers.

Whatever Happened to Juvenile Delinquency in America?

With all of the hoopla surrounding the juvenile delinquency epidemic in the 1950s, including the famous Senate Subcommittee that was featured so prominently in this book, it is worth revisiting this subject. Juvenile crimes were steadily increasing throughout the 1950s. This trend continued until the late 1970s before beginning to decline. Obviously, horror comics and their subsequent censorship had little to no effect on juvenile delinquency since the juvenile delinquency rates did not immediately plummet after the formation of the Comics Code Authority in 1954. Clearly the fact that we do not have to currently deal with wild mobs of out-of-control juveniles running amok on our streets today terrorizing the citizenry goes to show that something did eventually occur to stem the tide, though.

Juvenile delinquency is a complicated societal issue and as such has many different contributing factors. It also stands to reason that there have been many different contributing factors to the decline in the rates of juvenile delinquency as well. One of the largest contributors was the 1974 Juvenile Justice and Delinquency Prevention Act—a federal law put into place in that provided funds to states that followed a series of federal protections, known as the "core protections," on the care and treatment of youth in the justice system. The four "core protections" were as follows:

- The Deinstitutionalization of Status Offenders—Before the Deinstitutionalization of Status Offenders (or DSO) was in place, juveniles who were brought into police custody for status offences were processed into adult jail like any other criminal. Status offences are offences that are against the law strictly because of the age of the offender—so things like the underage consumption of alcohol, the underage possession of cigarettes, truancy, curfew violations, running away from home (prosecuted as disorderly conduct), and the famous "incorrigibility," which is really nothing more than a juvenile disobeying their parents. Once the DSO was in place, a juvenile could not be jailed for a curfew violation, running away from home, or being incorrigible. Instead, they would be remanded to the custody of their parents.

- Sight and Sound—The "Sight and Sound" separation protections prohibit contact between juvenile and adult offenders. Should a juvenile get arrested and jailed, they may never be in the presence of adult inmates.
- Jail Removal—The "jail removal" provision strictly prohibits the jailing of juveniles in adult jail facilities except under very limited circumstances. This provision was added to the Juvenile Justice and Delinquency Prevention Act in 1980 in response to finding juveniles incarcerated in adult facilities resulted in a high suicide rate; physical, mental, and sexual assault; inadequate care and programming; negative labeling; and exposure to serious offenders and mental patients.
- Disproportionate Minority Confinement—The Disproportionate Minority Confinement (or DMC) provision required states to address the issue of over-representation of youth of color in the justice system. This provision was added in 1992.

While the Juvenile Justice and Delinquency Prevention Act certainly helped reduce the overall juvenile delinquency rates, there are as many theories as to what caused juvenile delinquency rates to fall as there are theories as to why they rose. Changes in law enforcement, an overall increase in the number of police officers, and the formation of juvenile courts (so that juvenile offenders could be tried separately from adults) all were contributing factors. It also helped to have a societal change in the way adults viewed teenagers. In the 1950s the "teen-ager" was a relatively new phenomenon—too old to be a child, but too young to be an adult and not fitting into either world—to be a teenager was to struggle for identity. As the years have passed, society has grown to recognize the teenager as not just a stage in development between childhood and adulthood, but as a fully recognized stage of life. Teenagers are now an important demographic and specifically targeted by advertisers due to the fact that they have their own unique cultural identity and purchasing power and, let's face it, if you're targeted by advertisers you have officially "made it."

Chapter Notes

Chapter 1

1. Ron Goulart, *Comic Book Encyclopedia: The Ultimate Guide to Characters, Graphic Novels, Writers, and Artists in the Comic Book Universe* (New York: Harper Entertainment, 2004) 163.
2. *Ibid.*
3. *Ibid.*
4. Robert Overstreet, ed., *Overstreet Comic Book Price Guide* (41 ed.) (Timonium: Gemstone Publishing, 2011) 283, 571.
5. Ron Goulart, *Comic Book Encyclopedia* (New York: Harper Entertainment, 2004) 145.
6. Amy Kiste Nyberg, *Seal of Approval: The History of the Comics Code* (Jackson: University Press of Mississippi, 1998) 18.
7. *Ibid.* 18–19.
8. Les Daniels, *Superman: The Complete History: The Life and Times of the Man of Steel* (1st ed.) (London: Titan Books, 1998) 11.
9. Gerard Jones, *Men of Tomorrow: Geeks, Gangsters, and the Birth of the Comic Book* (New York: Basic Books, 2004) 201.
10. Ron Goulart, *Comic Book Encyclopedia* (New York: Harper Entertainment, 2004) 75.
11. Randy Duncan and Matthew J. Smith, eds., *Icons of the American Comic Book: From Captain America to Wonder Woman, Vol. 1* (Santa Barbara: Greenwood Publishing Group, 2013) 193–201.
12. Mike Benton, *The Comic Book in America: An Illustrated History* (Dallas: Taylor Publishing Company, 1989) 158.
13. Dan Nadel, *Art Out of Time: Unknown Comics Visionaries, 1900–1969* (New York: Abrams Books, 2006) 8.
14. George Kovacs and C.W. Marshall, eds., *Classics and Comics* (New York: Oxford University Press, 2011) 109.
15. Shirrell Rhodes, *A Complete History of Comic Books* (New York: Peter Lang, 2008), 71.
16. *Ibid.*
17. Bradford Wright, *Comic Book Nation: The Transformation of Youth Culture in America* (Baltimore: Johns Hopkins University Press, 2001) 166–168.
18. *Ibid.* 86.
19. *Ibid.* 173–175.
20. *Ibid.* 172–173.
21. *Ibid.* 181–182.
22. *Ibid.*
23. Will Jacobs and Gerard Jones, *The Comic Book Heroes: From the Silver Age to the Present* (New York: Crown Publishing Group, 1985) 34.
24. *Ibid.* 154.
25. Craig Shutt, *Baby Boomer Comics: The Wild, Wacky, Wonderful Comic Books of the 1960s!* (Iola: Krause Publications, 2003) 200.
26. Will Jacobs and Gerard Jones, *The Comic Book Heroes: From the Silver Age to the Present* (New York: Crown Publishing Group, 1985) 154.
27. *Iron Man* (Marvel 1968 series), The Grand Comics Database, https://www.comics.org/series/1867/ (Accessed November 2017).
28. Bradford Wright, *Comic Book Nation* (Baltimore: Johns Hopkins University Press, 2001) 249.
29. John Wells, "Green Lantern/Green Arrow: And Through Them Change an Industry," *Back Issue!* (December 2010).
30. Don Hayner, "Big bucks in rare comics—Classic find in '77 began a new era," *Chicago Sun-Times*, July 26, 1987.
31. Gerard Jones, *Men of Tomorrow* (New York: Basic Books, 2004) 335.
32. Shirrel Rhoades, *A Complete History of American Comic Books* (New York: Peter Lang Publishing, 2008) 129.
33. "Comics Publishers Suffer Tough Summer: Body Count Rises in Market Shakedown," *The Comics Journal #172* (November 1994) 13–18.
34. "Marvel Reaches Agreement to Emerge

from Bankruptcy," *The New York Times* (July 11, 1997).

35. Dan Brownell, ed., *Antiques Trader: Antiques and Collectibles Price Guide (27th ed.)* (Iola: Krause Publications, 2011) 343.

36. Katherine Noyes, "Marvel Comics Opens Portal to Its Archives," TechNewsWorld.com, https://www.technewsworld.com/story/Marvel-Comics-Opens-Portal-to-Its-Archives-60299.html?wlc=1257294826 (Accessed November 2016).

37. Greg Kumparak, "Amazon Acquires Digital Comic Book Store Comixology," TechCrunch.com, https://techcrunch.com/2014/04/10/amazon-acquires-digital-comic-book-service-comixology/ (Accessed March 2017).

38. Allison Chopin, "Record-breaking number of fans, cosplayers flock to Comic Con to let 'their inner geeks fly' in Manhattan," *New York Daily News* (October 7, 2017).

Chapter 2

1. Les Daniels, *Superman: The Complete History* (1st ed.) (London: Titan Books, 1998) 11.
2. John Gunnison, John Locke and Doug Ellis, eds., *The Adventure House Guide to the Pulps* (Silver Spring: Adventure House, 2000) ii–iv.
3. John Cheng, *Astounding Wonder: Imagining Science and Science Fiction in Interwar America* (Philadelphia: The University of Pennsylvania Press, 2012) 33.
4. John Gunnison, John Locke and Doug Ellis, eds., *The Adventure House Guide to the Pulps* (Silver Spring: Adventure House, 2000) ii–iv.
5. Michael J. Vassallo, *Marvel Masterworks: Atlas Era Strange Tales Vol. 1* (New York: Marvel Publishing, 2007) vi.
6. Ron Goulart, *Comic Book Encyclopedia* (New York: Harper Entertainment, 2004) 124.
7. Christopher Golden, Stephen R. Bissette and Thomas E. Sniegoski, *Buffy the Vampire Slayer: The Monster Book* (New York: Simon and Schuster, 2000) 146.
8. *Frankenstein Comics*, The Grand Comics Database, https://www.comics.org/series/428/ (Accessed November 2017).
9. Robert Overstreet, ed., *Overstreet Comic Book Price Guide* (41 ed.) (Timonium: Gemstone Publishing, 2011) 283, 483.
10. Ron Goulart, *Great American Comic Books* (Chicago: Contemporary Books, 1986) 314.
11. Ibid. 173.
12. *Eerie*, The Grand Comics Database, https://www.comics.org/issue/214564/ (Accessed October 2017).

13. Robert Overstreet, ed., *Overstreet Comic Book Price Guide* (41 ed.) (Timonium: Gemstone Publishing, 2011) 559.

14. *Adventures Into the Unknown*, The Grand Comics Database, https://www.comics.org/series/598/ (Accessed October 2017).

15. Ibid.

16. Robert Overstreet, ed., *Overstreet Comic Book Price Guide* (41 ed.) (Timonium: Gemstone Publishing, 2011) 749.

17. Ibid. 759.

18. Lawrence Watt-Evans, *"The Other Guys: A Gargoyle's-Eye View of the Non-EC Horror Comics of the 1950s," Alter Ego* #97 (October 2010) 9.

19. Robert Overstreet, ed., *Overstreet Comic Book Price Guide* (41 ed.) (Timonium: Gemstone Publishing, 2011) 440.

20. Ron Goulart, *Comic Book Encyclopedia* (New York: Harper Entertainment, 2004) 163.

21. Gerard Jones, *Men of Tomorrow* (New York: Basic Books, 2004) 254.

22. Ibid.

23. Ibid. 255–256.

24. Ibid.

25. Ibid. 257.

26. Bill Gaines, Al Feldstein and Otto Binder, *EC Archives: The Haunt of Fear, Vol. 4* (Milwaukee: Dark Horse Books, 2017) 98.

27. Bradford Wright, *Comic Book Nation* (Baltimore: Johns Hopkins University Press, 2001) 136.

28. Michael Dooley, "Ray Bradbury: 1950s Comics Illustrated Man," *Print* (June 15, 2012).

29. Bradford Wright, *Comic Book Nation* (Baltimore: Johns Hopkins University Press, 2001) 149.

30. Robert Overstreet, ed., *Overstreet Comic Book Price Guide* (41 ed.) (Timonium: Gemstone Publishing, 2011) 970, 972.

31. Ibid. 971.

32. Ibid. 970.

33. Ibid. 972.

34. Ibid. 614.

35. Ibid. 969.

36. Ibid.

37. Ibid. 649.

38. Ibid. 929, 983, 474.

39. Ibid. 983.

40. Ibid. 572.

41. Ibid. 992, 919.

42. Ibid. 918.

43. Ibid. 378, 377, 738, 675, 885.

44. Michael J. Vassallo, *Marvel Masterworks: Atlas Era Strange Tales Vol. 1* (New York: Marvel Publishing, 2007) vii.

Chapter 3

1. James Gilbert, *A Cycle of Outrage: America's Reaction to the Juvenile Delinquent in the 1950's* (New York: Oxford University Press, 1986) 69.
2. *Ibid.*
3. Amy Kiste Nyberg, *Seal of Approval the History of the Comics Code* (Jackson: University Press of Mississippi, 1998) 19.
4. *Ibid.* 20.
5. Allan Metcalf, "Birth of the Teenager," *The Chronicle of Higher Education* (February 28, 2012).
6. Amy Kiste Nyberg, *Seal of Approval the History of the Comics Code* (Jackson: University Press of Mississippi, 1998) 20.
7. David Hajdu, *The Ten-Cent Plague: The Great Comic-Book Scare and How It Changed America* (New York: Farrar, Straus and Giroux, 2008) 464.
8. *Ibid.* 106–108.
9. Bradford Wright, *Comic Book Nation* (Baltimore: Johns Hopkins University Press, 2001) 86.
10. David Hajdu, *The Ten-Cent Plague: The Great Comic-Book Scare and How It Changed America* (New York: Farrar, Straus and Giroux, 2008) 95.
11. Amy Kiste Nyberg, *Seal of Approval the History of the Comics Code* (Jackson: University Press of Mississippi, 1998) 31.
12. *Ibid.* 31–32.
13. *Ibid.* 32–33.
14. David Hajdu, *The Ten-Cent Plague: The Great Comic-Book Scare and How It Changed America* (New York: Farrar, Straus and Giroux, 2008) 113.
15. Amy Kiste Nyberg, *Seal of Approval the History of the Comics Code* (Jackson: University Press of Mississippi, 1998) 34.
16. David Hajdu, *The Ten-Cent Plague: The Great Comic-Book Scare and How It Changed America* (New York: Farrar, Straus and Giroux, 2008) 113.
17. *Ibid.* 129.
18. *Ibid.* 128.
19. Ron Goulart, *Great American Comic Books* (Chicago: Contemporary Books, 1986) 161–162, 172–183, 206–217.
20. Amy Kiste Nyberg, *Seal of Approval the History of the Comics Code* (Jackson: University Press of Mississippi, 1998) 35–36.
21. *Ibid.* 50.
22. Fredric Wertham, *Seduction of the Innocent* (New York: Rinehart & Company, 1954) 192, 234–235.
23. Bradford Wright, *Comic Book Nation* (Baltimore: Johns Hopkins University Press, 2001) 152–153, 161–166.
24. Gerard Jones, *Men of Tomorrow* (New York: Basic Books, 2004) 271.
25. Amy Kiste Nyberg, *Seal of Approval the History of the Comics Code* (Jackson: University Press of Mississippi, 1998) 51.
26. *Ibid.*
27. *Ibid.* 53.
28. *Ibid.* 54.
29. *Ibid.* 52, 54.
30. *Ibid.* 55.
31. *Ibid.*
32. *Ibid.* 56.
33. *Ibid.* 57.
34. Bradford Wright, *Comic Book Nation* (Baltimore: Johns Hopkins University Press, 2001) 161–166.
35. *Ibid.*
36. Amy Kiste Nyberg, *Seal of Approval the History of the Comics Code* (Jackson: University Press of Mississippi, 1998) 60–61.
37. Gerard Jones, *Men of Tomorrow* (New York: Basic Books, 2004) 276.
38. Bradford Wright, *Comic Book Nation* (Baltimore: Johns Hopkins University Press, 2001) 166–167.
39. Amy Kiste Nyberg, *Seal of Approval the History of the Comics Code* (Jackson: University Press of Mississippi, 1998) 61.
40. Bradford Wright, *Comic Book Nation* (Baltimore: Johns Hopkins University Press, 2001) 168.
41. Gerard Jones, *Men of Tomorrow* (New York: Basic Books, 2004) 277.
42. Amy Kiste Nyberg, *Seal of Approval* (Jackson: University Press of Mississippi, 1998) 63–64.
43. *Ibid.* 75.
44. *Ibid.*
45. *Ibid.* 76–77.
46. *Ibid.*
47. U.S. Congress, Senate, Subcommittee on Juvenile Delinquency, *Comic Books and Juvenile Delinquency*, 83d Cong. 1st Sess.–83d Cong. 2d Sess., April 1954.
48. Amy Kiste Nyberg, *Seal of Approval* (Jackson: University Press of Mississippi, 1998) 78.
49. *Ibid.* 79.
50. *Ibid.* 83.

Chapter 4

1. Amy Kiste Nyberg, *Seal of Approval* (Jackson: University Press of Mississippi, 1998) 110.

2. *Ibid.* 111.
3. David Hajdu, *The Ten-Cent Plague: The Great Comic-Book Scare and How It Changed America* (New York: Farrar, Straus and Giroux, 2008) 128–130.
4. The Comic Book Legal Defense Fund, "The Comics Code of 1954," http://cbldf.org/the-comics-code-of-1954/ (Accessed October 2017).
5. Bradford Wright, *Comic Book Nation* (Baltimore: Johns Hopkins University Press, 2001) 172–173.
6. Amy Kiste Nyberg, *Seal of Approval* (Jackson: University Press of Mississippi, 1998) 114–115.
7. *Ibid.* 117.
8. Bradford Wright, *Comic Book Nation* (Baltimore: Johns Hopkins University Press, 2001) 172–173.
9. Amy Kiste Nyberg, *Seal of Approval* (Jackson: University Press of Mississippi, 1998) 114–115.
10. Bradford Wright, *Comic Book Nation* (Baltimore: Johns Hopkins University Press, 2001) 172–173.
11. Emma Harrison, "Whip, Knife Shown as 'Comics' Lures," *The New York Times* (February 5, 1955).
12. Amy Kiste Nyberg, *Seal of Approval* (Jackson: University Press of Mississippi, 1998) 99.
13. *Ibid.* 99–100.
14. Bradford Wright, *Comic Book Nation* (Baltimore: Johns Hopkins University Press, 2001) 178.

Chapter 5

1. Robert Overstreet, ed., *Overstreet Comic Book Price Guide* (41 ed.) (Timonium: Gemstone Publishing, 2011) 651.
2. *Ibid.*
3. *Ibid.* 886.
4. *Ibid.* 675.
5. *Saturday Evening Post*, "Good Friends for Him … and Mother Too … in Dell Comics!" (January 10, 1953).
6. Robert Overstreet, ed., *Overstreet Comic Book Price Guide* (41 ed.) (Timonium: Gemstone Publishing, 2011) 553.
7. *Ibid.* 451.
8. *Ibid.* 942.
9. *Ibid.* 375, 755, 818.
10. Amy Kiste Nyberg, *Seal of Approval* (Jackson: University Press of Mississippi, 1998) 119–121.
11. Bradford Wright, *Comic Book Nation* (Baltimore: Johns Hopkins University Press, 2001) 176–177.
12. *Ibid.*
13. Digby Diehl, *Tales from the Crypt: The Official Archives* (New York: St. Martin's Press, 1996).
14. Bradford Wright, *Comic Book Nation* (Baltimore: Johns Hopkins University Press, 2001) 176–177.
15. Robert Overstreet, ed., *Overstreet Comic Book Price Guide* (41 ed.) (Timonium: Gemstone Publishing, 2011) 614, 638, 719.
16. *Ibid.* 949, 984.
17. *Ibid.* 474.
18. *Ibid.* 474, 749.
19. *Ibid.* 933–934, 510.
20. David A. Roach and Jon B. Cooke, *The Warren Companion* (Raleigh: Two Morrows Publishing, 2001) 37.
21. Tom Spurgeon, "Warren Case Moves Forward: Publisher Claims Numerous Violations in Case Against Harris Publications," *The Comics Journal* #210 (February 1999).
22. "The History of Vampirella," Vampilore.co.uk, http://www.vampilore.co.uk/history01.html (Accessed October 2017).

Chapter 6

1. Brian Cronin, "Comic Book Urban Legends Revealed," Comic Book Resources, https://www.cbr.com/comic-book-urban-legends-revealed-119/ (Accessed December 2017).
2. Don & Maggie Thompson, "Crack in the Code," *Newfangles* #44 (February 1971).
3. Robert Overstreet, ed., *Overstreet Comic Book Price Guide* (41 ed.) (Timonium: Gemstone Publishing, 2011) 929.
4. *Ibid.* 973.
5. *Ibid.* 615.
6. *Ibid.* 900.
7. *Ibid.* 615, 589, 837, 971, 972, 906, 552, 903.
8. Jon B. Cooke, "Lest We Forget: Celebrating Four that Got Away," *Comic Book Artist* #12 (March 2001).
9. Robert Overstreet, ed., *Overstreet Comic Book Price Guide* (41 ed.) (Timonium: Gemstone Publishing, 2011) 638, 832.

Chapter 7

1. Chuck Rozanski. "Returning to the Topic of My 1979 Visit to the Marvel Offices," *Tales From the Database*, MileHighComics.com,

http://www.milehighcomics.com/tales/cbg111.html (Accessed October 2017).

2. Amy Kiste Nyberg, "Comics Code 1989," TheComicsBooks.com, http://www.thecomicbooks.com/old/cca3.html (Accessed October 2017).

3. Robert Overstreet, ed., *Overstreet Comic Book Price Guide* (41 ed.) (Timonium: Gemstone Publishing, 2011) 750, 562.

4. *Ibid.* 533.

5. *Ibid.* 828, 641.

6. Dana Jennings, "MEDIA; At House of Comics, a Writer's Champion," *The New York Times* (September 15, 2003).

7. *Alias*, The Grand Comics Database, http://comicbookdb.com/title.php?ID=229 (Accessed October 2017).

8. Robert Overstreet, ed., *Overstreet Comic Book Price Guide* (41 ed.) (Timonium: Gemstone Publishing, 2011) 444, 643, 966, 921, 638, 1008.

9. *Ibid.* 733.

10. *Hellboy*, The Grand Comics Database, http://comicbookdb.com/character.php?ID=159 (Accessed November 2017).

Afterword

1. Digby Diehl. *Tales from the Crypt: The Official Archives* (New York: St. Martin's Press, 1996) 30–32.

2. *Ibid.* 150.

3. *"Biographies: Fredric Wertham, M.D.,"* Comic Art & Graffix Gallery, http://www.comic-art.com/biographies/wertham1.htm (Accessed October 2017).

4. Dusty Rhodes, "BAM! WAP! KA-POW! Library prof bops doc who K.O.'d comic book industry," *Illinois New Bureau* (February 11, 2013).

5. Don & Maggie Thompson, "Crack in the Code," *Newfangles* #44 (February 1971).

Bibliography

Adventures Into the Unknown, The Grand Comics Database, https://www.comics.org/series/598/ (Accessed October 2017).

Alias, The Grand Comics Database, http://comicbookdb.com/title.php?ID=229 (Accessed October 2017).

Alter Ego, Vol. 3, #54 (November 2005).

Benton, Mike, *The Comic Book in America: An Illustrated History,* Dallas: Taylor Publishing Company, 1989.

"*Biographies: Fredric Wertham, M.D.,*" Comic Art & Graffix Gallery, http://www.comic-art.com/biographies/wertham1.htm (Accessed October 2017).

Brownell, Dan, ed., *Antiques Trader Antiques and Collectibles Price Guide (27th ed.),* Iola: Krause Publications, 2011.

Cheng, John, *Astounding Wonder: Imagining Science and Science Fiction in Interwar America,* Philadelphia: The University of Pennsylvania Press, 2012.

Chopin, Allison, "Record-breaking number of fans, cosplayers flock to Comic Con to let 'their inner geeks fly' in Manhattan," *New York Daily News,* October 7, 2017.

"The Comics Code of 1954," Comic Book Legal Defense Fund, http://cbldf.org/the-comics-code-of-1954/ (Accessed October 2017).

"Comics Publishers Suffer Tough Summer: Body Count Rises in Market Shakedown," *The Comics Journal* #172, November 1994.

Cooke, Jon B., "Lest We Forget: Celebrating Four That Got Away," *Comic Book Artist* #12, March 2001.

Cronin, Brian, "Comic Book Urban Legends Revealed," Comic Book Resources, https://www.cbr.com/comic-book-urban-legends-revealed-119/ (Accessed December 2017).

Daniels, Les, *Superman: The Complete History: The Life and Times of the Man of Steel (1st ed.),* London: Titan Books, 1998.

Diehl, Digby, *Tales from the Crypt: The Official Archives,* New York: St. Martin's Press, 1996.

Dooley, Michael, "Ray Bradbury: 1950s Comics Illustrated Man," *Print,* June 15, 2012.

Duncan, Randy; Smith, Matthew J., *Icons of the American Comic Book: From Captain America to Wonder Woman, Volume 1,* Santa Barbara: Greenwood Publishing Group, 2013.

Eerie. The Grand Comics Database. https://www.comics.org/issue/214564/ (Accessed October 2017).

Frankenstein Comics, The Grand Comics Database, https://www.comics.org/series/428/ (Accessed November 2017).

Gaines, William; Feldstein, Al; Binder, Otto, *EC Archives: The Haunt of Fear, Volume 4,* Milwaukee: Dark Horse Books, 2017.

Gilbert, James, *A Cycle of Outrage: America's Reaction to the Juvenile Delinquent in the 1950's,* New York: Oxford University Press, 1986.

Golden, Christopher; Bissette, Stephen R.; Sniegoski, Thomas E., *Buffy the Vampire Slayer: The Monster Book,* New York: Simon & Schuster, 2000.

"Good Friends for Him ... and Mother Too. in Dell Comics!" *Saturday Evening Post,* January 10, 1953.

Goulart, Ron, *Comic Book Encyclopedia: The Ultimate Guide to Characters, Graphic Novels, Writers, and Artists in the Comic Book Universe,* New York: Harper Entertainment, 2004.

Goulart, Ron, *Great American Comic Books,* Chicago: Contemporary Books, 1986.

Gunnison, John; Locke, John; Ellis, Doug, eds., *Adventure House Guide to the Pulps,* Silver Spring: Adventure House, 2000.

Hajdu, David, *The Ten-Cent Plague: The Great Comic-Book Scare and How It Changed America,* New York: Farrar, Straus and Giroux, 2008.

Bibliography

Harrison, Emma, "Whip, Knife, Shown as 'Comics' Lures," *The New York Times*, February 5, 1955.

Hayner, Don, "Big bucks in rare comics—Classic find in '77 began a new era," *Chicago Sun-Times*, July 26, 1987.

Hellboy, The Grand Comics Database, http://comicbookdb.com/character.php?ID=159 (Accessed November 2017).

Iron Man (Marvel 1968 series), The Grand Comics Database, https://www.comics.org/series/1867/ (Accessed November 2017).

Jacobs, Will; Jones, Gerard, *The Comic Book Heroes: From the Silver Age to the Present*, New York: Crown Publishing Group, 1985.

Jennings, Dana, "MEDIA; At House of Comics, a Writer's Champion," *The New York Times*, September 15, 2003.

Jones, Gerard, *Men of Tomorrow: Geeks, Gangsters, and the Birth of the Comic Book*, New York: Basic Books, 2004.

Kovacs, George; Marshall, C. W., *Classics and Comics*, New York: Oxford University Press 2011.

Kumparak, Greg, "Amazon Acquires Digital Comic Book Store Comixology," TechCrunch.com, https://techcrunch.com/2014/04/10/amazon-acquires-digital-comic-book-service-comixology/ (Accessed March 2017).

"Marvel Reaches Agreement to Emerge from Bankruptcy," *The New York Times*, July 11, 1997.

Metcalf, Allan, "Birth of the Teenager," *The Chronicle of Higher Education*, February 28, 2012.

Nadel, Dan, *Art Out of Time: Unknown Comics Visionaries, 1900–1969*, New York: Abrams Books, 2006.

Noyes, Katherine, "Marvel Comics Opens Portal to Its Archives," technewsworld.com, https://www.technewsworld.com/story/Marvel-Comics-Opens-Portal-to-Its-Archives-60299.html?wlc=1257294826 (Accessed November 2016).

Nyberg, Amy Kiste, "Comics Code 1989," TheComicsBooks.com, http://www.thecomicbooks.com/old/cca3.html (Accessed October 2017).

Nyberg, Amy Kiste, *Seal of Approval: The History of the Comics Code*, Jackson: University Press of Mississippi, 1998.

Overstreet, Robert, ed., *Overstreet Comic Book Price Guide (41 ed.)*, Timonium: Gemstone Publishing, 2011.

Rhoades, Shirrel, *A Complete History of American Comic Books*, New York: Peter Lang Publishing, 2008.

Rhodes, Dusty, "BAM! WAP! KA-POW! Library prof bops doc who K.O.'d comic book industry," *Illinois New Bureau*, February 11, 2013.

Roach, David A.; Cooke, Jon B., *The Warren Companion*, Raleigh: Two Morrows Publishing, 2001.

Rozanski, Chuck, "Returning to the Topic of My 1979 Visit to the Marvel Offices," *Tales From the Database*, MileHighComics.com, http://www.milehighcomics.com/tales/cbg111.html (Accessed October 2017).

Shutt, Craig, *Baby Boomer Comics: The Wild, Wacky, Wonderful Comic Books of the 1960s!* Iola: Krause Publications, 2003.

Spurgeon, Tom, "Warren Case Moves Forward: Publisher Claims Numerous Violations in Case Against Harris Publications," *The Comics Journal* #210, February 1999.

Thompson, Don & Maggie, "Crack in the Code," *Newfangles* #44, February 1971.

U.S. Congress, Senate, Subcommittee on Juvenile Delinquency, *Comic Books and Juvenile Delinquency*, 83d Cong. 1st Sess.–83d Cong. 2d Sess.

Vamplore.co.uk, "The History of Vampirella," http://www.vampilore.co.uk/history01.html (Accessed October 2017).

Vassallo, Michael J., *Marvel Masterworks: Atlas Era Strange Tales Vol. 1*, New York: Marvel Publishing, 2007.

Watt-Evans, Lawrence, "The Other Guys: A Gargoyle's-Eye View of the Non-EC Horror Comics of the 1950s," *Alter Ego* #97, October 2010.

Wells, John. "Green Lantern/Green Arrow: And Through Them Change an Industry." *Back Issue!* December 2010.

Wertham, Fredric, *Seduction of the Innocent*, New York: Rinehart & Company, 1954.

Wright, Bradford, *Comic Book Nation: The Transformation of Youth Culture in America*, Baltimore: Johns Hopkins University Press 2001.

Index

Ace Magazines 141
Action Comics 10, 23; *See Also* Superman
Adams, Neal 13–14, 69, 76, 154
Adventures into the Unknown 28–29, 142
Afterlife with Archie 130
AfterShock Comics 114
Aguirre-Sacasa, Roberto 98, 130
Alias 93
All-American Publications 30
American Comics Group 28, 35, 142
American News Company 8
American Vampire 100
antihero 16
Archie Comics 130, 159
Argosy 24
Arkham Asylum: A Serious House on Serious Earth 101
Army of Darkness 126
Arrow Comics 91, 143–144
Association of Comics Magazine Publishers (ACMP) 42–44, 51, 60
Atlas Comics 29, 56, 142–143, 146
Avatar Press 127, 136
Avon Publications 27–28, 34, 144–145
Azzarello, Brian 106

Babyteeth 115
Barker, Clive 97
Batman 26, 45, 139
Batman: Haunted Gotham 102–103
Batman: Red Rain 101–102
Beasts of Burden 109
Beautiful Darkness 116–117
The Beauty 112
Bellin, Edward 27
Bendis, Brian Michael 93
Bissette, Stephen R. 124, 148
Black-Eyed Kids 115
The Black Monday Murders 112
Blade 95, 134
Blood & Kisses 125
Bradbury, Ray 34, 118
Briefer, Dick 26

Bronze Age of Comic Books 12, 80, 157
Brown, John Mason 40–42
Brubaker, Ed 113
Buscema, John 75–76, 155

Caliber Comics 91, 144–145
Chamber of Darkness 75
Chaos! Comics 126
Charlton Comics 29, 35, 74–75, 84–86, 146, 148
Child's Play 126
Chilling Adventures of Sabrina 130–131
Chronicles of Wormwood 128
Clean Room 103–104
Clendenen, Richard 48–50
Colder 110
comic book: independent publishers 91; as literature 14; origin of term 8; sale of banned 40, 44; speculation 17
comic book convention 15, 22
Comic Book Legal Defense Fund 159
comic book store 15, 87–89, 157; *See Also* direct market
Comic Media 146
Comics Code Authority 12, 29, 60–67, 76, 79, 81–82, 89–91, 93–94, 142, 155–159
Comics Magazine Association of America (CMAA) 60–61, 63–67, 155
Constantine 133–134
Conway, Gerry 75, 81, 84, 98
Corben, Richard 85, 108, 111, 154
The Courtyard 128
Craig, Johnny 29, 31, 53, 75–76, 154
Crawl to Me 120, 136
Creative Age of Comic Books 19
Creatures on the Loose 76
Creepy 75–77, 153–154
Creepy Comics 108
Criminal Macabre: A Cal McDonald Mystery 109–110
Crossed 127–128
The Crow 134–135, 145

169

The Dark and Bloody 104
Dark Ark 115
Dark Horse Comics 107, 135–136, 154, 158
The Dark Mansion of Forbidden Love 84; See Also Forbidden Tales of the Dark Mansion
The Dark Tower 97–98
David, Peter 19, 97, 134
Dawn of the Dead 123
DC 11–18, 67–68, 75, 84, 92, 94, 138, 147, 150, 152, 159; See Also Detective Comics
DC House of Horror 103
Dead of Night 83, 95
Deadworld 91, 145–145
Dell Publishing 8, 10, 43, 56, 65, 70, 146–147, 156
Delphine 117–118
Detective Comics 10, 147; See Also DC
Devil's Due Publishing 126
The Devil's Rejects 123
Digital Age of Comic Books 21
direct market 87–89, 158; See Also comic book store
Ditko, Steve 12, 69, 74, 143, 146, 152
Dr. Giggles 136
Doctor Occult 25–26
Doctor of Horror 118
Doorway to Nightmare 84
Dorkin, Evan 109
Dracula (Dell Comics) 70–71
Dracula Lives! 85
Drawn and Quarterly 116
Druid 96
Dylan Dog: Dead of Night 136
Dynamite Entertainment 78, 141

Eastern Color Printing Company 7, 8, 30, 146
Eastman, Kevin 91, 125
EC Comics 28–35, 65, 70–73, 79, 137–138
Eerie 75–77, 102, 148, 153–154
Eerie Comics 27–28, 144
Eerie Publications 78, 147–148
Elder, Will 31
Ellis, Warren 96, 105
Ennis, Garth 92–92, 95, 105, 115, 127–128, 133
Escape of the Living Dead 129
Evil Eye 118

Famous Funnies 8, 43, 60
Famous Funnies: A Carnival of Comics 8, 30, 146
FantaCo Enterprises 90, 123–124, 148–149
Fantagor 85
Fantagraphics Books 117, 138
Fatale 113
Faust: Love of the Damned 136
Fawcett 10, 35, 146, 148
Fawkes, Ray 113

Feldstein, Al 31, 73–74, 138
Flinch 93
Forbidden Tales of the Dark Mansion 84; See Also The Dark Mansion of Forbidden Love
Four Color Fear 118
Francavilla, Francesco 130
Freaks of the Heartland 108
Friday the 13th 129
From Hell 126, 132–133

Gaiman, Neil 19, 84, 92, 106
Gaines, Maxwell 8, 30
Gaines, William 30–34, 42, 49, 51–54, 56, 65, 71–74, 137–138
Ghost Manor 75
Ghost Rider 83, 86, 134
Ghostly Tales 74
Ghosts 84
Ghosts and Ruins 117
Gilberton Publications 27, 65, 70, 150–151
Gold Key Comics 70–71, 147, 150–151, 156
Golden Age of Comic Books 9, 23, 67, 148
Goodman, Martin 82, 142–143
Goodwin, Archie 75, 154
Gore Shriek 91, 124, 148
Gotham by Midnight 104
Grant, Brea 121
Grant, Zane 121
Grevioux, Kevin 135

Halloween 126–127
Harris Publications 77–78, 148, 154
Harrow County 108
Harvey Comics 29, 34, 151
Haunt of Fear 31–34, 118, 137
Haunt of Horror 85, 95
Haunted 74, 86
Haunted Love 85
Haunted Tank 93
Heck, Don 75, 146
Hell House 123
Hellblazer 92–93, 105–107, 133–134
Hellboy 108, 132
Hellraiser 97
Hellstorm: Prince of Lies 96
Hellstorm: Son of Satan 95
Hendrickson, Herbert J. 49, 58, 72
Hill, Joe 119
horror magazines 76, 85
House of Mystery 67–69, 92
House of Penance 110
House of Secrets 67–69, 81, 92
Howard, Wayne 84–85; See Also Midnight Tales

I Am Legend 123
I, Frankenstein 135

IDW Publishing 119, 145
Image Comics 111
In the Dark 123
Ingles, Graham 118
IZombie 92, 135

Jones, Kelley 102
Journey into Mystery 69–70, 143
Jughead: The Hunger 131
juvenile delinquency 36–40, 159–160

Kefauver, Estes 49, 53, 55
Key Publications 151–152
Kida, Fred 28
King, Stephen 97–98, 119
Kirby, Jack 12, 14, 69, 75–76, 143
Kirkman, Robert 97, 111, 132–133
Kubert, Joe 27, 153
Kurtzman, Harvey 41, 138

Land of the Dead 123
Lee, Stan 12, 33, 69, 75–76, 81–82, 85, 143, 146
The Living Mummy 83; *See Also* Supernatural Thrillers
Locke & Key 119–120
Lovecraft, H.P. 76
Lucifer 93, 106

Mad 79, 136–137
Man Thing 100
The Many Ghosts of Doctor Graves 74
Marvel Comics 10, 12, 14, 19, 69–70, 75, 81–83, 94, 143, 146, 151, 158
Marvel MAX 93–95
Marvel Monsters Group 85
Marvel Zombies 96–97
Masters of Terror 85
Matheson, Richard 123
Menace 85, 94–95, 143
Midnight Tales 84–85; *See Also* Howard, Wayne
Mignola, Mike 108, 132
Millar, Mark 96
Miller, Frank 15–16, 108
Milligan, Peter 92, 106
Modern Age of Comic Books 15
Moench, Doug 102
Monsters on the Prowl 76
Monsters Unleashed 85
Moore, Alan 15, 92, 126, 128, 132–133
Morrison, Grant 92, 101, 111
Murphy, Charles F. 60–61, 63–64, 73–74

Nailbiter 111
Nameless 111–112
National EC Fan-Addict Club 32
National Periodicals 25, 138, 147

Neonomicon 128
New Adventures of Frankenstein 26–27
Night Mary 121–122
Night of the Living Dead 124–125, 128–129, 149–150
A Nightmare on Elm Street 129
Niles, Steve 109–110, 119, 123, 133

O'Barr, James 134–135, 145
O'Neil, Denny 13–14, 75
Outcast 112, 133

Palmer, Tom 75–76
Pestilence 116
Phillips, Sean 113
Preacher 93, 100–101, 133
Providence 128
Pruett, Joe 114–115
pulp magazines 11, 23–25

Quality Comics 152

Rat God 108
Revival 112
Robert, Alan 120
Russo, John 129
Ryall, Chris 122

Saga of the Swamp Thing 90, 92
St. John Publications 34, 146, 152–153
Sala, Richard 117–118
Saw 123
Scary Tales 85
Schwartz, Julius 13–14
Sclavi, Tiziano 136
Scooby Apocalypse 107
Secrets of Haunted House 84, 86
Secrets of Sinister House 84
Seduction of the Innocent 11, 29, 44–46, 139–141, 147, 155
Seeley, Tim 112
Senate Subcommittee to Investigate Juvenile Delinquency 11, 12, 46–59, 67, 146, 155
Severed 113
Severin, Johnny 31, 154
Shadows on the Grave 111
Shaun of the Dead 123
Shuster, Joe 10, 23, 25
Siegal, Jerry 10, 23, 25, 155
Silent Hill 123
Silver Age of Comic Books 11, 12, 14, 67, 156
Simone, Gail 103
Skulan, Thomas 124–125, 148
Snyder, Scott 113, 114, 123
Species 129
Speculator Age of Comic Books 15
The Stand 98
Star Publications 153

status crime 36, 159–160
Steranko, Jim 76
Stine, R.L. 100
Strange Tales 69–70, 143
Superman 10, 12, 18, 23, 45, 139; See Also *Action Comics*
Supernatural Thrillers 83; See Also *The Living Mummy*
Swamp Thing 84, 134
Sword of Dracula 121

Tales From the Crypt 31–34, 118, 136–137
Tales of Ghost Castle 84
Tales of Screaming Horror 125
Tales of the Zombie 85
Templesmith, Ben 104, 119–121
Terror, Inc. 95–96
Texas Chainsaw Massacre 129
30 Days of Night 119, 133
Thor: Vikings 95
Tilley, Carol 141
Timely Comics 10, 142
Tobin, Paul 110, 123
Tomasi, Peter 110
Tomb of Dracula 83, 85
Top Shelf Productions 126
Tower of Shadows 76
trade paperback 20–21
True Blood 123

Underwinter 113
Underworld 123, 135
The Unexpected 75
Unholy Grail 116

Vallejo, Boris 85
Vampire Tales 85
Vampirella 77–78, 102, 148, 154
Vampironica 131

Vault of Horror 31–33, 136–137
Vertigo 92, 100, 133–134
Virus 135

The Wake 104–105
A Walk Through Hell 115
The Walking Dead 111, 132
War Is Hell: The First Flight of the Phantom Eagle 95
Warren, James 77, 153–154; See Also Warren Publishing
Warren Publishing 76–78, 147, 153–154; See Also Warren, James
We Will Bury You 121
Weird 78, 148
Weird Mystery Tales 84
Weird War Tales 84, 86
Welcome to Hoxford 120
Werewolf by Night 83, 102
Wertham, Fredric 11, 12, 41–42, 44–54, 60, 65–67, 72, 138–141, 147, 155
Whitman 150
Windsor-Smith, Barry 75–76
Wire Hangers 120
Witch Doctor 113
The Witching Hour 75
Wolfman, Marv 81
Wood, Wally 31, 76, 118, 152, 154
Wormwood: Gentleman Corpse 121
Wrightson, Berni 68–69, 75, 84, 154
Wytches 114

Ziff-Davis 34, 118, 154–155
Zombie 95
Zombie War 125
Zombies! Feast 122
Zombies Vs Robots 122
zuvembie 90

www.ingramcontent.com/pod-product-compliance
Ingram Content Group UK Ltd.
Pitfield, Milton Keynes, MK11 3LW, UK
UKHW042016140426
5217IPUK00015B/1203